THE VERY RI

D0005797

OTHER VOLUMES IN
THE CONCORD LIBRARY

Series Editor: John Elder

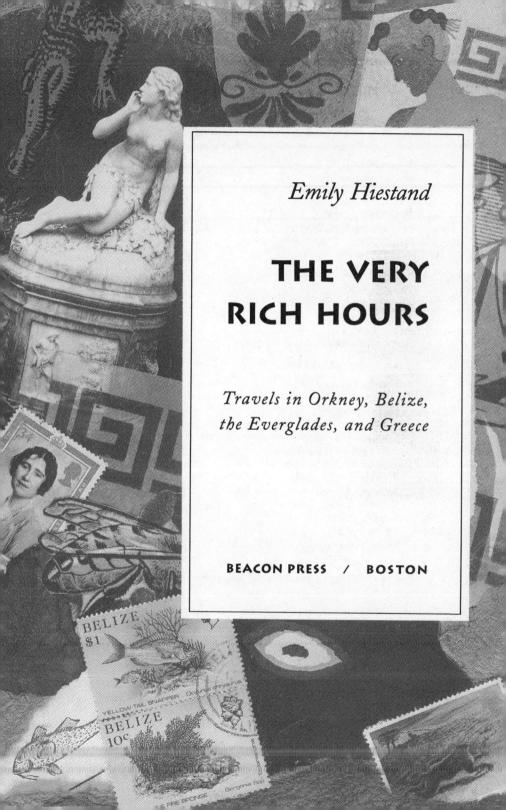

Emily Hiestand

THE VERY
RICH HOURS

*Travels in Orkney, Belize,
the Everglades, and Greece*

BEACON PRESS / BOSTON

Beacon Press
25 Beacon Street
Boston, Massachusetts 02108-2892

Beacon Press books
are published under the auspices of
the Unitarian Universalist Association
of Congregations.

© 1992 by Emily Hiestand
All rights reserved
Printed in the United States of America

99 98 97 96 95 94 93   8 7 6 5 4 3 2

Text design by Copenhaver Cumpston

Library of Congress Cataloging-in-Publication Data

Hiestand, Emily, 1947–
    The very rich hours : travels in Orkney, Belize, the Everglades, and Greece /
Emily Hiestand.
        p. cm. — (The Concord library)
    Includes bibliographical references.
    ISBN 0-8070-7118-8 (cloth)
    ISBN 0-8070-7117-X (paper)
    1. Hiestand, Emily, 1947–   —Journeys. 2. Poets, American—20th century—
Biography. 3. Voyages and travels. I. Title.
II. Series.
PS3558.I345Z468 1992
818'.5403—dc20
[B]   92-8153
                CIP

Page 225 constitutes a continuation of the copyright page.

A good traveler has no fixed plans
and is not intent upon arriving.

—*Tao Te Ching*, as translated
by Stephen Mitchell

CONTENTS

ACKNOWLEDGMENTS

The ideas in these essays come courtesy of rivers and peat moors, via mangrove roots, by way of fire corals and pelagic caves—phenomena without whose eloquence human language would be unimaginably different. No less essential are the contributions of three traveling companions: my mother, Frances Emily, who has given life at every stage of our journey; Katherine Jackson, whose literary perspicacity is matched only by her buoyant good humour; and Peter Niels Dunn, navigator and keel, a man who sings.

Deanne Urmy at Beacon Press generously made the ground in which a book might grow and guided its every page with grace and intelligence. Her assistant, Andy Hrycyna, was steadily helpful; Chris Kochansky copyedited the manuscript in such a way as to prove Blake right about Particulars; Lori Foley, Dan Ochsner, and Cope Cumpston ensured the book's physical beauty.

On my travels, numerous people showed me something of their lives and landscapes, many with such presence that they visit these pages—where I hope they find themselves treated with warmth and hospitality.

Such understanding as I have about habitation has been formed in conversation with poets, ecologists, archaeologists, naturalists, philosophers, and literary critics; accordingly, footnotes track through these essays, marking passages where my indebtedness is especially strong. Some themes have been nurtured by studies in the English Department and University Professors Program of Boston University, where Donald Carne-Ross, Robert S. Cohen, Rosanna Warren, Derek Walcott, George Starbuck, Linda Gregerson, David Wagenknecht, and Bonnie Costello encouraged and guided my inquiries. Three readers offered expert advice: Donald Carne-Ross, on the *Oresteia*; Clemency Coggins, on the Maya; and Jim Baird, about birds. Two naturalist guide groups, Wildabout Orkney and International Expeditions, generously shared their knowledge and field booklets.

A writer's award from the Mrs. Giles Whiting Foundation provided the time and peace of mind essential for sustained writing. Other sustenance has come from my brother, Partap Singh Khalsa, from my father, Sidney, and from two matchless friends, Jill Kneerim and Barbara Hindley. Finally, much of any art arrives from influences beyond the creator's awareness, and much soon belongs to readers who are the living habitat in which a book breathes.

To all of the above, I offer gratitude.

PREFACE

This is the story of several journeys, made in mid-life, to four remarkable parts of the Earth. All the landscapes were, to me, new and unfamiliar, so although I approach the places with the discipline of a visual artist and amateur naturalist, these pages do not recount old intimacies with beloved landscapes. Rather, these are tales of greetings.

I will hazard that the dislocations that prompted and allowed me to travel are a private instance of a transitional episode affecting our species as a whole. Any individual search for sustaining coordinates is linked to the conundrum of how humankind can make an enduring, respectful, and delightful habitation—a home—within our planet. These travels respond to an ancient, and newly urgent, recognition: that the Earth is a whole, that no rivulet or marginal field is outside our circle of concern. Naturally, none of us can tend, or visit, or even begin to grasp, the immense particularities of this planet, and often travel leads one toward modest plots, the watersheds of choice and fate. I immersed myself in the new and far-flung landscapes of Belize, Orkney, the Everglades, and Greece only to pose a question—what is right habitation?—and to listen for such answers as each place has to give.

Traveling to ask about habitation, I soon found, encompasses movement through more than physical space. By its very nature, the question involves moving among intellectual traditions; happily, the genre of the travel essay, so acquainted with range, easily accommodates poetry and science, philosophy and the painter's eye. And, too, there is always the possibility that one will enter the curious geography of which Black Elk speaks. Says the Oglala Sioux medicine man: "*The circumference is nowhere, the center is everywhere.*" The ecstatic excursions of shamans reliably lead to this knowledge: that the journey from the narrow self into watersheds, birds, bears, and constellations is the journey that links us with our world. But does Black Elk's utterance mean that physical travel is a needless activity? As Elizabeth Bishop puzzles, the entwined questions of home and travel are tricky and irresistible:

> What childishness is it that while there's a breath of life
> in our bodies, we are determined to rush
> to see the sun the other way around?
>
> . . . .
>
> *"Is it lack of imagination that makes us come*
> *to imagined places, not just stay at home?*
> *Or could Pascal have been not entirely right*
> *about just sitting quietly in one's room?*
>
> *Continent, city, country, society:*
> *the choice is never wide and never free.*
> *And here, or there . . . No. Should we have stayed at home,*
> *wherever that may be?"*

THE VERY RICH HOURS

FIELD NOTES
FROM BELIZE

One summer when the heartland of America dried up, from either the greenhouse effect or a convincing portent, when the eastern seaboard was washed with hospital wastes and heavy rains added storm-sewer debris to the toxic harbor of Boston, I traveled with my friend Katherine to Belize.

While we pack jungle boots and snakebite kits, our consorts, friends, and families give blank stares as they search mental globes and fail to find a country by this name. "It was once called British Honduras" stirs vague recollection, but no one places the nation on the limestone shelf that juts into the Caribbean and Gulf of Mexico, bounded on the north by Yucatán, on the west by the Petén forest of Guatemala. No one remembers its eastern shore as a swath of the Spanish Main, nor its interior as home to the Maya, whose world this was when Greece was having its Golden Age.

Living in forest villages away from the sea, small groups of Maya survive in modern Belize, each one speaking a different dialect of their tongue, raising black beans and maize as they did anciently, on small shifting plots called *milpas* after an Aztec word for corn. Many more Belizeans are self-described Creoles, African-Europeans descended from slaves who laboured for colonial timber merchants. Garifunas, descended from South American Caribs intermarried with Africans, live along the southern coast, where the women uphold traditional ceremonial life. A goodly fifth of the population are Mestizos of Mayan-Spanish roots. A small number descend from Spanish buccaneers and British colonials, and from Scotsman Peter Wallace and his fellow pirates, blessed in their raids on the Spanish Main by King James I, son of Mary Queen of Scots. There are trace elements of Chinese, Lebanese, and Eastern European people. Near Orange Walk in the north dwells a sturdy Mennonite community with barns that look like Ohio and members who speak an archaic form of German.

In a fine understatement, one student of Belizeans has said, "It is clear they do not subscribe to a common culture, ideology, or value system."[1] On an average day one encounters byl-ups of cassava roots and fish; roofs built by Scots to withstand the snow loads of Inverness; Rastafarians moving like bees in amber through fragrant ganja swirls; clerks with racks of stamps to certify the formidable paperwork of a postcolonial bureaucracy; the Maya god of writing, who is a monkey that roars like a jaguar; schoolgirls in navy-blue uniforms and white knee socks; bargain funeral parlours in the port city, each small interior an encrusted catacomb of drying flowers and plastic crosses flanked by burning candles; Mestizo boys tattooed in honor of their pirate ancestors; a nine-foot boa constrictor run over by a car in the downtown shopping area; mom-and-pop stores where if you are low on cash you may buy one cigarette from a pack or a cup's worth of corn flour on credit, where an elder's African authority silently pulses from behind the counter, light creeps through a dusty window, and a child sits on a stool, learning by watching.

To my eyes, as yet unschooled in things Belizean, it appears that this rich combinatorium of humanity manages to conduct life without resorting to any very rigid organizing principles. When journalist Norman Lewis traveled to what was still British Honduras in the 1950s, he found "wraiths of old English thatched cottages" and a population moving about aimlessly or else "fallen asleep in the attitudes of victims of murder plots." Belize City is still a spectacularly tatty world in which the traveler, if not the inhabitant, is reduced to a bewildered, pleased wandering through streets heated to the melting point. Since all members of this society descend from cultures with highly organized values, aesthetics, and economies, one can easily guess that some X factor accounts for the disarray. Perhaps Lewis meant only to convey the general street scene, but his observation about crime is right in a larger sense, as British Honduras was one of the slave-based "New World" economies. Not only obscure but anomalous, the tiny land is the only English-speaking nation in Mesoamerica, more kin to the Caribbean countries than its contiguous neighbors; but in the eighteenth century the sail to Belize from the British West Indies was a long one, the barrier reef in the Bay of Honduras daunting, and a struggle for control between Spain and England further dissuaded either power from fully settling the territory. As a result, Belize was not only exploited but considerably more neglected than a standard colony; one is surprised not that the infrastructure is yet tenuous, but rather that veins of cultural wisdom have survived.

In one of the ironies that is history, it is largely due to the particulars of their dreadful past that Belizeans occupy their land in a sound ecological manner. With a tiny human population—the lowest population density in Central America[2]—no industrial pollution to speak of, and low-impact subsistence farming, the region appears very much as it did in earlier British accounts: "Approach to the coast is through the islets known as cayes, and through coral reefs, and is both difficult and dangerous. For some miles inland the ground is low and swampy, with mangroves and tropical jungle. Next succeeds a belt of rich alluvial land, seldom more than a mile in width, beyond which, and parallel to the rivers, are extensive tracts of sandy, arid land called 'pine ridges' from the trees . . . with which they are clothed. Further inland comes the less elevated 'broken ridge' country, of mixed scrub. These tracts are intersected by what is called 'Cohoon ridges,' with a deep rich soil covered with myriads of palm trees and broad savannas, studded with clumps of trees which are threaded by streams from the mountains."[3]

At the close of the present century, Belize is blanketed by palm trees and broad savannahs interlaced by lagoons, mangrove swamps, and gallery forests that line streams and rivers. Limestone spines of fossil coral reefs fold through the northern half of the country, shaping jungle-covered ridges whose valleys hold the Nuevo and Hondo rivers. In the days when the territory was a backwater Crown colony, mahogany was the economic staple, but some tall red trees remain in the rainforests of the moist south, where lianas and epiphytes also swag over Mexican cedars, balsa, silk-cotton, and mayflower trees, and the vegetable canopy soars one hundred and twenty feet and disappears into clouds. The jagged-toothed Maya Mountains create the Cockscomb Basin, where a preserve protects jaguars, pumas, ocelots, and coatimundis. The coastal savannahs and sedge marshes are home for osprey and laughing falcons, snowy egrets, white-crowned parrots, and Tennessee warblers. Dense mangroves cloak the mainland coasts. Clusters of cayes shelter the mainland and in turn receive shelter from the barrier reef of the Caribbean, a coral wall that grows six to twenty-one miles wide and stretches one hundred and sixty miles up the Yucatán peninsula— after Australia's Great Barrier Reef, the largest coral being on the planet.

To those sobered by the current state of the planet, Belize appears as a hopeful, nearly prelapsarian land, a place where sustained-yield conservation principles might outpace conventional development and keep the ecosystems healthy. Among the species that teem in its rainforests, marshes, and reefs must be counted a near tribe of conservationists, ecologists, and enlightened natural-resource planners, converging especially from the United States, Great Britain, and Canada. Naturally, to marina and motel builders, land speculators, and cattle ranchers of the old school, Belize looks ripe for the picking. To refugee farmers from neighboring Guatemala, Honduras, and the Quintana Roo state of Yucatán, the tropical forests look like next year's *milpa* fields. Belizeans themselves come to nationhood and modern technology at a time when not only the goods but the devastations of industrialism have unfolded for all the world to see. It is hard to say whether an emerging tropical country can forgo immediate income from pesticide-based agribusiness and forest-destroying cattle ranches, but the innate worth of their land is not lost on Belizeans: through private and government efforts, they have placed nearly one third of their country in reserves and sanctuaries, and welcomed many plans that marry ecological wisdom with economics, notably Programme for Belize, which conserves an enormous land tract in the Río Bravo River area and hopes to generate income through natural history tourism, research, and selective agro-forestry. Economically fragile, as yet unable to feed itself, Belize has staked its future on an ecological agenda that includes the view that tourism can evolve from a force of environmental damage to one for conservation and sustainable development. Here, the Minister of Tourism is also the Minister of the Environment; says Mr. Glenn Godfrey in an open letter to travelers, "We are unwavering in the protection of our environmental treasures . . . [and] you will derive considerable satisfaction from knowing you are making a positive contribution to [our natural wonders] simply by visiting them."

So abundant are professional environmentalists in this hospitable climate that Katherine and I cannot get from airport to inn without meeting one. We share a taxi with a British coastal ecologist studying the destabilizing practice of clearing mangrove for home sites along the Belize River and, as the rattling vehicle hurtles by the olive brown river, are briefed in detail on the role of *Rhizophora mangle* (red mangrove) in protecting against hurricanes. The lecture is interrupted when the driver brakes to a sudden stop in the middle of a single-lane bridge and stares at the cloudy water. The mighty fish that Lewis's driver sought at this spot cannot be alive decades later, but apparently some ritual cæsura is. No traffic nears, so we get out, lean over the rusting iron railings, and study the river. Does a shape laze along the bank? Afterwards (having alerted us to the elusive) our driver hies us into Belize City, where within days we meet a Canadian engineer who is researching expansion of the port city's primitive sewer system; the U.S. Aid for International Development officer for environmental projects in Belize; a senior political scientist researching forest management techniques; the director of the Belize Center for Environmental Studies, who is planning a conference of herbal healers; and one especially bonny field researcher whose card reads "Institute of Biological Control, West Indian Station, Trinidad, W.I., with compliments, Graham Breen."

Graham Breen's mission is to locate plants that repel insects, plants that could be used to diminish the use of chemical pesticides. We meet on the veranda of a guest house with no vacancies and share a ride to another where the room card says that here one can, "at the most reasonable rates, enjoy bi-fo-time olde Belize Creole hospitality and breakfast in a dis-ya-time modern Belizean home." Breen is on his biweekly return from the *Freshening up from the wild* rainforest for an indoor shower and city food, and before zipping out to scour the nearby roadside for insect-repelling plants, he suggests dinner. In the 1950s, Lewis found roast tapir, roast armadillo, and roast paca being served as delicacies in the dining room of the nearby Fort George Hotel. He describes the paca, the only exotic speciality he was able to try, as "a large edible rodent, in appearance something between a rabbit and a pig." And, he said, "as usual in the case of such rare and sought-after meats, the flavour was delicate to the point of non-existence." Endangered species acts now keep these creatures off the menu entirely, and during our stay offerings are, for unknown reasons, further distilled. Usually shrimp, many fishes, and conch are plentiful, but this July the only first course is lobster cocktail and the only entree, "mixed seafood grille," is composed entirely of the local spiny lobster. Thus, lobster followed by lobster with a lobster salad is the standard dinner.

As we submit to this diet, we discover that even in decline the British Empire turns out youth who find a discussion of mind and nature stimulating whilst freshening up from the wild. As one would expect, this sometime forest dweller has an active and intimate affection for the tropical woods, for its creatures and calls, the light that filters through tangled lianas, and the salmon-hued *amapolas* that relieve the many greens. He often falls asleep to rain drumming the leaves, wakes to the full-throttle songs of birds, feels at home weaving among the tree trunks whose bases spread like the shaggy fetlocks of workhorses. What I didn't expect a plant-and-insect man to say was that razing these forests for commercial interests is acceptable. Scientific data about the role of the forests in climate regulation dissuades many from this opinion; moreover, one hopes that visceral experience of forests also leads to a far different conclusion. Animated conversation reveals, however, that our young friend does not trust his keen sense of beauty. Indeed, professionally he disowns it, noting that "it doesn't come up that much in science." The ravishing Landsat photos are among thousands of images that say otherwise, but what Breen means, correctly, is that for the habits of mind that characterize idealized science thinking, aesthetic insight does not have the status of fact, nor does it figure in the famous five-step scientific method.

In common parlance, *objective* means an account of the world uncolored by the variable tinctures of emotional and sensual intelligence, which, by contrast, produce an imaginative, subjective version of the world. However, as philosopher Erazim Kohák notes in *The Embers and The Stars*, his eloquent inquiry into the moral sense of nature, "the opposite seems far closer to the truth. . . . It is what we are used to treating as 'objective reality'—the conception of nature as a system of dead matter propelled by blind force—that is in truth the product of a subject's activity . . . a highly, sophisticated abstraction. It is, undeniably, a highly useful construct for accomplishing a whole range of legitimate tasks. Still, it is a construct not an experiential given. In a real, though not customary sense, it is what we mislabel 'poetic imagination' that is 'objective,' a spontaneous experiential given."

As scientists themselves were among the first to notice, the sophisticated, useful abstraction called objective reality rests on the fantastic belief that mind and nature are separable phenomena, and on the corollary that such things as forests are objects, while such things as people are subjects. Although the senses, by drawing us into communion with tidal pools and butterflies, suggest such a rigid separation is a false notion, knowledge from the senses— arising from syntheses of aesthetic, emotional, empirical data—has long been suspect in both religious and scientific doctrines of the West: either it led to damnation, or it was untrustworthy, or both. Nevertheless, as poet Susan Griffin notes in her essay on Newton's *Optics*, we can make a very different interpretation of sense knowledge: "Instead of believing that we are deceived by matter or our senses . . . we can assert, since we *do* experience colour, that in our experience of colour we have entered into a union with what we perceive. That together with matter we create colour." In this view, beauty is evidence of a joyful connection, one that French mathematician and physicist Henri Poincaré discerns at the very heart of the scientific quest: "The scientist does not study nature because it is useful: he studies it because he delights in it, and he delights in it because it is beautiful. If nature were not beautiful, it would not be worth knowing, and if nature were not worth knowing, life would not be worth living."

In his study of the place of beauty in physics, Fang Lizhi goes so far as to say that science "arises from the search for and the creation of beauty," and that since nature "has the property that all truths are necessarily beautiful, . . . [t]he pursuit of beauty will inevitably lead to the discovery of truth." Among Lizhi's examples of this heuristic are Copernicus, who put the sun at the center of the solar system not because heliocentrism better fit current empirical observations but because he found its image "more perfect in form," and the English physicist Dirac, who, on the strength of its beauty and against all evidence, held to his equation for symmetry between positive and negative charges in nature until the positron that satisfied his theory was discovered.[4] Surely champions of objective fact are right when they claim that the senses can distort and obscure, and yet, curiously, this flaw does not diminish the vital role aesthetic knowledge plays in our conversation with the world.

Nearly forty years ago, during the beginnings of the independence movement in Belize, Mr. Leigh Richardson was a leader of the reform-minded People's United Party. In his desire to hasten independence, Mr. Richardson sought to purge British Honduras of all things colonial: its name, the game of cricket, above all, tea drinking. Happily, independence came and tea remained. One can get a fragrant pot of tea, named for the likes of Earl Grey or the Prince of Wales, without throwing the establishment into a dither. So pleasant are Graham Breen's manners that by the time we take tea he is not so much agreeing with the hypothesis about sense knowledge as cheerfully alternating between two minds: one that communes with a sensual, living forest, one that objectifies the forest as inert products-to-be. It is not unusual to find both forms of knowing struggling within one person, although one hopes that these capacities twine affably together like strands of the DNA double helix to produce our most illuminating ideas. Most of us hold conflicting ideas about nature; our minds curate an unsettled alliance of literary images, fragments of physics, spiritual doctrine, vestigial animism, and contemporary ecological theory. As a result we call our surround the world, the planet Earth, a mechanism, the biosphere, Mother Nature, fallen matter, wilderness, the ecosphere, the natural resource base, and, of course, nature. But these are not perfectly interchangeable words; each carries with it a different implied philosophy about how our species might inhabit the earthly phenomenon. Over and over, one learns that any two humans who care about the Earth rarely mean to offer their affection to the same being: is the multiplicity of human language and belief merely consonant with the complexity of the world, or is it a sign that humans are but loosely connected to the rest of nature, free in our floating languages to make now this, now that, appear?

Eventually one biologist and two poets come to accord on this point: that present human activities, if continued, will lead to collapse, not of nature *per se*, which will surely continue its experiments in other forms, but of the life that presently comprises the planet. A surprise solution is proposed by our dinner companion, the man of many parts. He is one of the souls who evenly acknowledge the likely demise of the Earth's systems but claim that all is not lost because human beings can colonize space! At just the moment Breen suggests an escape to space biosphere stations, we are offered dessert by a Belizean with a radiant smile. We are distracted by her skin glowing red-brown in kerosene lamplight, and as we have only just met, I check the impulse to ask Graham whether, on some far star-world, he hopes to see raindrops silver a leafy canopy.

A short hour later, the first notable tropical wildlife is spotted— a specimen roach skittering down the wall of my dis-ya-time room. In a loud, high-pitched voice, I invite the house entomologist to race upstairs to identify it. Although G. Breen arrives on the double in his dinner costume of fatigues and combat boots, the specimen has escaped. Nevertheless, Breen discourses on the tropical forest roach and the coastal roach, helpfully pointing out that the main difference is size—the forest roach obtains to eight inches while the coastal roach (with distinguishing swirling pattern on the back) reaches only to six inches. Since I judge the room roach to be twenty to thirty inches, we cannot make a positive identification. It has been a long day, during which the destructive impulse I have upon regarding a giant insect viscerally instructs me in why our species determined to objectify and control nature in the first place. Head swirling in a distinguishing pattern, I close my eyes on day one in the tropics.

By day three in the unrelieved humid midsummer heat of Belize, enough disorienting events have occurred that Katherine and I suspend conversation on the modes of human cognition. It is quite enough, at day's end, to get to an eatery, gaze at dim lanterns, sip cold, bubbling water with lime, and be grateful for ceiling fans. These milder activities are pleasing accomplishments when one has broiled upriver in a skiff, searched for crocodiles and manatees, walked in the forest with numberless mosquitos and the fer-de-lance snake. The tropical landscape is a powerful, spectacular system in which lifeforms multiply in profusion. But the tropics incubate the offspring of the human brain at a stately pace: one becomes content to observe more than to claim.

Mangroves,
manatees

Going upstream on the Haulover Creek that is the last four miles of the Belize River, we are tracing the river's route back from the salt bay and port city through brackish veins and mangrove swamp toward its headwaters in the Petén rainforest to the west. At the river's mouth in the bay, we pass the local fleet of shallow-draft barges, muscular boats with big, open decks, sides swathed in strips of old rubber tires. So shallow are the waters at the port that cargo ships must rest at anchor a mile offshore while their holds are loaded and unloaded onto the barges. Always ships shimmer on the eastern horizon, tankers reduced to minute ghost-grey silhouettes. The congestion of the port causes us to sidle next to a small wooden *pitpan* hauling bundles of mahogany. Short reddish logs are stacked on the boat's decks and poke from the cabin windows; blue smoke sputters in a thin trail from the engine. The crew is a Maya family—a mother, father, girl, and two boys, all settled here and there on log bundles under a canvas shade tarp. The oldest boy is at the helm; the mother wears a flame-red chemise for the trip into town. As our boats pass, they slightly graze and squeak, causing the boy pilot to grin. Along this urban stretch, the riverbanks are shored with metal and wood reinforcements that give the appearance of a canal. Square wooden houses on stilts are built directly up to the water's edge; high as they are, the houses catch such breezes as come from the ocean, and each has a small veranda laden with drying clothes, rocking men or waiting chairs. Roofs are corrugated zinc; the walls glow even under grey skies in a medley of peeling paint—lime green, blue, coral, and white. Built Belize is worn, flaking and rusting away in layers of color, with the tops of ragged palm trees swaying above, sometimes brushing, the sheets of metal.

Beyond the port, our boat travels under clearing clouds. The houses thin, then disappear, until we are moving beneath an arch of thick green mangrove trees. Slender aerial roots drop from the high limbs of the trees, dangling in midair, taking gravity's patient path toward the mud bottom. Enormous dark brown nests, three feet around, swell in the crooks of trees, the cradles of jungle termites whose trails lead up and down the trunk from nest to water line: closely observed, the bark is alive with wavering golden-brown lines, the insects glinting in what sun comes through the tangle of trees. The river surface itself glows with flotillas of leaves, some yet green, many turned bright yellow and brown. We are floating in the local ecological nursery, a seamless cycle that goes like this: continuously shed mangrove leaves decompose, filling the estuarial rivers and coastal waters with slurries of phosphorus bits that appeal to local shrimps and crabs, who feed on the phosphorus, filtering the particles from the water, placing them in a marl from which the phosphorus is released by mud feeders to grasses and planktons, who feed the fishes, whose droppings are taken up by the trees and other plants as delicacies and who (along with crabs and shrimps) are eaten by people, who contribute methane gas, and possibly other attributes, to the whole.

The boat we have hired has a brilliant turquoise hull that flaunts itself against the dull green river. Later, when we take the boat into the bay and toward the mangrove cayes, we reach water where the hull perfectly matches the color of the sea, and this we realize must be the young boatman's power spot. His name is Bandula, after the name of an elephant in a children's story, and he makes a living from his boat, from fishing, and by selling jewelry that he smooths from corals, whelks, and coconuts. He is jaunty and stylish, redolent with self-sufficiency, his forearms tattooed with mermaids whose red hair and green tails flicker in the light dappling through the shiny river mangroves. Further upstream, where the mangrove stands are eighty feet high, Bandula turns off the motor; the engine noise dies away, revealing the deep, minor-key hum of insects that rises, a curtain of sound, from the forest. We drift for a while in the current, searching for manatees. The story that Spanish sailors mistook manatees for mermaids strains credulity when you see what lumpish blimps the sea cows are, large placid creatures with bristling whiskers, so peaceful that they are thought to be the only mammals that cannot be goaded into fighting. Although the bond between a cow and her calf is strong, manatees will not fight even to defend their babies, and perhaps this is because until the Spanish arrived and found their meat and oil desirable, the world had not presented them with enemies. More recently, speedboats have come to coastal shallows where manatees graze on vegetation just under the surface of the water and, to make a very sorry story very short, the propellors carve up the animals. It is rare to see a manatee whose hide has not been sliced by the whirling knives that leave scars resembling geometric patterns broken, then randomly reassembled. Although we come close to the river village of Manatee, we don't see manatees this day, and perhaps it is just as well. They are so shy that even the slow boats of admiring observers can alarm them and disrupt their placid well-being. Bandula's tattooed mermaid—old emblem of ambivalence, of the human imagination animated, fooled, encouraged, and perplexed by its world—will be the catch of the day.

Winil At the guest house where we first stay in Belize City, a decorative wrought-iron grille and a heavy carved wooden door are locked behind every guest, and mahogany-slat blinds over the front windows keep the sun from entering the cool marble foyer. Inside, it is Winil's world. Born in Belize, she inherited the stately white house on Barrack Road from her parents and a decade ago converted it into a guest house that she calls Glenthorne. Is she forty-five, fifty? She has radiant skin, a slightly rangy form, and a queenly aura that make speculation moot. Evenings, she entertains a handful of friends in her private sitting room on the second floor; as her guests glide up the stairs, one has a glimpse of men in white embroidered shirts, women from whose ears sway elaborate shell and silver earrings. From the window onto the street comes the faint clink of ice in their glasses and the tumble of Creole, the English dialect similar to Caribbean patois. Occasionally Winil and her guests effortlessly shift into a nearly Jamesian

English rhetoric no longer produced even by Oxford, and like most Belizeans they all speak fluent Spanish as well. Mornings, Winil arrives in the breakfast room in a flowing formal dressing gown, urging us to nibble the toast points, kippers, muffins, and marmalade arranged on salvers and bone china plates on a table under the slow ceiling fan. There are two other guests at the Glenthorne, but by the breakfast hour Graham Breen has long been in the countryside, and the young Canadian woman in the room whose poster bed is swathed in a purple gauze fantasia will not rise until afternoon, when she will set out on rounds to discuss hydrological schemes for the new sewer system. Katherine and I sit alone with our hostess, taking bits of smoked fish and toast, trying to rise to what is a formal morning tea.

From the other end of the guest parlour comes the muted monologue of an old and enormous television set mounted on the wall. Belize produces radio but no visual broadcasting of its own. The curvature of the Earth and international broadcasting regulations combine to allow the signal from just one television station to reach Belize; CTV9 from Chicago beams into the region, and a young entrepreneur catches (that is, pirates) the signal on several satellite dishes mounted in his backyard, then relays it to all of Belize for a fee. Television screens flicker throughout the city, permanently on, alerting residents to ice storms and winds over Lake Michigan and the perennially sad news about the Cubs. The woebegone team of ever-doomed innocence and underdoggedness has gripped the affections of Belizeans; a program guide in the weekly newspaper lists Cubs games (this week with the Padres, Expos, and Phillies) in bold type under the heading *Please Take Special Note*. Pointedly, there are no listings for cricket, nor for the Maya ball game once played for keeps in the nearby pyramid cities of Caracol and Lamanai (more properly *Lama'an/ayin*— "The Submerged Crocodile").

When she was ten, Winil followed her brother to school in England, returning summers to Belize or traveling with her parents. "In the theatre" is how she describes her mother and father. One morning Winil brings out a box of souvenirs of their performances in the thirties and forties: there are playbills limp with humidity and thick pasteboard posters printed in faded black and orange inks, the images of Hamlet, Puck, Othello, and Titania mottled by tropical molds that have spread across the paper. Winil first settled in Europe, married, and moved for a time to California, where a daughter studies at Berkeley. About the decision to return to Belize for good, she supplies only a framework of delicate hints in a regional language that, like Japanese, makes indirection an art form. A death was involved, and above all, one knows, the disappointments that must come, in white America, to an aging black woman with a memory of bi-fo-time Creole hospitality.

After breakfast Winil goes downstairs to oversee the washing. Her housekeeper, Mrs. Welch, has sorted the laundry from three large baskets into piles and has begun the first load in a small washing machine that hums and sloshes, shaking slightly side to side. The smells of Twenty Mule Team Borax and a lemon soap mingle and rise in the humid room. Winil is still in her morning gown; Mrs. Welch wears a long deep-purple scarf around her head, the shape towering like a headdress. Through an open door to the interior courtyard, a stand of Royal Poinciana trees shine in the sun, the last of their flame flowers fading. I meant to linger a moment in the laundry room door, pausing on my way to look for wonders in the jungle. The two women gently wrap me into their morning chat. They say that when they were girls and young women, the thing to do was to dance the quadrille. Yes, the quadrille—do I not know it?

As they begin to reminisce, the sheets hang in the women's hands, and soundlessly my knapsack comes to rest on the floor. The women are soon gone, their smiles not so much for me, nor even each other, but to some much larger, vanished audience. The conversation is itself like a dance, each woman supplying phrases and figures of speech as they resurrect the world in an old dancehall whose gleaming cedar and rosewood floors were logged from forests to the south of the Cockscomb Mountains. The dances were held on Sunday afternoons and into the early evening. The young Creole men and women of the capital city came in finery; older people came as matchmakers and chaperones. To begin, the men formed one long line, the women another; as the music commenced, they processed in concentric rings around the hall, advancing at a signal toward their chosen partners and forming the squares of six couples each in which the quadrille is danced. It is of French origin, the five figures and the finale of the *quadrilles des contredanses* derived from the ballet: *Le Pantalon, l'Été, La Poule, La Trénitz, La Pastourelle*. It is not hard to believe that, as Winil says, the dancers were light on their feet.

They are hardly on the ground now, and when the music of their conversation comes to its last strains, the women land with a soft thud in the laundry room. They see Katherine and me there, gradually swimming into view with our polite questions. No, there is no more dancing the quadrille, they say, the music fading completely. Have I seen the discos in Belize City? Cheap places with fights, drinking, drugs, the music too loud, and—worst of all—everyone dancing alone. The woven figures of elegant order have disappeared from the dance floor. But "Oh," the women say, not willing to be curmudgeonly, "it is what they are like now." And Winil goes further, bravely admitting about the discos, "I do not attend very often, but if you want to dance, . . ." Mrs. Welch, older, more conventional, glances at her employer with aghast admiration, and I see how Winil transforms reality with a single word here and there: to "attend" a disco is to alter its nature, bringing to the beery din the rustling of concert programs and skirts, nods of recognition between personages in a room.

I n the earliest human account of this landscape, the limestone sponge is said to be the flat back of a crocodile resting in lily pads. The people telling the story are themselves made of maize dough after attempts to fashion them in mud, wood, and flesh each failed. Itzamná, the lizard god, links heaven and earth; a young man with almond eyes is the perennial god of maize; frogs and tortoises sing to help the *chac*s bring rain; the unfaithful moon, Ix Chel, weaves and heals. The people love chocolate, and its beans are money. Very prized are the four long, green, iridescent tail feathers of the quetzal. Settled by the mangrove estuaries, the inhabitants collect oysters, turtles, and crabs. They like the eggs of iguanas and keep stingless bees in hollow logs. In the sky, the North Star is the god of travelers. The god of the underworld smokes a cigar; deities abound—for beekeepers, poets, and tattoo artists, for lovers and fishermen. In fields and kitchen gardens grow calabash,

Ways of traveling

sweet manioc, beans and chilis, pumpkins, papayas, and custard apples. In time, the maize-made people engineer the *tintal bajos* (swamps) into fertile land and terrace fields with canals. Fish can be numbed and caused to float into their weirs. Shields are made from tapir hides. They think of zero, and each number is divine. From the swirling, elegant glyphs they have left behind are parsed only fragments: "it had existed," "he entered the sky," "the child of," "he let blood." For some six thousand years, they evolved with the forest and estuaries; between 150 and 950 A.D., the Maya way of life became one of the great experiments.

Thirty miles north of the modern port city, near Corozal Province and a scant six miles from the sea, the Maya of 200 B.C. began to build what would become a small ceremonial and trade center that linked their southern lowland region with the far city of Teotihuacán (northeast of modern Mexico City). At the ruin of Altun Ha, Katherine and I are met by the custodian, a dignified middle-aged man named Louis, who wears a machete at his waist and, despite the heat, knee-high rubber boots. Dr. David Pendergast of the Royal Ontario Museum of Canada and the team of archaeologists who excavated Altun Ha in the 1960s long ago returned to their universities and museums; since they went home, it has been up to Louis and one teenage helper to keep the rampaging foliage from swallowing up the stout pyramids again. Beyond the area of Louis's patrol lies another mile and a half of soft green mounds: temples, dwellings, and urban structures yet uncovered, by now even more grown over than the models for Frederick Catherwood's moody engravings of crumbled cities with trees erupting from broken steps, the pyramids covered in mats of roots and vines quietly crushing the stone—images that stoked the nineteenth-century idea of ruin as a romantic *tristesse*.

During our walk up, over, and among the several pyramids that enclose a central courtyard, Louis is ever on guard for weeds, which he dismisses with a flick of his steel-blue blade. Even when we stand atop the largest crumbling structure, Louis hacks away at the stubborn rooted wildflowers and grasses that spring from every crevice in their will to turn the stone into soil. From this point three pyramids are visible, their bulk and wide bases enclosing several large green plazas, and here we pause for a long while to study the enigmatic scene. No kiva, longhouse, or sweat lodge in the North remotely resembles this staggering rubble; even the earthmounds of Alabama, though similarly shaped, are of an utterly different scale, mere mud pies compared to the present site. As Katherine's notes recall, attempts to elicit information about the ruins from Louis go like this:

"Did they worship the sun god here?"

"They buried the priest over there."

"Oh, priests were buried inside the pyramids?"

"The jade treasure from the tomb was stolen."

High up on the pyramid, the world spilling away on every side, Katherine and I squint in the sun, peering into the air, light, and surrounding jungle as though there we might see what the Maya did on this spot and in the chambers below. Quite suddenly, Louis announces that he will now take us to the pond. What pond? A Maya pond? Questions have thus far proved futile, so we silently follow Louis into the woods, giving him clearance for swinging his machete at green tendrils invading the black-earth path. Giant fern fronds sway overhead and the woods to either side are limitless. The walk itself grows endless, and as the path descends it gradually elides into sludge. Louis trudges on and on without explanation, giving us ample time to wonder what we are doing two thousand miles from home in the jungle with a stranger who seems perfectly kind, but who has a machete . . . when, at last, the pond! Louis looks extremely pleased.

"Is the pond very old?" Katherine ventures.

"A farmer dug it for his horses."

"There must be wonderful wildlife here," I suggest.

"I don't use mosquito repellent; I just swat them."

And then Louis turns and leads us back through the mud and mosquitos and swaying fronds in a companionable silence. From the trees and lianas comes the call of the bill bird, the keel-billed toucan, whose steady *crick crick* carries through the forest. Back at the ceremonial center, we buy a booklet (c. 1970) that rivals the pedagogy of Louis: it says that B—1 may have been more complex than A—4, that B—4 may be the site where copal and jade were cast into a blazing fire, that the shape of structure B—2 suggests a palace, but we can never be certain, that the glyph writing is not yet cracked, and that the true name of the city is unknown.[5] *Altun Ha*, we learn, is the modern Mopan Maya equivalent for "Rockstone Waters"— the pond! (which is partially clay-lined, indicating ancient engineering). Sometimes mystery is best left that way, and sometimes it sends you tumbling into the minds of archaeologists and other diggers. As it turns out, what we were standing on when we presumed to stand in cotton tee shirts on the nameless pyramid of the city newly named for a water hole, is at once a structure to focus and manifest divine energy for the human world and a means to move from earthly to celestial geography—surely a phenomenon into which every self-respecting traveler must inquire.

For a novice, tiptoeing even very circumspectly over the threshold into the ancient Maya world is to find oneself in a vast, endlessly rich reality, an experience curiously like the one the Maya meant to embody via their pyramids. They had noticed that the Earth was a thin band of existence, and so they constructed gateways into the fullness of the universe. The pyramids are special points, intersections of the vertical and horizontal planes through which the sacred *ceiba*, or silk-cotton tree, may grow from the underworld to the Earth and onward into celestial regions, a route by which the Maya expressed the continuum between the natural and numinous worlds. To link worlds, naturally, the geometry and siting of the pyramids must be precise; each is aligned to one of the four cardinal points of Maya space, which was—like time for Einstein—as much an autonomous, pervasive force as an abstract measuring device. The four points are visibly marked by *ceiba* trees and guarded by four invisible figures, the *Bacab*s, whose task it is to hold together time and space. The resulting architecture and landscape do not so much symbolize as embody the structure of heaven; just so, the steps that sheath one side of a pyramid mark days of the year, and, moreover, embody the unique quality of each day, which like every other thing and creature of the ancient Maya universe is animate and brimming with significance. Scholars often speak admiringly of the economy of Maya symbols, and suggest that the pyramid, in its densely packed meanings, served as an "index to the complicated natural ciphers" of the world.[6]

Sitting on the seawall back in Belize City, Katherine identifies the huge black birds soaring on eight-foot wings over the bay.

"Magnificent frigatebirds," she says, and it takes a little Abbot-and-Costello "who's on first" go-round for me to realize that *magnificent* is part of the bird's actual name, not an adjective Katherine is supplying. What an exemplary naming technique, by which token we would study Splendid Brown Bears, Astonishing Bacteria, Incomparable Honeybees. As we watch the birds, with their sharp, pointed wings and red gullets, sailing wind currents out to sea then back to shore, Katherine and I begin to grasp the meaning of the Maya constructions: in the conjunction of space, time, and matter, what were they making if not a unified field theory, a version of the modern physicist's dream of the Theory of Everything? Moreover, the Maya theory included the union of spirit and matter: the pyramids were often tombs from which rulers launched their souls' arduous journeys through the afterlife.

At Altun Ha, we innocently climbed the *axis mundi* of an unseen *ceiba* and stood in the main doorway to time and space, and on the crest of the pyramid that our booklet calls A–1, we instinctively turned toward the four directions, easily led by the architecture to view the surround in the quadrants that characterize all Amerindian geography. To the East is birth and vitality; to the North, maturity; to the West, old age. And in the South—ignorant of the implications of traveling, even facing, to the Maya South, we looked directly into the jungle thicket that grows where a soul may become lost, unable to return to the center, place of birth and rebirth.[7] While gazing out on the landscape of life, we stood above the chambered tomb of some elite person who was buried with mounds of jade carvings, shell necklaces, jaguar claws, a folding book written on bark from the wild fig tree (by now a powder), and a cache of stingray spines used in ritual bloodlettings. Accounts from the 1970s begin to emphasize the long known fact that the Maya were not an entirely peaceful theocracy, rather a society that knew both war and secular power, whose citizens engaged in self-mutilation and sacrifice, carving hearts from souls held spread-eagled on altar stones, placing the warm organs in gourds and offering them to prime the pumps of the *chac*s, benevolent but thirsty gods of rain. As usual, the wet season this year began on May 3 and should last until December. But for weeks in July there has been no rain. Sometimes it happens that rain ceases for a month in midsummer, a dry blue spell called the *canicula*. What we count lucky weather would have occasioned a bargain with the *chac*s, and as strangers, we would have been ideal candidates for the ritual, along with slaves, bastard children, and conquered warriors.

We had asked Louis why the central Maya ceremonial centers had been abandoned in the late tenth century. "The route to the sea is this way," he replied, pointing his wiry hand to the east. Reasons more commonly offered are diseases, drought, the unintentional creation of savannahs (which, lacking the plow, the Maya could not till), but in his suggestion Louis is in good company. Of the abundant theories of collapse, Algar Gregg has said that "guessing the reason for this failure of social organization is a favourite pastime for archaeologists in Central America."[8] While the collapse was drastic, it was not complete. Construction in some centers, Altun Ha for one, continued for a century after the fateful changes elsewhere, and after Maya migrated north into Yucatán, the region they called the Land of the Turkey and the Deer, their ceremonial centers endured into the thirteenth century. By the time Francisco Fernández de Córdoba's conquistadors arrived in Yucatán in 1517, Maya in many parts had been subdued by a Toltec/Mexican people, but the latter had greatly absorbed Maya culture. At Chichén Itzá, the Mexican lords were dismissively described by Maya citizens as those who "speak our language brokenly." In their remotest Yucatán dwellings, the Maya rebuffed the Toltec and Aztec and were still holding out against Porfirio Díaz in the late nineteenth century. At some abandoned sites to the south, the stone stelae that recorded annual events continued to appear well after the tenth-century disintegration, although the monuments were often erected upside down or in the wrong kinds of places. "These aberrations," archaeologist Patrick Culbert muses, "look not so much like impiety as like efforts [to] continue the stela cult by people who had lost the knowledge of the proper way of doing things."[9] More propriety disappeared when sixteenth-century Spanish missionaries burned the Maya books; and yet, a millennium after the classic Maya culture collapsed, one can come upon a bowl of copal burning at the base of a stone stair in the jungle, the incense smoke twining thinly and bluely through the leaves, giving off what the Maya call the "odour of the center of heaven."

The loss of their intellectual records is especially sad for a people whose supreme deity is Itzamná, inventor of writing, patron of learning. For centuries this people has been so resistant to our understanding that the late dean of Mayanists, Sir Eric Thompson, conceded of encounters with them: "[T]ravelers . . . return from their journeys, physical or mental, curiously unsatisfied." Now, even as we walk the old forest home of the Maya, their glyphs are yielding to the epigrapher's art. Taking the view that the marks are both phonetic and logographic signs (capable of representing words and syllables), scholars Linda Schele and David Stuart are beginning to read and pronounce the plump, convoluted marks. Glyph T539, says Stuart, speaks of "co-essence," the Maya knowledge that such as ocelots and comets can "share in the consciousness" of a human being.[10] This is spine-tingling stuff, signaling a phase in Maya research that Schele, alluding to the decipherer of the Rosetta stone, names "the time of Champollion."[11] And yet, so much was burned by friars and dissolved by humidity that Thompson is still right and may always be.

His famous books are full of burro rides, fleas, hammocks strung in bat-filled temples, questions coming in the middle of Yucatán nights. He uses the word "quest," and thinks it is relevant to write down his feelings about the unusual intellectuals of Mesoamerica. Sir Eric is fun to read and he is scrupulous, modestly introducing his own theory about the collapse (peasant revolt) by recalling Hilaire Belloc's reflection on all theories: "Their whole point and value is that they are not susceptible to proof; . . . what makes them amusing and interesting is the certitude that one can go on having a good quarrel about them, and the inner faith that when one is tired of them one can drop them without regret."[12]

In his search for a way to do science and shape a story, Thompson engages a riddle that is surely something of what drew him to the Maya. In their combination of exactitude and elusiveness, the Maya are a model for the tantalizing play between the known and the unknowable. To say anything about them, not only the raw amateur like myself but the specialist must step onto the trembling earth where what one deems reasonable is an admixture of accepted fact (changeable) and the medley of free will and fierce socialization we so casually refer to as the self. Recent scholarship of all sorts relies on the methodology of professional pointillism, an apparently cautious but after all radical approach to knowledge that rests on faith that one's dot of research, added to innumerable other dots, cumulatively yields. . . . Tunneling into a narrow region to find, in miniature, firm ground is as dizzying an approach to knowledge as it is respectable, and the eternally deferred meaning of orthodox skepticism appears in centrifugal as well as reductive form: Italo Calvino sympathizes with modern novelists who cannot make an ending and with Proust, whose net of reality grows and grows, beyond human comprehension, presenting the mind with signs that "knowledge . . . is attained by suffering this intangibility." The Maya teach us about this suffering; after the theories and facts, there remains the quietness of stones.

They dared to conduct civilization on a thin, poor soil with few water reservoirs, and the most suggestive of current theories is that the collapse was precipitated by strains laced into the very success of a rainforest culture. the clever, intensive, forced-field agriculture led to a population increase, to a rise in building programs and new standards of leisure among the elite. Inevitably, the human expansion overwhelmed the fragile ecology, soil depletion and malnutrition arose, management failures and violence between the great cities of Tikal and Caracol ensued, and a desperate demand for labor soured the bond between the peasant and elite classes. Patrick Culbert believes that, once degraded, "the ravaged land offered little potential for repopulation," and notes that "the rain forest home of the Maya still remains an unpopulated wilderness."[13] It could be that the Maya were not surprised by discovering the limits of their way of life. Ptolemy Tompkins finds that in myth they foresaw "the dangers and contradictions of human progress" and told themselves the story of evolving from village life "plagued with . . . guilt and ambiguity," warning themselves that a culture growing in scale courts the loss of knowledge about how to properly live on the Earth.[14] Certainly, modernity echoes their anxiety; by now, the difficulty of guarding against the loss of Earth wisdom would seem roughly analogous to the task presented to Louis and his blade by the persistent foliage on the excavated pyramids of Altun Ha.

Mercifully, a handful of Maya sacred texts were translated, by

Mayan speakers, into Spanish under the supervision of sixteenth-century friars. Though these translations weave strands of Christianity into Maya cosmology, they comprise some of our most reliable clues about ancient Maya thought. From one of the books, known to us as the *Chilam Balam of Chumayel*—that is, *The Book of the Jaguar Priests of Chumayel*—comes this observation:

> All moons, all years, all days, all winds, reach their completion and pass away. So does all blood reach its place of quiet, as it reaches its power and its throne. Measured was the time in which they could praise the splendor of the [divinities]. Measured was the time in which they could know the Sun's benevolence. Measured was the time in which the grid of the stars would look down upon them; and through it, keeping watch over their safety, the gods trapped within the stars would contemplate them.[15]

In the Maya measure, time flows eternally from past into future, a conception that sounds plausible enough to our minds. But our linear notion of history is alien to their view that the past recurs in cyclical, specified time periods. In such a reality, history is prophecy; thus, the three interlocking Maya calendars are numerical grids by which learned squadrons might mark returns of time periods and predict life's events. The time frame observed is very long indeed: the Maya measured in days, months, and *tuns* (a three-hundred-sixty-day unit) in *katun* (about twenty years), *baktun* (four hundred years), *pictun* (eight thousand years), *calabtun* (one hundred fifty-eight thousand years), *kincultun* (three million years), and *alantun* (about sixty million years). Thompson marvels at the Maya ability to compute perfectly day and month positions three hundred million years in the past and moreover at what this suggests about their vision. Theirs was, he says, "an appraisal of the ages which would have been utterly inconceivable to us even today, had not our minds been conditioned to their vastness by the writings of the astronomers and geologists of the nineteenth century."[16]

That a numerical count was not the only Maya idea of order can be known from a glance at any pot or stone serpent's head: some have found in the teeming, convoluted imagery the terror of empty space, and some have praised the proliferation of form, but no one doubts the plasticity the artwork embodies. Roger Fry finds nothing in Europe to match the Maya "power to suggest all the complexity of nature." A "dynamic imbalance . . . leads the eye restlessly along," says Michael Coe. Here is the ceaseless drama that saturates beetles and civilizations, in whose reverberation nothing endures save energy and change; in art and myth, the Maya gracefully yield to the fundamental contradictions of being. Perhaps the rigid, predictive calendar and the immensely fluid, elastic art represent two veins of the Maya soul, and perhaps under the strains of population explosion and ecological depletion—stresses we can well appreciate—the balance was lost.

By the sixteenth century, Maya society had evolved again. The priestly astronomy and fine mathematics were long lost, and life had returned to the calendar of maize and calabash in fields ringed by shining pepper plants. In what would become Belize, villages were situated along the fertile coast and central lagoons and were, predictably, devastated by Spanish weapons and diseases. Although the Maya sometimes appeared to yield to the beliefs of their oppressors—expediency, diplomacy, curiosity, and similarities between Christian and Maya thought are some of the reasons—they quickly discovered the foreigners' lack of reciprocal tact.[17] By the time British loggers arrived, in the middle of the seventeenth century, coastal Belize was empty of human settlements. As a poem from the *Chilam Balam* laments, Maya who survived violence and pandemics had melted into the forest interior:

> On that day, the tender leaf is destroyed . . .
> On that day, three signs are on the tree,
> On that day, three generations hang there . . .
> And they are scattered afar in the forests.[18]

The Maya tactics of retreat and resistance, as well as the influx of Yucatec Maya, have resulted in northwest Belizean forests lightly dotted with villages named Yo Chen, Chunox, Patchchacan, and Xcanha.[19] In these places artisans weave an old cosmology into shirts and blankets: white for North, red for East and blood, yellow for the South and maize, black for the West and war, blue for sacrifice, green for life. Here, too, villagers seek the traditional healing arts practiced by the *H'men*, an old word that means "those who understand and can do."

T hose who understand and can do is most definitely what Katherine and I are not while maneuvering in this tropical reality. What happens when we attempt to visit one of the old *H'men* is typical. Outside San Ignacio, near the western border of Belize, an herbalist named Rosita Arvigo studies medicine with Don Eligio Panti, the renowned ninety-year-old *hierbatero,* or herbal healer, of the Cayo district. En route to San Ignacio, the back axle of our hired car cleaves in twain on a road more properly called a pothole that occasionally lapses into a surface patch. We have the means to change a flat tire but not to weld an axle, so we wait on the dirt road for three hours until a truck laden with sacks of beans stops and ferries us back into the port city. Spending a late afternoon on the scruff of a pineland savannah is not regrettable; vines and *craboo* grow up to the road, green skinks dart here and there, blue butterflies flutter over the dusty leaves, and as the heat abates, birds begin to appear, most prominently a bevy of ruddy ground doves. We chat about Eugenio Montale's poetry, the heat, whether or not to get out our snakebite kit. The key is to utterly abandon expectations. Everywhere travel is an exploration of the relationship of plans to surprise, but no other land has so thoroughly taught me surrender to unpredictability.

While in Belize, we have one chance to participate in a controlled plan: a well-regarded naturalist tour occurs during our stay, and the field guide kindly invites us to join his expedition for a day. The night before, we sit in a hotel lounge with the thirty official members of the expedition and watch a slide show during which cheese and fruit is served. The hotel wall glows with pictures of macaws, orchids, and heliconias. The guide names and describes all species and terrains that we are to see the following day and outlines the itinerary: at seven o'clock in the morning the well-stocked minivans will roll toward the rainforest. When that hour arrives, we are fast asleep, guided by some inner dream to forgo the shred of order that might have tinctured our experience.

Another day, we determine to prowl the seamier parts of Belize City. Advised by Winil to stow tickets, checks, et al. in money belts worn under our skirts, we struggle into the contraptions and, pleased with ourselves, strike out. Soon I notice the sash string of Katherine's money belt dangling from under her floral skirt, frisking along the street like the discreet tail of a city mouse. We nose around until we turn up the in-town address for Dora Weyer, the legendary naturalist who founded Parrot's Wood Biological Station, on the Sibun River. Ringing the bell in midafternoon, we are politely admitted to a cathouse whose inhabitants are lazily painting their toenails red and silver, languishing on dark Spanish chairs and settees that stand, heavy as grandees, on a crazed, painted tile floor. The women hoot and chortle outright when we ask for Ms. Weyer, and we slink back down the stucco stairwell. Settling for simpler outings, we head for the Philatelic Office to collect some of the gorgeous local stamps, among them shimmering yellow-tail snappers who swim, mouths open, across a rectangle of blue water, eternally moving toward the tiny head of Elizabeth II that stares, grey as stone, from the corner. The office is closed and no one can say when it will reopen. We hope to make a copy of a playbill Winil has shown us, but the machine in the single copy shop serving the nation is broken, awaiting a crucial part from a factory in Connecticut. At a department store, we purchase dozens of locally manufactured matches whose box covers are extravagantly printed with keel-billed toucans, the huge beaks flaring in green, orange, red, and blue inks over bright yellow breasts, black bodies, and blue claws. Quite soon we discern that Belizean matches do not burst tamely into a flame, but reliably explode into small missiles that blast about the room, lighting curtains and bandanas. Although our minds have largely been fashioned by a culture that reveres rationality, Katherine and I generally imagine ourselves capable of greatly modulating that principle. But as lucidity recedes ever more completely in Belize, we suspect the slippage arises as much from our inability to recognize the prevailing order as from the ephemeral infrastructure that so little resembles Western industrial schemes. To what extent is such evidence of the limitations of human manipulative powers a desirable aid to sustainable habitation? Physicists must lodge some experiments in Belize: there can be no finer place to test the notion that equilibrium can spontaneously give rise to disequilibrium and that form can grow out of randomness.

ad we reached Don Eligio's small shack outside San Ignacio, chances are we might not have found his disciple,
Mrs. Arvigo, in residence. These days she sometimes
travels to the New York Botanical Garden, where she teaches
ethnobotanists what she has learned from *el mero*, the real one, who
himself learned medicine from a healer who kept the old ways, such
as turning himself, when required, into a jaguar. In a letter to
Sanctuary magazine, Mrs. Arvigo describes her typical day with *el
mero*. At dawn, she and Don Eligio set out to gather roots, leaves,
bark, and vines from the *campo*; by afternoon, they are back at the
medicine shack, where they reduce the plant materials into potion-
sized chips. Each year, she says, they must walk farther and farther,
past newly parched, cleared areas to get to the *campo* and the source
of healing plants. One day, as Mrs. Arvigo and Don Eligio were
passing a field of watermelons blanketed white with insecticide, the
hierbatero had this to say about agribusiness developers: "They are
fooling themselves, and the earth will make them pay for this cruel
treatment. They have slashed and poisoned their own mother and
sent her out to sell herself in the markets of the world." Still
pondering their peculiar economics, he later added, "I cannot see
why people of today do not understand that the soil is like a bank
account. You must put in and put in and wait for the interest to
grow before you start making withdrawals. Who has a bank account anywhere where you can only withdraw and never deposit?"

In his appreciation for precise accounting and his long view of
the Earth's economy, Don Eligio invokes the time that is eternal
and interwoven. Of elders like *el mero*, ethnobotanist Mark Plotkin
has said, "Every time one of these medicine men dies before
someone can capture his knowledge, it is as though an entire library
has burned down." Elaine Elisabetsky has described why the intellectual property of traditional healers deserves the status afforded
the results of industrial research:

> To transform a plant into a medicine, one has to know the correct
> species, its location, the proper time of collection (some plants are
> poisonous in certain seasons), the part to be used, how to prepare it
> (fresh, dried, cut in small pieces, smashed), the solvent to be used
> (cold, warm, or boiling water; alcohol, addition of salt, etc.), the way to
> prepare it (time and conditions to be left on the solvent), and, finally

posology (route of administration, dosage). Needless to say, curers have to diagnose and select the right medicine for the right patients.[20]

On her farm named for the healing moon, Ix Chel, Mrs. Arvigo works patiently to conserve and respect the value of Don Eligio's archive. But what, one wonders, can be done with his knowledge if the habitat that provides healing plants becomes grazing pastures and citrus groves? One idea, well underway, is to store the genetic material of otherwise extinct plants in laboratories where it is available for chemists to analyze in order to duplicate useful pharmacological properties. One quibbles but softly with well-meaning efforts, and yet . . . even if it were possible to analyze the vast forest pharmacopoeia before it disappears, the blue-hooded euphonia and the warbler, who were wont to sing to gaudy flowers and rainspeckled leaves, are unlikely to be moved to delirious trills by a beaker of genes. Nor can a laboratory restore us with its cool shade or by the curiously healing fact of merely knowing that a wilderness exists. Naturally, in Don Eligio's view the scheme is nonsensical; fundamental to his medicine is a prayerful approach to the forest, a consciousness inseparable from the bioactive properties of plants. Not only does the plan overlook these matters, it appears unlikely that species characteristics are salvageable in the lab. These qualities rely on large breeding populations to cull for beneficial genes, and they emerge from the long cycles of nature. Now, unless we were dropped here from space as a lethal alien virus, we have also emerged from the long cycles of nature, as fully members of this world as the heroic and mild pearly-eye moth. So why *are* we progressively destroying our earthly home? "Ah, solving that question," as poet Philip Larkin says about the mystery of days, "is what brings the priest and the doctor, / In their long coats, / Running over the fields."

A selected gazetteer of official standard names of Belize

Aguacaliente Swamp, Almond Hill Lagoon, Andersons Camp, Baboon Creek, Bakers Rendevous, Baking Pot, Beattie Estates, Betty Creek, Big Eddy, Bight Swamp, Black Creek Indian Reservation, Boatman, Bob's Creek, Bomba, Boom Creek, Boom Town, Bound-To-Shine, Cabbage Haul Creek, Campa Negro, Carib Girl Fall, Carib Reserve, Cashew

Tree, Catfish Bight, Chan Chen, Chan Chich Creek, Chequbul, Rio Chiquibul, Churchyard, Cobweb Swamp, Cockscomb Peak, Cocoa Plum Cay, Colonel English Creek, Cool Shade, Cowboy Camp, Crique Sarco Indian Reservation, Curlew Cay, Cut and Throw Away Creek, Dancing Pool, Darknight Cave, Dog Flea Cay, Dolores, Egypt, Eldorado, El Tigre, Esperanza, Fabers Lagoon, False Branch, The Flat, Flour Camp, Forest Home, Gallon Jug, Gentle Work, Glory Caye, Gladden Spirit, Good Living Camp, Go-To-Hell Creek, Grace Bank, Gracias A Dios Fall, Happy Home, Harry Jones Caye, Hellgate Run, Hen-and-Chickens Caye, Rio Hondo, Iguana Creek Forest Reserve, Indian Church, Isabella, Jacinto Landing, Joe Goff Barquedier, Kaxil Uinic, La Milpa, Lands of Goshen, Las Lomitas, Lucky Strike Camp, Macal River, Macaroni Creek, Machaca Indian Reservation, Manatee Bar, Meditation Rapids, Monday Morning Ridge, Monkey Shoal, More Tomorrow, Mosquito Caye, Punta Mother, Mountain Cow, Naranjal Burgos, Crique Negra, Negroman, New Boston, New Egypt, New Home, New River, New Town, New Windsor, Never Delay, Oak Burn, Old Harry, One Man Caye, Orange Walk, Otoxha, Pachacan, Paradiso, Placencia Point, Plantation Creek, Plenty, Pork and Doughboy Punta, Puhui Zibal, Pull Trouser Swamp, Quebrada de Oro Camp, Revenge, Rice Station, San Felipe, San Heron, San Jose, San Lazaro, San Pablo, Santa Maria Creek, Santa Teresa Creek, Savanna Bank, Scotland, Shipstern, Shipyard, Silk Grass Camp, Skiff Sand, Snook Eddy, Spanish Lookout, Tiger Run, Tobacco Reef, Trinidad, Tum Tum Creek, Tulec, Tu-Tu Camp, Tzimin Kax, Tzokotz, Uncle Sam, Usbentun, Vaqueros, Victoria, Ciejo De Belice Rio, Viper Rocks, Wee Wee Caye, Wild Cane Caye, Xaxe Venic, Xcanha, Xpicilha Village, Yalbac, Yo Chen, Young Girl, Zuniga Creek.

Only excursions into history allay the bafflement this land arouses in a traveler; soon one realizes that after the Maya there was yet another failed experiment. The tall, red, fine-grained mahoganies sought, and almost entirely found, by seventeenth-century British woodcutters were found growing abundantly in Belize because fifth-century Maya farmers had planted them in great bands to cool the soils of their permanent

Sub
Umbra
Floreo

terrace fields, recently invented to feed the growing population of the ceremonial centers.[21] After the cities declined and Maya farmers returned to shifting-field *milpa* farming, the mahoganies grew until Europeans made them the raison d'être of British Honduras, whose coat of arms was a shield held by a brace of woodcutters, axes in hand. (Chippendale highboys and sideboards, panelled railroad coaches.) Spain and England endlessly bickered about the valuable forests, finally agreeing that British woodcutters could harvest trees but could not own land. To reach this solution, neither empire consulted Guatemala, and until quite recently maps on the walls of Guatemalan diplomats clearly showed *Belice* as the easternmost province of their country. The arrangement did please the British loggers and export merchants who were keen not to settle the mosquito-ridden land but to extract from it their fortunes. Even after the British drove the Spanish away in a naval battle off St. George's Caye and could theoretically have started satisfactory communities, the settlements of Baymen (as British loggers called themselves) remained raw frontier camps. The niceties of the only formal code of behaviour, drawn up in 1765 by Rear Admiral Sir William Burnaby on a visit from Jamaica, may be judged by Rule Number Five: "No kidnapping, that is, press gang methods of recruiting, except for pilots for one trip only." The Burnaby Code prevailed until 1840, when, partly in response to conditions that prompted from visitors words such as "anarchy," the territory was made a Crown colony with a legislature and a motto. *Sub Umbra Floreo*—"I flower in the shade"—is a haunting, poignant phrase that seems to refer (half-consciously, as if in *umbra*) to the shady, flowery forests, to the marginal state of the colony relative to London, and to the dark, deathly conditions by which this, and all colonies, produced their flowers.

Finding no indigenous labour force, the logging merchants followed the model of West Indian plantations. Slaves were brought from Jamaica as early as 1724, most likely from the Niger and Cross Delta regions of present-day Nigeria, and from the Congo and Angola. As slave loggers, their work took place in remote forests from which escape to Yucatán and Guatemala was possible, and as a result, the timber captains created conditions somewhat less brutal than those in the West Indies. "There were no

Negro whip drivers, and the liberties found in forestry work, the isolation and lack of constant control, contrast sharply with the labor gangs on the sugar estates."[22] A history published in 1968 by Her Majesty's Stationery Office claims that a "rough comradeship existed between black and white" in British Honduras, that "a free man could not live better than the well treated slave."[23] On this subject, the definitive judgement was made by the slaves, whose responses to their life condition included suicide, frequent escapes, high abortion rates among black women who chose not to bring babies into such a world, numerous revolts, and, after abolition, migration in hearty numbers over the borders.

To keep the skilled Creole labourers in the region after abolition, logging companies began to offer relatively high wages, and some former slaves continued woodcutting as free men. For another century the territory remained an extractive factory organized around mahogany profits. A thoughtful colonial administrator would now and then propose that in a climate with a long growing season agriculture would seem plausible, but timber merchants fiercely thwarted such diversification even after the mahogany trade declined, and, after a brief recovery, declined again.[24] As their profits flowed entirely toward foreign investments, no capital remained in the colony to create schools, hospitals, theatres, or roads. With only rivers to ship produce to the market port, farm costs were too high to be viable; the only planting occurred on small family plots and in the flurry of underfunded attempts to start banana and cacao plantations which resulted, above all, in the Chinese-Belizeans who trace their ancestry to labourers imported for these failed schemes.

At the turn of the century, the mahogany market remained sluggish and logging was mechanized: the prolonged failure to create an infrastructure, a diversified economy, a social order—a livable human world—came home to roost. In response to widespread unemployment, the colonial government created a few small relief programs, but as absentee merchants controlled the legislature, relief monies were commonly distributed for such things as building new sawmills. Only with the rise in the 1950s of a working-class independence movement did a government emerge that took as its mission the well-being of local inhabitants. Now the past will be but slowly shed. In 1991, ten years after independence, agriculture is one of the most promising sources of national income, but although Belize has high unemployment (thus many potential agricultural workers), centuries of colonial laws that hindered planting and denied land to Creoles have produced a great number of citizens who have no traditional knowledge of farming. Agriculture is further arrested because a handful of absentee foreign owners hold fifty percent of the arable land and choose to leave it idle. A land tax, meant to stimulate such landowners to sell or develop their land in ways beneficial to the country, had disastrous results. Owners elected an exemption for "improving" a fraction of their holding; virtually no tax was produced, and one "improvement" was the clear-cutting of the handsome forest that bordered the Hummingbird Highway.

The danger in telling such histories is an easy outrage, but diagnosing an earlier generation's disease rarely protects us from the comparable thing embedded, as an acceptable norm, in our own way of life. Rarest among us is John Newton, on the Atlantic with a human cargo in his hold, taught by the amazing grace of a storm to look again, to see himself out of time, and to change. As for the logged-out mahogany stands of Belize: in what seems a minor ecological fable, Algar Gregg tells of the Kekchi Maya farmers near the Chiquibul Forest Reserve who are now restoring mahoganies to the forest. Along with corn, they drop mahogany seeds into their planting rows; several years later, when they abandon the fields, saplings are rising above the harvested stalks.

From a hotel window   Situated across from the seawall in Belize City is the hotel Château Caribbean. It has served as a private home and as a hospital, and now its broad Victorian verandas and wide entrance cause the wilted tropical traveler to sigh with relief. Two old parlours downstairs comprise the lobby, an unutterably clumsy word to apply to the airy rooms with tall slender side doors that give onto the verandas and frame views of white balustrades and a hulk of pelicans. The surface of this sea is what prompted Elizabeth Bishop—an epistemological skeptic, and therefore one of the best poets on the solace of seeing—to say that "the sea is 'all a case of knives.'" Face to face with this sea, one realizes that it is entirely without malice. Although as glittering as knives, it simply is the sea, an enormous fact that requires of us certain respectful approaches, no more or less arduous than the approaches of friendship or romantic love. This hotel architecture embodies such an approach: narrow windows punctuate the dim interior and operate on the brilliant sea like narrow-slitted Eskimo snow glasses on a blinding expanse of white, allowing just a tolerable slice of the gleaming blade into the hotel.

The room upstairs is air-conditioned, fiercely so, by a jumbo, rusty metal box that dangles out the window overlooking a city park. By six o'clock in the evening, the sun has backed off a little. The sand lot with wind-worn palm trees is now inhabited by three social groups. Handsome young men are playing soccer, many of them Rastafarians with dreadlocks flying and the lion of Judah on their chests; girls are learning what is ostensibly a cheerleading routine, but which one instantly recognizes as an old dance, some vestige of which has movingly survived among the population. The girls range in age from about ten to sixteen, with one toddler toddling the distinctive syncopated rhythm of the dance. It is a subtle, elegant dance whose theme might be stated as "the older girls teach the younger girls how to move." Like most African-Caribbean dances, this one is discreet, the hesitations contain the sensual knowledge, and an occasional full body ripple reveals the joy of being alive, supple, and female.

While the young men pursue a soccer ball and the young women synchronize their hips, they are framed by an unsteady pair, one on either side of the great dance—an old man and his grandson playing a kite game that goes like this: the old man holds the reel of an airborne kite, the boy runs with his hand around the string, bringing the kite close to the ground, turns, and looks gravely at his grandpa. With huge smiles and gestures, the old man encourages the boy to release the string. The kite leaps into the sky like a jack-in-the-box, whereupon both players collapse in hilarity. The rule is that the game goes on indefinitely, for as long as boys want to run down kite strings. Seeing these three ancient games in a bleached-out park just before sundown, I feel not far from home. (Of course, colonizing space is terribly exciting, as are the silver cadet suits we would wear. Heaven knows, every barefoot summer of my youth, I scanned the constellations, inviting a saucer to glow down on the damp backyard grass.)

Pictures of the scarlet tanager, magnolia warbler, and rose-breasted grosbeak plainly appear in field guides to the birds of eastern North America, and in New England we think of them as *our* birds. In truth they are tropical creatures who live eight months in the Central American rainforests, visiting our area only to breed. It is a good scheme, for in the tropics food is steadily present but never plentiful, while in New England the abundant food needed for nesting is available, but only during the summer. By their ingenious adaptation, winged creatures have long grasped that tropical forests and northern meadows are interrelated habitats, and lately our clever species has begun to gain the bird's-eye view. Do we all have this view as children? The family globe sat on our father's desk, lit from within by a small bulb. I was seven the night I sat turning the light on and off, watching continents shed national borders, seeing mountains unite and rivers and canyons define the puzzle shapes of the world. The globe had lured me into the long conversation; it was the beginning of wondering about representation and being, scale and magnification, parts and wholes, and whether ideas and political lines are natural no less than beeswax and whales. The conversation has by now suggested to me, as to many others, that while the eccentric theatres called nation-states and their divers customs are the human equivalent of rainforests and barrier reefs, there are no national solutions to aligning the humans with a seamless planet.

This was Jim Baird's view when he and Jerry Bertrand launched Programme for Belize from a dell in Massachusetts, saying, "It does no good whatsoever to protect the areas in Massachusetts where wood thrushes nest if when the wood thrushes leave here, they have no place to go." The two men were vice president and president respectively of the Massachusetts Audubon Society, which had been assisting its Belizean counterpart for several years, helping the group become a stronger voice for conservation in the land where New England birds overwinter. When Audubon leaders realized that a conservation project was welcome in Belize, they initiated negotiations between the government and private landowners, a patient effort under Jim Baird's guidance that has led to three hundred thousand acres of adjacent forest preserves. Inspired by the global eye, such schemes occur squarely within political lines. An editorial that appears in *The Belize Times* just days after we arrive in the country reminds one how carefully wrought must be projects that negotiate between firm political lines and invisible ecological borders:

> It seems that some organization in Massachusetts is going around the USA begging for money from children or anyone else it can catch to raise money to purchase . . . land in Belize. . . . The intention of these gifts may be perfectly altruistic. The generosity of these givers must indeed be rewarded in heaven. But something seems to be wrong when foreigners are donating Belizean land to Belizeans. Something must be wrong when our farmers are short of land and need to accept from people in another country gifts of land in their own country in order to make a living. There is something undignified and degrading and shameful about all this. Does our government care nothing for the dignity of our people and the reputation of our country?

Three years later, in his backyard in rural Massachusetts, I ask Jim Baird about the editorial and how the Programme has fared. As we talk, Belize City is filled with parades, dancing, and speechmaking; four beautiful stamps have just been issued from the Philatelic Office, naming as heroes men who led revolts and hastened freedom. It is September 21, 1991, the tenth anniversary of independence. Jim tells me that the editorial touched a deep nerve of indignation among Belizeans, namely the historical control of their land by foreigners, but was largely a political jibe against the opposition party. When the People's United Party, which issued the editorial, returned to power it not only continued but strengthened the Programme, which has become a Belizean-run enterprise. The Programme has a fifteen person staff and a research station, and is attempting to discover just what sustained-yield management of a tropical forest *is*. The former editor of the *National Geographic* has proposed a regional plan called *La Ruta Maya* that will link parks in Guatemala and Mexico with the Río Bravo lands, creating something comparable to East Africa's Serengeti Park. Such plans have altered regional dynamics and helped prompt Guatemala and Belize to settle their centuries-old border dispute.

While in Belize, I so viscerally felt that everyday life warrants material change that upon return to Cambridge my reaction was palpable relief: joy to find roads with signs, telephones that work, bathtubs without large insects, boat and bus schedules that mean something. Now, as Jim and I reflect on Belizean realities, something rises in me to praise the dotty unpredictability that speaks of another force in life. Staring at the doubleness of my reactions, I recognize the old play. One can see the conundrum for those of us who fancy ourselves friends of the Earth. Belize offers a living three-dimensional riddle about order: what it really is, what place it has in our affections, what ideas of human order most beautifully align with our surround. A merely tenuous human order is doubtless not a viable scheme; at present, Belize exists in a flukish window between the collapse of two successive, non-sustainable orders and the delayed imposition of another. (Who is not given pause by knowing that this tropical landscape has shed so many ideas of human order?) Now, the more astute of the emerging countries wonder out loud whether economic development means acquiring the ecological and psychological wounds of the West. And while no one denies that by industrial standards Belize is poor, as forests, animals, plants, clean water and good air begin to vanish, they are newly included in the definition of wealth. By this gauge, Belize is already rich. Programme for Belize, which responds to these puzzles as well as any effort can, is asking the huge questions about humans on the Earth.

It is surely one of history's symmetries that Jim Baird is a full-fledged Scot, born in Glasgow, that four hundred and fifty years after pirate Peter Wallace launched the European misadventures in Mesoamerica, another Scotsman, working at the top of his game, has been able to touch the region with a healing hand. The scale of Baird's work notwithstanding, there is nothing grandiose about the man. He conveys a natural refusal to consider his efforts out of the ordinary, embodying the daily decency, *la decenza quotidiana*, that the poet Eugenio Montale rightly names "the hardest of all virtues." As we talk into the afternoon, I am also given a glimpse of his attention to modest particularity. Every hour on the hour, Jim gets up from his chair, slings binoculars over one shoulder and sets off at a brisk clip. "Want to come?" he asks each time. I always do, following him through late-August meadows heavy with gold-enrod and fading grasses, past the compost heap from which volunteer tomatoes flop, to the edge of a woods where he has strung three Japanese mist nets. The nets are a fine, supple black material with folds that fall into pocket-like troughs where a bird that flies into the net will be briefly trapped for banding. No birds appear in the nets any of the hours during my visit, but if there was a bird, Jim would cup it in a carrying case and take it to his banding shack, where two simple scales hang from the ceiling, each with a small leather cone into which the bird to be weighed is briefly tucked. The slender, dark leather cones are something from Brueghel paintings and you cannot look at the pointed cones without feeling the bird's fast-beating heart, its certain confusion. Not so, says Baird. "If considered anthropomorphically, you would have to say that a bird lives in a state of constant apprehension arising from ever present dangers such as being et by hawks." Baird tells me that while a bird experiences modest trauma during banding and retains a brief memory of its experience, the impact is minimal. "When I release a bird," he says, "it is almost as good as when I caught it."

Over the banding table dangle what appear to be rare African necklaces but are long strings of bird bands in two sizes: tiny and much tinier. The worktable also holds a small black notebook in which Jim records data about each bird: size, weight, date of banding, age. How does he know the age of a bird? On a scrap of a brown paper bag, Jim draws a bird's skull, a quick, precise drawing in cross-section, handsome in its search to understand. One thin pencil line marks the outer arc of bone; another line indicates an inner arc of bone beneath the surface. Finally he fills in the space between the two bone arcs with marks that make the whole skull assembly resemble a suspension bridge. The sequence of marks traces the sequence of development of a bird's head. It seems that a young bird's skull is at first comprised of the single outer layer of bone. As the bird matures, a second layer grows, and then pillars of bone grow between the two, connecting and reinforcing, making a skull that is thick and strong and at the same time very light. The ossification takes place centripetally—that is, growing inwards from the outer edges of the two hemispheres of the bird's brain. By fall, only a small window of unossified skull remains. Another feature of bird anatomy allows one to observe the status of the head bones. Underneath its feathers, the skin of a bird's head is transparent: merely by wetting the tiny head and parting the feathers with his finger, Jim can see inside the skull. If he sees tiny white dots, he is observing the ends of strengthening pillars in the skull of a mature bird. If instead he sees a pink field of tissue, he is looking directly at the brain of an immature bird.

When we leave the banding shack, it is about three o'clock in the afternoon. The sun warms; the air is squeeky as an apple and alive with hints of the coming fall; crickets and wind rustle through the bending grasses, but no bird calls from any of the oaks and sugar maples that encircle the hut. The small notebook gives the news: from the middle of August through early September, not a single redstart has come to the net; one red-eyed vireo flew by, one black and white warbler, and six ovenbirds. These numbers record a stunning decline of our New England/Central American song-birds, losses traceable to forest cutting on both ends of the migratory route as birds seek and do not find the trees in which they have previously nested.[25] The flights of banded birds and the numbers they yield are markers in a welter of data that joins continents, maples, silk-cottons, and seasons—a mingling of species' intelligence that culls along the lines of a shared reality. Interpreting the songbird numbers, Jim Baird uses the phrase "imminent collapse," speaking in the even timbre that rises from immersion in the hardest of all virtues.

At the station Skiffs leave Belize City for the offshore cayes at unpredictable times from moorings next to a Shell marine fuel station on Haulover Creek, whose water at this point is black as the asphalt and shimmers with the same rainbow of oil as the pools spilled near the station pumps. The city's open sewage canal runs alongside the shed at one end of the station and empties into the river at just this point. A foul odour emanates from the canal, but drizzling rain brings most passengers under the roof of the shed and under the canal's noxious thrall. None of us dares leave the station for even a moment; such folly would only prompt the skiff to arrive in our absence, so we steadily endure the afflictions of tropical weather and each other. Waiting for skiffs this morning are a platoon of off-duty Canadian sailors who are beginning to crack beers, and two women in paramilitary camouflage pants, hunting knives on their belts, tee shirts announcing the days of males are numbered. On the other side of the station, outside and near the river, under the marina's tiny roof overhang, is most of a Maya family: the mother and five shiny children arrayed around her full cotton skirts like a set of nesting dolls. Over the many hours that we all wait for skiffs, the children never once cry out or run around the station; even the toddlers are patient as old animals, brown eyes luminous under straight, dark bangs, closing at times in sleep. There is also an assemblage of bare-chested young Creole men in oil-stained pants who want to jive someone, anyone, especially the two gay women. There is a character out of a Graham Greene novel, a seedy man with a faintly Canadian accent, whose story, one feels instinctively, has something to do with a racetrack and bourbon. There are two young Mestizo boys, about twelve, in short-sleeve dress shirts, carrying knapsacks from which protrude books and fishing gear.

The atmosphere in the marina station is moody, oily, and raw. For solidarity, Katherine and I gravitate toward the other two traveling women, and are well into a conversation about their adventures in the Guatemalan jungle (matriarchal socialism among the ruins is the general idea) when the two leap up, responding to the Creole men's taunts by unsheathing knives and a venomous rhetoric. The men reply by swaggering closer in a lewd line dance. As the two camps bare their teeth and advance, Katherine pales and sinks to the ground, an unpremeditated act which—surprisingly—diffuses the situation. Everyone puts their knives and egos back in their cases, and though they clearly need no physical protection, we persuade our fierce sisters to "take some fresh air" and resettle with us on the sea wall, not far from the twelve-year-old boys who have mastered the trick of being left alone.

An hour passes with neither skiffs, nor torrential rain, nor gender wars. The sun comes out; the Maya children stare silently at the river. We turn to books to pass the time. Katherine reaches for her volume on Rome—brought as a stay against the tropics—adjusts her eyeglasses at the same time, and promptly knocks the latter into the open sewer of the river.

"Well," she says, "I am blind."

"Blind?" I ask.

"For all intents and purposes," she says formally, with the calm of the suddenly, catastrophically resigned, "blind. For example, I cannot make out where the river is. Can you see the glasses? Are they floating?"

They are not floating. We stare sadly, me into the murky soup, Katherine into something murkier yet. Everyone, save the tactful, insular Maya, gathers to laugh, commiserate, or just see what will happen. From the gang of bobbing Creole men emerges one scrawny, barefoot fellow, maybe twenty years old. All morning he has been the butt of jokes by the other men, who consider him a pest not worthy of inclusion in their circle. His name is Cecil and his face has the waxy, innocent look of some very brilliant, aging scientists, or of people who have been ill for a long time. He prances up to us, announcing that he will dive into the river of sewage and search for the glasses.

"Is it safe?" we ask.

He puffs out his chest. "I will do it."

Even the bullies are quieted by Cecil's proposal. He strips off his shirt and slips into the filthy gruel, here about four feet deep. Someone throws him a pair of underwater goggles. After ten minutes of diving, feeling with his feet, diving again, Cecil comes up with Katherine's glasses in one hand, his body dripping with dank sediment. Everyone cheers and laughs; even the Maya are smiling and Katherine seems about to swoon again—with happiness. Cecil struts up to her and proudly presents the dripping glasses as the wharf rats give their grudging approval. We thank Cecil profusely, glad to help his elevation. He has not asked for money, but we expect to offer him some, and he now hovers as artfully as a hotel porter. On the way to the station washroom, where we insist that he rinse with hot water and soap, he names his price and we pay it. We praise him again in front of the still-watching gang and make him promise to go to a doctor for an antibiotic. He points out that medicine will cost more money; we give it without hesitation. Katherine washes her glasses in the washroom for about an hour, and when she comes out the skiff to Caye Caulker arrives.

Some days later, back in Belize City, Cecil comes to our guest house and shows us an envelope of small red pills that the doctor has given him so that he will not get sick from the water. The pills are very expensive, Cecil says, looking theatrically mournful. The choice is between seeming to be mildly duped or abandoning someone who did us a great favor because he was lowest on the pecking order and who would never have considered such a thing if he had anything resembling a promising hope in life. It is not much of a choice. We give Cecil twice what he asks for and tell him to get more pills if he needs them. Traveling in places like Belize offers one a steady stream of ethical conundrums. Perhaps we have encouraged Cecil to consider future Americans as dimwitted customers? But surely we forfeited the right to resist his pleas and to another kind of relationship the instant we allowed him to dive into the open sewer? Yet stopping him would have been tantamount to patronizing him? And so on. We see Cecil one more time just before we leave Belize; he comes for a visit on the veranda and we can tell at once that he has come only to bask one more time in rare praise, to hear us use the word "hero" again. To have stumbled into this drama while waiting for the boat to Caye Caulker is especially instructive because the people of Caulker have organized a fishing cooperative that brings them economic well-being and independence from unwanted influence.

T he two young boys at the marine gas station are natives of Caye Caulker, on their way home. They settle next to us onto the plank seat of the skiff and are pleased to tell us about their island for the duration of the boat ride. The water is choppy and a storm is brewing—the skies massing with dark, charcoal-grey thunderheads, glints of silvery light at the horizon, the first rain in a month. The skipper heads the boat straight for the caye, twenty-one miles northeast of Belize City, eleven miles offshore, and keeps his boat at full throttle hoping to outrun the storm. The wind flattens our hair and the unmuffled decibel level palpably inhabits the skiff. Used to the sea and boats and engines, Bepo and Thomas converse as though we are in a parlour. They tell me that they are native islanders, *jicaqueños*, and like most islanders they are Mestizos. They don't say so, but this means that they are

On the caye

descendents of refugees who fled from *la guerra de las castas*, the mid-nineteenth century misadventure by the remaining Maya of Yucatán to reassert their territorial heritage, which began with a massacre of their Spanish Creole and Mestizo neighbors. The boys speak fluent Spanish, English, and Creole. Thomas is studying to be a mathematician and he loves computers (to practice his skills he will likely join the brain drain that routinely robs Belize of skilled technicians, educators, and managers); Bepo likes fishing. Both boys have the grace and self-confidence characteristic of their community. When we reach the caye, they direct us to a minute shack with a room to let—where a pet monkey nearly bites the traveler's ear off by way of greeting—and they invite us to meet them after evening church services, when they will introduce us to their Uncle Rojilio.

The caye on which we are walking is a coral outcropping, a place where the top of a coral ridge has emerged above the surface of the sea. By the action of plants, oxygen, and animals, the bony coral surface has developed a layer of soil and the momentary geological appearance of something more solid than the surrounding wash of tides. By five o'clock in the afternoon, the storm has passed, and when we emerge to circumnavigate the island, we encounter several young girls walking barefoot in clumps along the sand paths, carrying tin pans of their mothers' powder bun biscuits and chocolate-coconut tarts to neighbors' houses, the warm breads and sweets wrapped in cotton cloths. The round metal pans are dented, and the sides burst with light from the sliding red sun. As we pass the girls they nod to us calmly, moving like dancers down the sand, with a baked perfume streaming behind them. Sand paths are the only streets on the island, two long ones that make Front and Back streets, on the windward and leeward sides of the island respectively, and several short paths that cross the main ones. Sand muffles our footfalls. There are no motor vehicles; the only sounds are from the wind rustling palm fronds, women calling their children, the evensong of birds. Houses are very like the mainland houses along the river: wooden and squarish, raised ten feet off the ground on stilts, with zinc roofs and paint that lingers in uneven thin sheets over exposed, weathered wood. Beside each house is a large wooden rain barrel; underneath the houses are such things as washing machines and baskets full of fishing gear and clothes. After nightfall, as we set out for the church, the paths are cool and the dark sky is framed by yet darker, blowsy palms scratching roofs as a wind sweeps across the island.

The church is a small cement-block building whose main room has perhaps nine short pews. The congregation has dispersed save for a few souls standing in the doorway, talking, with prayer books under their arms. From the path where we stand, the interior glows with a yellow-orange light against the black streets and thicket of bushes. The boys appear and show us to the outdoor café, where we drink coconut sodas and wait for their Uncle Rojilio. From the café kitchen comes the evening programming of Radio Belize—tonight fundé drums of a lanky reggae, deceptively simple pressure drops from Kingston, at times punctuated by a melodious voice broadcasting news of deaths and local events from one region of the land to another. In the café, people do not pause in conversation to hear the notices, but elsewhere islanders listen closely to the bulletins. Rojilio arrives, sixtyish, white-haired, and, because the boys have told him that we are poets, with his copy of *The Star Apple Kingdom* by the Caribbean poet Derek Walcott. We order local Belikan-brand beers and more coconut sodas for Bepo and Thomas. "I have only one theme," Rojilio says, reading from "The Schooner Flight,"

> The bowsprit, the arrow, the longing, the lunging heart—
> the flight to a target whose aim we'll never know,
> vain search for one island that heals with its harbor
> and a guiltless horizon, where the almond's shadow
> doesn't injure the sand . . .

Derek himself is an unsurpassed reader, but even he might defer as his poetry rolls into the air twenty feet from the sea, the night before the full moon, from a fisherman's lips:

> My first friend was the sea. Now, is my last . . .
> I try to forget what happiness was, and when that don't
>   work, I study the stars.
> Sometimes is just me, and the soft-scissored foam
> as the deck turn white and the moon open

a cloud like a door, and the light over me
is a road in white moonlight taking me home.

It is an impeccable welcoming gesture; here as elsewhere in
Belize we are moved by the delight in learning that gives rise to an
astonishing literacy rate of ninety percent. When the talk turns
from poetry to the fishing cooperative of which Rojilio is a member, I wonder aloud, "How do islanders come to be so indepen-
dent?" "It is the way we are," he replies, artfully suggesting that my
question is backwards, that autonomy is the original state. It also
helps that this peppercorn of a caye is so remote as to have been
invisible to colonial merchants, and that it is located amongst some
of the most plentiful lobster-fishing grounds on the planet. "Bugs,"
Rojilio calls the clawless, spiny lobsters that resemble the crayfish
who swam through the cold creeks of Tennessee and into my
youthful collecting jar. At first, fishing for bugs was only a supple-
ment to work on the coconut plantations, but by the 1920s workers
could make a living selling lobster to foreign exporters in Belize
City.[26] In the 1950s, when an American company named Del
Caribe Fisheries bought out other exporting companies and fixed
prices below market rates, the fishermen remembered Father Ga-
ney. A decade earlier the Jesuit priest had suggested that the
jicaqueños start a fishing cooperative, and now they saw that the
time had come. In the summer of 1960, the fishermen boycotted
Del Caribe and demanded their own export license from the colonial government. They had a powerful ally: Bucher Scott of Baymen Fisheries in Belize City kept their lobsters fresh in his freezers
until the fishermen prevailed. Since that time, the cooperative has
gained control of processing, packing, and marketing its fish and
lobster catches; it sends likely members to management programs
and produces healthy incomes for islanders. It would seem that
sand streets and modest houses are choices made by people who
believe themselves to be among the wealthiest communities in
Central America.

It is a happy story, and yet in his account Rojilio does not
mention something that anthropologist Anne Sutherland noticed
in her years studying and admiring the island. The economic well-
being of Caye Caulker is entirely controlled by men; there are no

women in the fishing cooperative and until the recent increase in tourism made it profitable for women to let rooms to guests, island women have had no economic independence. One man, whose son chooses not to fish and whose daughter is naturally gifted with boats and lines, told Anne Sutherland rather sadly, "She loves to work with me when I go out. She handles the sails and loves to fish. Too bad she can never make a living from fishing."[27]

Bepo and Thomas are asleep with their heads on the table. We say goodnight and poke back to our landlady's shack along a dim sand road. As we walk, scuttling sounds issue from the foliage along the paths, and we glimpse backs and legs of large crabs whose claws scrape the dry underbrush. In our room there are two cots, one chair, a hurricane lamp, a mosquito coil, and a small mirror. We fall asleep to an antiphonal chorus of changing rhythms made by the least of creatures rubbing their thousand wings through the night, perfectly in synch.

A t the glimmer of dawn the throaty, full-textured, tropical morningsong of the birds lets loose—lunatic calls of an operatic soprano rushing up and down the scale, vast choruses of twittering small birds, and rogue contraltos and tuneless wonders on sound escapades of their own. Birds sit directly outside the wooden shutters, in a miniature forest of coconut palms and papayas and one lime tree swaying over a sprawling hedge of blooming bougainvillea. Rojilio has warned us that boats to the nearby reef leave early, so we stumble down the windward path; along the way we pass a woman raking her sandyard, smoothing the grains into grooved patterns that resemble a meditation garden. From the open windows of the neighborhood come smells of fried dough breads called journey cakes, and the slap slap of flour tortillas being shaped. Here and there, a stream of shower water flows from the bottom of a house, just as it did during our own morning showers, into a catchbasin on the ground. (Later in the day, our landlady will reuse the water for her small terraced jungle.) The house we are looking for is a tiny, weathered shack with a large painted sign leaning against the porch rail: YOGURT, TAPES, GAMOOSA'S MASK & FIN RENTALS. Inside there is Martha, who sells us a breakfast of homemade yogurt and cups of tea. The yogurt is an

Gamoosa and Martha

inedible custard, the tea so strong it bolts my spine upright. Martha is an expatriate American, eager to wax lyric about island life, a dream (she says) compared to New Jersey where her parents live, the ones who disowned her for moving into this shack with Gamoosa, but that is their trip and life in the U.S. is frantic and expensive and a person cannot be really free like you can here where the ocean is just outside the door and where really you have everything you need. Martha pauses briefly to sweep her hand around the room.

One wall is floor-to-ceiling cassette tapes, another is formed entirely of radios and speakers, with wires dangling from one to the other in intricate swirls and loops. Off the main room is another, divided from it by a tie-dyed sheet, from behind which comes the pleasant smell of marijuana.

"Mart—" a deep voice calls from behind the pattern. Martha leaps from her chair, smiling conspiratorially at us.

"That's Gamoosa," she says unnecessarily. As she pulls the curtain aside to enter, there is a quick view of a tall man sprawled on a couch.

Instantly Martha is back, turning the reggae volume, already booming, up another notch. She sits down again at the table in her print housedress, asks if we would like the recipe for the clotted yogurt. Agreeing with Martha about the desirable nearness and beauty of the sea and the satisfactions of the community, we cannot shake the first-blush impression that her domestic situation closely resembles that of a 1950s housewife in, say, New Jersey—Briarwood pipe and proffered newspaper transmogrified into spliffs and reggae. We instantly like Martha and are astonished by this instance of the human mind's ability to make the French right, that is, *plus ça change,* . . . After carefully copying the yogurt recipe into our notebooks, we rent fins and masks and make our way down to the dock. It is still early, the air is cool, no one is in sight. We sit on the end of the dock and look out toward the reef.

Partly due to the voracious feeding habits of the crown-of-thorns starfish, many parts of the Great Barrier Reef of Australia are dead; one veteran naturalist in Belize thinks that makes the Caribbean's the largest living reef on the planet. Moreover, he speculates that since the polyps that make up a coral reef are best understood as one interrelated organism, the Caribbean reef is the largest living thing on the planet. Biologists find this idea provocative and controversial; there is new uncertainty about what exactly constitutes an organism, ranging from the view that the physical outlines of an organism are the extent of its being to the notion that the planet itself has some properties of an organism. We are pondering these points when the skipper arrives—to our surprise, the risen Gamoosa. We are even more surprised when fifteen vacationing American college students straggle down the dock and clamber aboard his small, wooden, handbuilt sailboat, whose heavy canvas sails are an ivory color, stitched along the sides in patches like an old quilt. At ten o'clock we set sail on what Gamoosa describes as "a three-hour cruise." (When he says it, the phrase does not recall for me the theme song from "Gilligan's Island," but by midnight, as the sparse lights of the Caye Caulker dock are faintly coming into view again, we have had ample time to remember all the lyrics of the shipwreck sitcom and to ponder other disasters at sea.)

Our disaster involves a boatload of young persons to whom the idea of swimming about what is possibly the largest living thing on the planet is not sufficiently thrilling without large doses of other stimulants.[28] As the students drink tequila, pass spliffs, and swallow an assortment of white tablets, Katherine and I gradually become the only two clear-eyed persons aboard. Gamoosa and his helmsmate Kavo had arrived at the dock mildly stoned, but from observing Rastafarian ways on Jamaica and elsewhere, I considered their condition neutral to good, the permanently mellow Rasta mind that gets on well enough. Kavo spends the seaborne hours languishing supine (half-hidden in the small hold, apparently dead or dying, like the figure in Homer's "Gulf Stream" sloop, only his forearm and an occasional flash of an eye visible), but on the reef he comes alive, a kindly guide and master of tapping one gently on the arm to point out a shy Hamlet or harlequin pipefish. Gamoosa has no trouble navigating his boat to the three-thousand-acre Hol Chan Marine Preserve, where fish are protected and have responded sensibly by swarming there in luscious schools of color. But the expedition is vastly prolonged when Gamoosa yields to our shipmates' pleas to stop on Ambergris Caye to load up on more substances, and made very sad by the eventual collapse of one youngster in an overdose. We do what we can to help revive him, and then we sit on the deck under a full and luminous moon watching the black sea.

How easily one thing turns into another, yet only grudgingly do I exchange my hopes of a naturalist's idyll for the unfolding reality. The day and night of Gamoosa's reef trip demands from us grueling diplomacy, pained endurance, and reliance on imaginative resources. As ever, the latter are liberally supplied by Katherine. My favorite moment occurs when a young woman, who has been stranded a hundred yards off Ambergris Caye on her windsurfer, is hauled aboard our ship, and Katherine cautions her, sotto voce, that she is "boarding a Melvillian nightmare," that far from delivering her, the ship is "a Coleridgian fate." The young woman, apparently not a student of the sea, stares blankly at Katherine with eyes like those of a well-fed puppy. "Say what?" she finally replies in a broad Texas drawl before turning away and brightly announcing to the others that she is "here to party." Only the presence of Gamoosa and Kavo make us feel that we will not be thrown to the sharks by this effluence of our own dear country.

A fraction of the voyage resembles my expectations—two hours at the reef itself in waters clear as air, whose colours wash memory cobalt and turquoise, magenta and rose-red. We drop anchor to swim near the reef crest, where the lagoon floor rises from twenty feet to only inches deep. Beyond this zone, the floor drops four thousand feet into what the Caye Caulker fishermen call, simply, "the blue." These contrasting depths indicate the geomorphology of a barrier reef and the lagoon created between reef and shore. Shallow just offshore, the water grows slightly deeper before becoming shallow again as the reef rises; once past the reef crest, the breaker zone called the *palmata*, the floor slopes abruptly down terraces and escarpments of the fore-reef, finally plunging down a vertical cliff.

Over the barely submerged *palmata* crest corals, combers roll in and break with full force, snapping brittle elkhorn corals during storms and always creating a surreal surfline that from any distance crashes for no apparent reason on no apparent shore. When a large wave breaks, a rush of water pulses through the underwater architecture, ruffles the sandfloor, swirls the waving arms of plants, and easily hurls a human body into the nearest coral skeleton. When such a wave seems imminent, it is wise to swim free of the branching alleyways of elkhorn coral and to hover, somewhat more safely, in the rubble zone over the large, freestanding grey-brown lumps called brain corals—roundish beings that look just as you would imagine, surfaces roiling in convoluted patterns. Less beautiful and prickly than their brilliantly coloured kin, they nevertheless produce a fine souvenir: the brain coral scar on my knee, obtained while twisting between thick outcroppings of staghorn corals—trying to avoid fire corals, remembering that the human body is too large to trigger a barracuda's feeding instincts, trying to breathe through a tube and not gasp at the sight of harmless nurse sharks—in order to get close to a school of huge fish, serene, platter-like beings, each one three feet long, mere inches thick, coated in yellow-green scales shimmering with flecks of red and azure blue. As they swim, all five turn as one, gliding adroitly as sheets of paper through the intricate corridors of coral structures.

Nothing on either side of the border where air and water meet is more astonishing than the demarcation itself, a line both fluid and firm, depending on whether one is a ray of light, a sailfish, a sponge, or a harlequin brittle star. Position the eyes of the air-loving, briny body at the line: a hairbreadth upwards blue meets blue in a calm expanse, down a mite swarms the baroque panoply not predictable from the tranquil surface. The human talent for likening is everywhere in the given names of what we admire growing, swimming, oozing, and undulating underwater. Here are merman's shaving brushes, fans, feathers, puddingwives, cucumbers, eggs, and urchins, stiff pens, whips, umbrellas, wasps, walnuts, girdles, and encrusting colonials. Corals are named for fingers, cacti, stars, pillars, flowers, elks, starlets, stags, plumes, candelabras, boulders, deadmen's fingers, lettuce leaves, and sun's rays. Sponges are black chimneys, orange softballs, stinking pillows and vases, chicken livers, and lavender tubes. Like their dry namesakes, underwater brains can be common, large-grooved, depressed, or tan. Worms are elegant, magnificent, luminescent, Christmas, and Medusa. In the lavish waters, we see no phytoplankton, and would not even if our snorkeling masks were fitted with microscopes; how startling to learn that the blue clarity of tropical waters is a sign that the nutritious green algae are but sparsely present in the water itself, that to find the "meadows of the sea," we must go to temperate and polar waters.[29] How can it be that the vibrant reefworlds exist without this vital biomass of clorophyll? A mystery was solved when the brothers Eugene and Howard Odum found that on tropical reefs, biomass occurs in sand-dwelling bottom algae, in the algae that encrusts dead coral, and in the coral polyps themselves: by one of those arrangements that suggest humans could learn a thing or two about inventiveness, an algae named *zooxanthellae* inhabits the coral polyp, feeds it, and becomes nearly half its weight.

Living national treasure

There is another boat to take in Belize, namely the surplus skiff that glides through the waters of Crooked Tree Wildlife Sanctuary, skippered by John Jex (pronounced "Jakes"), a man who, if he lived in Japan, would be named a "living national treasure." One needs good, trained eyes in the lagoon and Jex's eyes are better than binoculars. As we pass stretches of unrelieved green jungle, apparently only vines and tangles of vegetation in truly alarming profusion, Jex slows his skiff, now to point out a rare black-collared hawk astride a treetop, then a clump of trees where, dotted like shadows among the green, sleeps a troop of what Jex calls baboons. With the motor turned off, the boat drifts silently under the limbs where the creatures languorously droop and sprawl. When we are just underneath the troop, two baboons wake up and swing closer to gaze back at us. Natural history nomenclature in Belize, even more idiosyncratic than most local lexicons, arises from a mingling of diverse languages of settlers and pirates, from memories of distant floras and faunas, and from mistaken identities. Here, jaguars are tigers, moths are bats, bats are rat bats; the boa constrictor is a wowla, great blue herons are Toby full pots, green-backed herons are poor Joes; storks are Turks; grackles, blackbirds; the tapir is a mountain cow; the basilisk lizard is the cock makala; agouti are rabbits, scaley-tailed iguanas are wish-willys.

And what to official taxonomy is the black howler monkey (*Alouatta pigra*, the agile New-World primate unrelated to the larger Old-World baboon) is to Belize a baboon. Black howlers are uncommon, found here and there, in patches, in northern Guatemala, southern Mexico, and Belize, especially in low rainforest regions, in the central river forests, and the Maya Mountain foothills. As these awakened ones swing toward our boat, they make no sound save the light thrashing of branches. If we want to hear the calls that give rise to their standard name, Jex says we must come back late in the evening, in the early morning, or when a rainstorm batters the forest. At those times, he says, the lagoon reverberates with a sound that, in full-grown males, is less a howl than a roar, a bone-chilling sound that novices routinely mistake for tigers—that is, jaguars. They live in small family groups, four to ten members each, and primatologists speculate that the roars that pour from the resonating chambers in the throats of males are signals between rivals and relations, a way of placing each other on a map of sound.

Jex laughs at the youngest howler in this group of six, so sleepy that it seems in danger of sliding off its limb. These monkeys have long endeared themselves to local humans because of their play, their expressive faces, and the adults' devotion to their babies. A thousand years ago, Maya artists were painting the monkeys on ceramic pots as images of divine writing: shaggy hands scribbling on bark paper. Coming from the people who created the most sophisticated written language in the Americas, this image of divinity is either a high compliment or an irony worthy of those modern linguistic theorists who stress the arbitrariness and play-fulness at the root of language. Modern Belizeans are so fond of their baboons that thirty miles southeast of Crooked Tree, Creole farmers and local landowners who live along the Belize River run a community baboon sanctuary. Jex tells us that one thousand howlers live along the riverbanks among stands of figs, hog plums, and sapodillas that comprise the baboon diet. The sanctuary began in Bermudian Landing and has spread to include the villages of Double Head Cabbage, Willow's Bank, Big Falls, Isabella Bank, and Flowers Bank. Ecologist Carolyn Miller reports that there is a waiting list of local landowners who wish to pledge use of their lands for the sanctuary, ensuring that the monkeys have the range and aerial pathways they need for forest travel.[30] It is a sweet-spirited success, the boon of a longstanding rapport. "Baboon ya de fu we," is the local sentiment as expressed in Creole—"Baboons, we are for you!" As Jex moves his boat away from under the howlers' sleeping-tree, a large male in the troop swings down from a branch, balances himself by his prehensile tail, grasps the trunk with his front hands, stretches his shaggy head toward us and opens his mouth, impressing us with two remarkable teeth that jut from his lower jaw at rakish angles. Jex waves and moves away, yielding the territory.

Returning, our boat follows serpentine strips of clear water that thread through water hyacinths and dense mats of overlapping lily pads. Hundreds of red-brown jacanas poke along the thick green pads on thin legs; as we pass, they rise up en masse in clusters of beating wings, a froth of yellow as late sun illuminates the delicate flight feathers of their wings. The motion of the flocks rising and falling back to the lilies is a great breath of the lagoon, inhaling, exhaling. After poking through the waters for hours in the sun, we are now cooling under a shade tree across from the village store, drinking cold sodas and pressing the icy glass to our temples. There are several modern, unpainted cement-block houses nearby (structures that please the villagers and have, to my eye, roughly the charm of a chain-gang barracks), and there is one older-style bush house with a roof thatched with palm leaves and secured by liana vines, "tie-ties," Jex calls them. He is pleased that we have seen the black-collared hawk—*Busarellus nigricollis*, a Belize Audubon field guide tells me. We are lucky, he says. Sometimes birders come from the north, from America, he means, and search the lagoon for a week without seeing this handsome hawk. Jex's tone and expression tell that he is amused that the rare one shows itself to a novice, to someone too ignorant to be astonished. He is a subtle man who favors haiku-like gestures, and he is amused by all of it: the avid birders from an avid culture, the lucky beginner, the unpredictable bird, himself for noticing.

It is early evening, and children are coming to the store for tins of evaporated milk, breads, and fruit to take home for dinner. Passing by our bench, each child gives a courteous nod of the head, saying, "Good evening, Mr. Jex," whereupon the village elder pauses in his story about the woman he calls Miss Dora to reply, "Good evening." Certainly Dora Weyer must consider John Jex a living treasure. She and her husband came to Belize from America in 1960 to research tropical birds, and soon began to envision a sanctuary in the Crooked Tree lagoon, an especially lush area that is wet the year long. She asked Jex to show her the Belize River, Black Creek and Revenge Lagoon, Calabash Pond and Crooked Tree Lagoon itself—the great green and silver maze that Jex knew intimately from a life lived close to the inland waterways. If she was impressed by his knowledge, the compliment was returned. Of these boat trips, Jex says, "Miss Dora called to the birds and brought them to the boat. She whistled an ivory-billed wood creeper right to the boat." After several scouting trips, Jex acquired three skiffs and this cobbled-together arrangement: Dora Weyer lined up naturalists, mostly American birders, to visit Belize, and sent advisory notes ahead of time. As there was then no road into Crooked Tree, Jex picked up the adventurers at a designated time and place along the river, and they set out through the teeming waterways. After many years of this shoestring labor of love, the boat tours for intrepid birders have resulted in sixteen thousand acres being designated the Crooked Tree Wildlife Sanctuary—a going thing with a headquarters building, a brochure, and an outhouse where just as a body sits down a massive frog jumps out of a shadowy corner.

Even at Crooked Tree, Mr. Jex occasionally finds a skinned Morelet's crocodile or its dried skeleton on a sandy bank of the lagoon. Beyond the sanctuary's borders, as throughout the tropics, the poacher's catch-of-the-day will be a crocodile hide, or tropical fish, parakeets, and parrots for sale to pet stores and collectors. Because the scarlet macaw is among the gaudiest beauties of the jungle, it has been hunted down to about one hundred birds. "This Is Their Land Too" read posters tacked up in gas stations, post offices, and little markets throughout Belize. Under a picture of a piglike tapir or a parrot, the words say that it is illegal to kill this creature or to smuggle it out of Belize. At the airport, customs officials take this latter possibility seriously, and my duffel bag, which could conceal a twenty-inch coastal roach, is inspected as though it might contain a tapir. Anyone who dares come to the airport with things packed in boxes might just as well label them ENDANGERED PARROTS INSIDE, so strenuously are they scrutinized by immaculately dressed customs officials whose carriage alone declares that trouble will not be brooked. The only things I bear away are boxes of the death-defying Belizean matches and a brain-coral scar, a fine thing to have on one's knee as a journey shades into the past, and something that elevates one's person in the eyes of small nephews. About three inches 'round, and a precise imprint of a brainy pattern, the wound is less a cut than a brand. Three weeks after my return to New England, the mark has not entirely disappeared, and when I swim in the warm saltwater bay of Peconic on the north fork of Long Island, it comes back to life, leading one to surmise that the controversial, very large living thing has established a new colony.

FOLLOWING
HERMES

That night, as soon as her husband fell asleep, Psyche lighted the lamp and crept to his side. When the light fell on his face she trembled with happiness. There lay Eros, fairest of all the Gods! The longer Psyche gazed at him the more she trembled, and suddenly a drop of oil spilled from the lamp onto Eros' shoulders. He opened his eyes and looked at her sadly and left the palace without a word.

—*The First Book of Mythology,* written and illustrated by Kathleen Elgin

This news first came to me in 1956, in a child's book with endpapers delineating the family tree of the Mediterranean gods. In a full-page illustration opposite the story, Psyche was a wan blond of the times, simpering in a cowl-necked, ruffled gown. But sleeping Eros was timeless, with blue-black curls, chiseled lips and chest. At nine, growing up in a little Southern town in the deceptive stasis of the decade, I neither wondered nor thought to wonder why the picture fairly glowed, drawing and drawing again my gaze. How simply it begins; from household shelves come tumbling Ithaka, golden boughs and pomegranates, democracy, islands of poetry, contrapuntal grace, a domain of the Muse. . . . For a traveler from the West, Greece is finally so saturated in myth, history, art, and ideals that one inevitably journeys in spiritual as well as physical geography, easily entering into *physis*—that indispensable Greek word meaning the active force in nature. Has every traveler to Greece felt this creative power? Perfectly proper people who have will ask a Greece-bound traveler, "Is it your first time?" and the faint nuance in the question is just right. Greece is soaked in, and one reliably encounters the cosmic eros that permeates the silky Aegean, colors blossoms the yellow of monk's robes, and animates the quirky affair that is the human city.

I first set out for the Mediterranean cradle in the summer of 1989 with another peripatetic poet, my friend Katherine; our consorts Peter and Tony are to follow. On the *Olympic Flame*, the other passengers are predominantly Greek-Americans returning to the homeland, and immediately after dinner, they erupt from their seats to roam the aisles patting arms, laughing, showing wallet-crumpled photographs, talking blistering Greek. By the tones of voice, one knows that these passengers are not old friends, nor even acquaintances greeting each other on holiday; rather, the fact of return has made an instant airborne nation of the citizens of the diaspora. Two hours ago, they were morsels in the melting pot, suspended and dilute among tens of American tribes. Now they are the concentrate of a people: the interior of the plane is a homogeneous swath of black shiny heads and dark pools of eyes.

Zooming into the night across the Atlantic, we are already on an island of Greece; when children shriek in joy or misery, their cries are full-lunged, loud, unleashed, unabashed, prolonged Greek wails. One cannot imagine such children aboard Swissair, or KLM, where they would be firmly, gently, humorously, but surely in some way, quieted. In the Greek sky, the mothers and fathers and the surrounding villagers neither wince nor in the mildest way admonish the expressive young citizens, and one sees that the mature social gestures of the roaming adults rest on this base: the piercing, exuberant, announcement of self cultivated in the smallest child. Days later, on the ground in Athens, the fruition of the training will be demonstrated when each night for three successive nights—streaming from the countryside and from all parts of sprawling Athens through the city's alleys and avenues to Omonia Square and Syntagma Center, with Theodorakis music pulsing from enormous walls of audio-speakers, with military and news helicopters circling and beaming light into the polyrhythmed, chanting beast—the *vox populi*, one million Greeks in peak democratic form, prepares for election day.

To picture the Olympic Airways female flight attendants, you must think of the JAL flight attendants, all grace and exquisitely nuanced deference become an art form, and then you must think of the opposite. The Olympic women roll through the aisles snapping seatbacks into full upright positions, hurling food trays, simmering, glaring at, then ignoring requests to locate an air nozzle, to secure a blanket. Eight hours in the air with them recalls how tenuous was the ancient plan by which the Furies are renamed the Eumenides, "the Gentle Ones," and buried beneath the patriarchal city. And now, judging from this glimpse of winged Greek female fury, not resting easy. It would be comfy to have a blanket, and sweet-tempered souls wafting through the pressurized cabin, making it seem more like a living room and less like a flying *hybris* with a slight aluminum skin between humans and the sub-freezing void. Yet, equally to be relished: gorgon-coiffed females in four-inch heels blasting away gracious servitude as when a bomb tears open the side of the plane, sucking out seats and blankets, the little cocktail napkins and complimentary soft drinks.

The short telescoped night of east-bound transatlantic flight occurs: old rosy-fingered dawn blushes outside the windows, and on the Athenian tarmac, five dark blue shuttle buses, each the length of a city bus and staffed with armed military personnel, slide alongside the jumbo jet to convey the passengers a slight twenty yards to the terminal gate. Up to this moment in my life, I have not seen one machine gun. By the time the shuttle bus reaches the terminal I have seen eight Uzis cradled in the arms of eight military troops, serious young lieutenants with taut torsos bolt upright, legs braced apart in the stance of backwater policemen, caps far down over their foreheads. On the armed shuttle a woman, perhaps twenty and from the countryside, has settled onto a molded seat with her infant. This is a mother and child for whom the phrase "tender and mild" is sung. Birth has barely divided their union, and, still symbiotic, they embrace, each permeable skin breathing life into the other. When a grizzled man beams at the unit, the madonna dimples, smiles, still smiling ducks her head, collects herself, then looks up with demure triumph, choosing, one sees, to share her happiness like a good queen. The perfume of the elemental tableaux dizzies the air of the shuttle bus, out whose open windows rest the cradled Uzis. To watch is to have one's head pulse like it will after wine.

These days the journey to Greece is often to sun-'n'-fun resort compounds that hope to eliminate what one Greek resort owner unabashedly calls "the problems outside the hotel"— by which, presumably, he means Greece. It *is* a land of frightful toilets, reckless young men aiming motorcycles at pedestrians, extravagant litter. One eminent classicist whose lifework is an investigation of pre-Socratic literature, will simply no longer actually go to Greece, where the old, sacred sites are overrun by tourists and sullied by misapprehension, where the ancient sounds are lost even to the Greek tongue. In the way of milkweed seeds and nomads, Hellenism is elsewhere. I admire this scholar and his mature, resigned belief that we can neither restore the old pious ways of habitation nor mend our modern world with present technology, that the most we can do is bear witness to a loss and, perhaps, make a clearing in which something new might arise. Still, I have packed Richard Geldard's *Ancient Greece*, in which he dares to say that "the gods have not vacated the holy places. . . . If there has been any vacating, it is our own 'vacation' from the myths of sacredness within ourselves." Traveling with neither a Hellenist's pure vision, nor the wish to loll on a tethered raft in a sanitized compound, I have come to Greece to see what this land has left to say about right habitation. The question has a special charge in Greece because it was here that Western culture proposed not only answers but whole traditions of how to ask.

That the geographies of place and spirit are inseparable is clear from the very beginning. After a hot taxi ride from the airport into Athens, Hermes—the trickster guide to the underworld and god of all travelers—promptly appears. At our hotel the dim lobby has a sepia-toned frieze of archaic figures and fish which runs along the wall just below the ceiling. Along the bottom of the wall runs a living frieze of ripstop nylon duffels and a row of tourists who are not jumping bulls acrobatically but are slumped on suitcases and wearing white sneakers. The desk clerk, Rafael, who booked and twice confirmed our rooms by overseas telephone, is wearing a sweet cologne that fills the room and a humble-pie, fatalistic smile—the kind of smile a traveler does not want to see on a hotel clerk. He says it right out: "I have no room for you." I like the way he does it. It's not an apology, nor in the least cavalier. It is a fact that he delivers, with the dignity and finality of a fact that has been visited upon us all equally by a fact-making apparatus located elsewhere.

Somewhere outside the lobby, in that brilliant sunlight, there exists a deus ex machina who has ordained that Rafael cave in to Greco Tours and give away our reservation. Rafael gets to the better news: he has arranged for a room in a hotel down the street and he will carry our luggage there. Rafael is thin, a Fred Astaire gone to seed, mid-sixties; I think he is wearing a pretty good hairpiece, and he doesn't look like he can carry our luggage even one block. We make a slow procession through the old city at the base of the Acropolis, on the north side. Tired, prickling hot, disappointed, we are just civil to Rafael, and trudge up to the substitute room on the top floor of the small Hotel Plaka, a structure composed of gleaming wood and deep blue paint. Opening the door, we enter the best room-with-a-view in Athens; perfectly aligned with the Acropolis, it has tall casement windows that open wide and frame the temple complex. As we stand mute before the close shimmering marvels, Rafael gives a slim smile and glides away. In a long, ambient sleep from afternoon until early the next morning, we see the temples out the window at every half-waking turn. In the sun they are bleached white; at dusk, the stones meld into the grey blue sky; by night, the limestone hill and marble sanctuaries are flooded in bursts of diamond-bright gold and red light. From eleven until three in the morning, a light rain of songs—music floating from the tavernas outlined in strings of lights and terraced into the slope of the Acropolis. With dawn, the temples are flushed rose, and the Greek flag is being raised.

A thens is toxic with pollution, and not merely ugly but a study in ugliness, a life-size monument to the wretched idea that seized whole cities in the 1950s like an infestation of gypsy moths, stripping the lovely and the old, the settled and the eccentric, leaving behind hideous grey concrete modular cells. The Athens built during the thrall of urban renewal is a city whose poured-concrete architecture calls to mind the solacing observation of Le Corbusier: "There is enough ivy in the world to

Parallel universe

cover all the bad buildings ever built." One delicious patch of the old city was left, like a meatbone thrown to a good dog. This zone is called the Plaka and surrounds the Acropolis in a square mile of the stucco and red tile structures, narrow winding streets, and over-hanging trees and vines that once comprised all of Athens. Here are pale butter-colored dwellings, wrought-iron stairs spiralling up the sides of houses, purple-blue painted doors, flowers spilling from old olive cans and from cracks in the stonework—the great accre-tions.

Outside this oasis, the city is hard to admire. In the face of hideous Athens, I recall the well-known post-travel experience of returning to one's home city and seeing some familiar street as though for the first time. How common, even bleak, the fences, variety stores, and local parks can appear. Between brutalized Athens and this recollection of some raw streets back home springs the arc of an hypothesis, to wit: *the ugliness of an unknown city is greater than the ugliness of a known city.* Perhaps this is because in the known city we are far beyond the hyper-alertness needed in a new place, the need to inscribe each potentially vital navigational and sociological detail. Once one's survival kit reaches a workable level, one may suspend scrutiny of the present scene in favor of the shopping list, latest romantic travail—the endless possibilities. One begins to visually edit a blighted passage for a bolt of beautiful cloth or strip of neon that appeals; one may allow the shop scents of cumin and thyme to color dull walls. And, too, many a lackluster road leads to someone or something whose fair image overlays the physical route. By such familiar alterings are the seedy and sad transformed into the fond known, which is not ugly.

The unknown city, as yet unrelieved by buffers and cushions of memory, gives us a great gift: it opens the senses wide to an undifferentiated, uninterpreted flood. Continually orienting, ab-sorbed, surprised, and by end of day utterly spent, a traveler resem-bles a child. By such ordinary travels on Earth, this kind of child may readily collect evidence for the theory of parallel universes. Gradually the peering and marvelling at "the other" (still hauling goods by mule!! votive shrines in airports!!) smoothly, quietly elides into the quintessential traveler's knowledge: that one's own way, as well as that large assumption *the self*, are as curious, arbitrary, and inevitable as the odd Other. Traveling in some parts, it is even possible for the self to become an other.

Our initial quest is to an appliance store. Athens is a jumbled city, whose merchandizing style has a strain of the middle-Eastern bazaar: sandals, rugs, tables of books, pyramids of food, inexplicable carts of steaming hot charred corn peddled in ninety-degree heat, and racks of clothes take up the slender sidewalks, on which few Athenians walk anyway, most preferring the streets, where they weave among traffic, screaming destinations into the windows of taxis with fares, hoping to piggyback—a custom that sounds energy-efficient and is only horrible, adding to the hustle, making another bit of city life a predator/ prey suspense. Like New York, Athens overstimulates and disorients. Overstimulated and disoriented, returning from the appliance store with a Black & Decker world-wattage blowdryer in hand, we see the tiny shop in whose window is this beguiling display: two skulls—one human, one cow—a basket of tall dried herbs, two candles in the shape of roses, a hefty stack of beeswax and votive candles, a rack of paperback books with illustrations of women and devils licked by flames, and a book on aerobic yoga. We go right in. The shop is cool, dim, eight feet wide, maybe fifteen feet deep, with one long wall lined from top to bottom in dark mahogany drawers, the other wall composed of open shelves stocked with candles, incense, and books. Three women tend the βοτανα (*vo* tahnah), women for whom the word *crone* originated. Ancient they are, stooped, wrinkled, and gnarled, survivor women far beyond the temporal concerns of the young or the middle-aged, or the merely old. All three crones turn ever so slightly to take us in as we enter and then continue what they were doing, which is weighing and measuring amounts of dried and powdered plants into small brown paper bags. Along the back wall are five chairs on which are seated three silent customers. The preparations proceed at a deliberate pace; the crones collect substances from drawers, crush them in a mortar, funnel them into bags, occasionally ask one of the customers a question. The latter, two men and one pale, thin woman, answer in a few, almost inaudible words. The crones look terrifically angry.

The Blowdryer and the βοτανα

Beeswax candles smell like bees and honey, and are the color of honey; they are thin and pliant and sold in banded bundles of one dozen. When I pick up two bundles, the crones give me a hard look, turning slowly in concert to glare uncannily like the three deadpan musicians of Sid Caesar's enigmatic Nairobi Trio. Of the whole dried plants stacked loose in large boxes on the floor, some are recognizable—branches of bay leaves (also called daphne), long wands of oregano, bunches of thyme—and some are unfamiliar. One unknown, labeled only as "mountain tea," is sweet and heady with a tincture of fennel. I select some of these plants to buy, gently prying the stems and leaves from the heap. The crones glare. Bracing myself, I take the herbs up to the crones to be wrapped. Store packaging in Greece is a cultural study in miniature: either the goods are dropped into the thinnest, cheapest possible poly-plastic bag, or they are hand-wrapped, carefully, in a strong paper, often one printed with a floral pattern. If a store hand wraps, even a purchase of five post cards is wrapped as though it were a gift, the paper's ends folded into a triangle and secured with a small square of tape. When one crone finishes compounding her remedy, she takes the candles and herbs from my hands and begins to roll them in heavy pink-brown butcher's paper, making a big bundle flared like a bunch of lilies from a florist.

Bumping so immediately into the βοτανα, I assume that there are many herbal medicine shops in the city. Later, when I mention the βοτανα to a native Athenian who teaches urban planning and architecture at the Polytechnic, she is quite interested. Could I tell her how to get there? She knows of no such shops. I'm surprised the shop is as rare as all that, but it is no surprise that herbalists have become scarce. Plant lore emerges from intimacy with the land and, like great basketball teams, relies on a large, predictable pool of youth who are capable of assuming, perhaps improving, the prac-tice with each generation.

Like traditional healers in all parts of the globe, the βοτανα crones curate a vestige of a paleolithic moral order in which the Earth was alive, figured as a goddess who made the land fertile, received the dead, and caused life to be renewed. Her two great emblems were the serpent and the tree, and in the Mediterranean world her name was Gaia. That something of Gaia lives on, and fiercely, in the βοτανα crones is beyond question. Perhaps the balmy air, light, and waters of southern Christendom have been more tolerant of the *pagani*. Yet everywhere now the survival is slender; while the likes of Henry David Thoreau and John Muir were articulate witnesses of the natural miraculous, such talk has been carefully abandoned by environmentalists as they make their case to a pragmatic, materialist society.[1] As the twentieth century closes, we have no common, respected vocabulary to name and cultivate the experience of an innately valuable Earth. As this being is not recognized by our prevailing worldview, it is difficult to shape language with which to honor and defend it. Even much of ardent environmental talk reduces the planet to a storehouse of raw materials for human use and assumes that value is determined by human needs. We are urged to care about rainforests because they supply sources of medicine for us, because they help keep the Earth's climate congenial for us—though, paradoxically, when the Earth's value is determined merely by changing utilitarian values, the planet and source of our well-being remains at risk of degradation.

Merely standing in this old shop among the crones' pungent plants, one can feel a residual infusion of an older, more intimate rapport with the land. From the drawers of powders, tawny stems, roots, and drying flowerheads rises a subtle, spicy, musty aroma. The quiet meditative mood of the room is a property that mute, generative plants reliably bring to human beings. Rousing myself, I realize that even if I were fluent in Greek, it might not be possible to tell the crones of the βοτανα why they are so moving to me. The very fact that they *are* is an index of the distance between our worlds. Between their furious glares as they sift powders, and my tentative smile is a space of some two thousand years of consciousness. It is our first day in Greece; my only Greek is "F. Harry Stow," a phonetic device for the Greek word for *thank you*. "F. Harry Stow," I say to the crones, who glare, press the flared package of herbs and candles into my hands, turn their stooped collective back, and abruptly Katherine and I are out of the gum-sweet, dark shop, into the grey light of downtown Athens. In hand, we have two lovely products of *physis*: a cone of fragrant, healing herbs which we plan to use along our journey, and a plastic travel blow-dryer, a high-tech artifact that may tame the Gorgona in our appearances.

Acropolis

Much attention is given the marble temples—their scale, grace, and endurance—but compared to the rock on which they rest, the buildings are a delicate filagree. *Acropolis* means "outcropping," and the temples are built on the outcropping because it is an astonishing geophysical event: a mass of coarse semi-crystalline limestone and red schist that abruptly rises five hundred feet from the surrounding plain of land and forms a vertical wall of overhangs and clefts, the summit inaccessible save on its southwest slope. *Chthonic* is the wondrous, onomatopoeic word that my first classics professor used for the forces that produce such upheavals of the Earth. From the city below, the great rock may be seen by chance at any time of the day or night: as one turns a street corner, looks up from the newspaper, sinks into a taverna chair. The hill and its temples are an inescapable constant, dignified even during the gaudy light show that recalls the Venetian powder-keg explosions that reduced the Parthenon to ruins. The rock radiates silently, shimmering above the murmurs of the Plaka and the relentless bouzoukis of the tourist trap cafés, above juntas and mad political coalitions of conservatives and communists, above the clucking evil eye.

For ancient Athenians, the rock was an ideal plateau from which to invite the sky gods into their city. At this time of year, citizens would be approaching the culmination of months of activities that prepared a soul to meet the divinities, the annual summer pilgrimage called the Panathenaia. It was a spectacular procession during which the fierce summer sun might help intensify and shape consciousness for the passage through the Propylaia, the gateway structures which draw the eye steadily upwards.[2] Katherine and I wend up the rock outcropping along the dusty old processional path, putting bundles of bay and sage leaves on likely rocks and retaining walls, where the herbs appear perfectly at home. As we rise, Athens recedes to a patchwork of blinding lights, reflections from hundreds of solar hot-water panels mounted on the flat roofs of the city. The hillside path of the sacred way is strewn with cola cans and sticky popsicle papers crawling with delirious ants. Along the whole route, olive trees twist their trunks in writhing patterns, the sun is unbearably strong, the *maquis* aromatic with scattered pines, rosemary, oleander, and roseberry spurge buzzing with bees. Up close, shrubs reveal large snails, the color of deer, clinging to the inner, shady limbs.

Among the temples, not even a spare-needled pine shades against the sun, and to admire the Parthenon the head must be constantly tilted upward toward the light. It was easier to study this grandeur in the slide lectures of art school, where the temple was a wall-size rectangle of light glowing in the dark. Beside the edifice, one feels off balance, dwarfed, in danger of falling backwards, the body a minute irrelevance. Properly awed, I am more drawn to the small Erechtheion, the sanctuary whose south porch is supported by the six famous stone women, the Karyatides. The image of endurance, these statues weathered two thousand four hundred years of time, invasions, and the blasphemous use of their pagan temple as church, harem, and military powder magazine. When they succumbed it was to the lightest medium; in the 1960s, Athenian air grew so corrosive that their eyes, noses, gowns, and thick braids were dissolving. Replicas were installed, and the original statues removed to a climate-controlled exhibit case in the Acropolis Museum. It is a familiar story by now in cities with great marble and limestone heritages; one should not be surprised to see a numinous being turned air-conditioned artifact, but I am brought up short all over again by the instance of the Karyatides, with their strong arms, neck-bolstering braids, and calm, penetrating eyes. To the south and east of the replica Karyatides and close by Athena's urbane temple stood the two-winged stoa that was the sanctuary of Artemis Brauronia, the wilderness goddess. Greatly honored in the gorges and forests of Greece, especially in Arkadia on the Peloponnese, she was also judiciously invited into the heart of the human city, a gesture that suggests with what suppleness the pair "wild" and "civilized" were understood. Today, in the rubble of the stoa, a Japanese camera crew is filming a scene; how disarming, considering that Artemis, a most ancient divinity, entered Greece from the East.

You may
not see her
face to face

These days in mid-June are the longest of the year, and one afternoon in the remaining light, we drive first south to Poseidon's Temple on the bluff of Sounion, and then north again through the olive groves and vineyards of the Messogia Plain to Brauron on the eastern coast of Attiki. Near the sea, with the Erasinos River nearby, the road goes uphill, then downhill into a forested valley. The entrance to the excavated site at Brauron is closed; we are several hours too late. Nearby, off the road, half-hidden by tangled vines and woods, stand three columns, insubstantial as a private, tumbled-down porch. We stand for a while in the failing light peering at the slender evidence. I know there is a fountain at Brauron, and a crack in the wall of the sanctuary behind which lies the tomb of Iphigenia, the Argolid princess who was either (according to Aeschylus and Euripides respectively) slain by her father or saved at the last minute by Artemis and brought by her to Brauron to live as Mistress of the Animals. If rescued, Iphigenia lived in the dormitory as one of the little girls called the *arktoi*— "the bears"—who slept on wooden beds, ate at little stone tables, and served Artemis as acolytes in her sanctuary. In the scruffy field before us, small marble statues of the *arktoi* have been found, delicate carvings like the one called Bear With a Bird—a child cradling a dove in the folds of her gown.

On journeys it has happened many times before that something I especially desire withholds itself. Travel is like knowledge: much remains unknown and imperfectly seen, a situation not always remedied by checking museum hours, which are, in any case, changeable. And, too, the direct gaze, for all its virtues, can obscure: some things can simply not be seen head-on in the sun's glare. Here at Brauron, dusk is coming cool, covering the fields with gauze. We peer into the field until dark, and then we drive back toward Athens, stopping along the way at an empty taverna by the shore, where tables, legs sunk in sand, are scattered through a grove of olives that grows nearly into the sea. In a strong, clammy wind, the leafy olives are a froth of silvered green. The wind whips the paper tablecloth, held but tenuously with an elastic band. Hurricane lamps glow on the tables, and in the harbor, lights pulse on inside the cabins of boats. They shine through the trees and bob on the water, and the lines between sky and water, trees and tables grow indistinct.

Having eluded our eyes, the shrine to Artemis at Brauron has shown something essential of this goddess. Even if we are comfortable intimates of nature, many faces of the wild remain elusive. Of the wilderness goddess, her most luminous *arktoi*, the princess Iphigenia, says, "None of us ever sees Her in the dark or understands Her cruel mysteries."[3] Historically, Artemis is an aspect of the Earth goddess, not fecund Gaia herself, but the goddess of inviolate nature, the wilderness that is virgin in the old sense of being "unto itself." Artemis is "otherness"—that which cannot be fully possessed, known, or controlled. Of all the divinities, she is the most solitary and the most contradictory: she carries a quiver of arrows, her name means "she who slays," yet she also tends the mother in childbirth and protects the tender green youth of the world. Although she is the twin of Apollo, she is his complement: while her younger brother rules in the sunlight of the patriarchal city, she moves in moonlight. Have we seen her?

T he problem of statue noses dissolving and human eyes burning in Athenian smog is the sort of thing Droussoulla Vassiliou Elliot plans to remedy. Droussoulla and her husband, *Greening Athens* Sloane Elliot, are publisher and editor in chief respectively of *The Athenian*, the English language magazine of Greece. They are a nearly imperial couple. Sloane is slim and erudite, a dry wit, a watcher of Greece by profession and by marriage. Droussoulla is kindly and intellectual—able to effect city-wide campaigns from her desk using only natural grace, a telephone, and a web of people as complex as a coral reef. Her family has lived in Athens for centuries, and I am not surprised when three people from the UN Global Cooperation Project show up in Droussoulla's office saying that it is their Greek headquarters. I have turned up in her office to talk about her idea to—as she puts it—"green" Athens. (Although we are most familiar with the word as an adjective, *green* as a verb is hoary: it dates at least to 1000 A.D. and is a common early-modern usage. "The new lands, already weary of producing gold, begin to green with vineyards," writes Stevenson in *Silverado Squatters*; "He has begun greening his breeches' knees among the hazel bushes," says R. S. Surtees; and Mrs. Raffald claims, in the *English House-keeper* of 1769, that "nothing is more common than to green pickles in a brass pan.")[4]

Ten years ago Droussoulla Elliot launched a children's nature club that has by now greened the first batch of what she hopes is a generation of ardent naturalists. Recently Droussoulla has been helping to organize a campaign to protect the Mediterranean sea turtle. But the scheme dearest to her heart is to cover the buildings of Athens in living flora. (Corbu lives!) From her large office window, Droussoulla can envision the ubiquitous balconies of all the cement high-rises, apartment houses, hotels, and offices draped in a lush hanging garden, vegetation spilling from every sill and rail. This, Droussoulla declares—quite correctly—would greatly purify the air. The green plan is the response of a woman who looks out her window every day to see haze drifting across bleached, dry-as-bone buildings whose hot balconies bear only the rare plastic chair, and it is not, in her powerful hands, a quixotic idea. Over lunch, Sloane Elliot tells me about another means of tending what one loves, and at first I am surprised that it should be this urbane intellectual who teaches me about the evil eye.

Twenty years ago, when the Elliots were traveling in New York with their new baby, the infant's temperature suddenly soared. A doctor treated the baby, but his temperature did not drop. Droussoulla called her sister in Athens. The sister asked only if the baby had been in crowds. Yes, they had stood in front of a theatre where people had admired the baby and chucked its chin. Well, obviously the baby had been given the evil eye. Over the transatlantic cable, Droussoulla's sister led her through the ceremony to remove the curse; immediately the baby stopped crying, and his temperature dropped to normal. In Droussoulla's family, knowledge of how to give and remove the evil eye has been passed from a grandmother to an uncle to a sister, who will pass it on to a son—always woman to man to woman to man. Sloane tells me these things with the tone of someone who only discovered ice cream as an adult and is just never going to get over the fact of ice cream in this world. We are lunching at a taverna situated only inches from street traffic, and as the waiter brings fragrant bean soups, a car ruffles the tablecloth.

Undisturbed, Sloane advises me on how to recognize the evil eye: you must suspect it if things are going badly, if you are sick or unlucky for a long while. Still, you may just be sick, or having a normal streak of bad luck. How can one tell? It's quite simple.

Take a glass of water and pour a small amount of oil on the surface. If the oil gathers together in one floating island, as it would normally do, things are just going poorly, but if the oil stays scattered on the surface of the water, then you do have the evil eye. A second way to know is to say a passage of Christian liturgy quickly: if you can say the liturgy fluently, you are just having a bad time of it; if you scramble the words, it's the evil eye. Curse removals can be performed by an Orthodox priest or a lay healer, and prevention is also possible: wear a blue bead painted with an eye and, when in situations that invite the evil eye, pretend to spit. "Pwppitt," Sloane says, pretending to spit into traffic. If only the New Yorkers had taken this simple precaution when cooing over his new baby, they could have convinced the wicked spirits (mean but apparently dimwitted) of their utter disdain for lovable babies.

The evil eye is respected by all classes of citizens in Greece and it is caused by envy. Societies based on cooperative ventures like fishing and farming especially value the equitable distribution of goods, but nature is ever inequitable, and humans, children of nature, are inequitable, and these facts produce social unhappiness. It is this unhappiness—born of natural injustice, and the limited powers and desires of human beings to remedy it—that is attended to by the evil eye. It seems a brilliant bit of psychology to help level things in the community. Belief in the evil eye both allows and discourages envy. It locates the sources of envy: first, in the successes of the fortunate, and secondly in the longings of the less fortunate. It instructs the successful to bear the burden, the potential curse, of their success, and suggests that they guard against the evil eye by tact and discretion, and by plowing their good fortune back into the community so that others are not so tempted into envy but more often grateful. At the same time, those vulnerable to envy are given a powerful ritual to constrain the destructive emotion, to anticipate it, to protect others from it, even to purge themselves of it. The belief acknowledges the variations in awareness that people bring to social life: some maliciously convey the evil eye; others unwittingly infect their circle; still others learn to purge themselves of envy and dispel curses. By all these means, the ritual modulates the imperfect scales of fate. Behaving like nature itself, the evil eye is neither entirely beyond, nor entirely within, human influence.

Wealth I defy you to find poverty anywhere in Greece as wrenching as what you see on Washington Street in downtown Boston, any hour of the day." Kostas Gavraglou makes the claim in his quiet professor's voice, at the Taverna Psarra, where Katherine and I are about to be treated to untempered Greek hospitality. Kostas and his wife Anne have been alerted to our arrival by a mutual friend, a philosopher of science with whom Kostas and I have both studied in America; the courtliness the Gavraglous shower on us is an extension of their regard for him. One goes to a taverna for dinner not before eight-thirty at night. Nine is better, ten o'clock prime time. Out of deference to our recent arrival from Boston where restaurants often *close* at ten o'clock, the Gavraglous come to our hotel at eight and lead us on a winding walk up the hill, through courtyards, shops, and tavernas seamed together by stairs, arbors, and strings of lights, until we reach the Psarra.

The name means fish. Outside the fishing villages, where, as we ooon learn, the price scarcely shows up on the hill, fish is quite expensive in Greece. But Psarra is a rare city taverna that serves fresh, affordable fish. In other ways, too, Psarra betrays village roots, its clock slow as a sleepy town. It is the one taverna in the foothills of the Acropolis that makes no special appeal to the tourists flowing up the hills, leaving to other eateries the practice of lining the cobbled streets with soi-disant suave men who perform like crosses between maitres d'hotel and carnival barkers, calling out price, quality, and invitations in whatever tongue they suspect a visitor might speak. At the Psarra, a sloe-eyed, plump fellow subliminally notes one's arrival from his chair by the door, nods (possibly in sleep), and sometime later lumbers over with the standard taverna issue: paper tablecloth, a basket holding the mediocre bread and silverware wrapped in napkins. To call the bread mediocre is no slur against Psarra. All the bread in Greece is mediocre—of refined flour, white, neither textured nor flavorful—and this is a surprise in a country of village-scale agriculture. In America, we have watched the migration of good whole-grain breads into the boutique markets for the rich, and the peddling of something called "Wonder" to the poor, but I had imagined alive and satisfying bread to be a birthright of a people who live close to the land.

A vast tree grows in the center of the Psarra cafe: the roots have erupted between stones, causing the sloped dining plateau to be forever uneven. Limbs and leaves shade thirty tables, the kitchen structure, and nearby leather shop. Logging and stock-grazing severely deforested Greece as early as 300 A.D, and since these practices have relentlessly continued and there is today but slight interest in (and neither government nor private money given for) reforestation, tree and spring are welcome events on the landscape.[5] Within hours of driving down the eastern prong of the Peloponnese, one knows viscerally why shade and water, and their sources, are revered and have been since the time of the bucolic and pastoral poets. It is an excellent sign when a taverna, or anything else, is located under a tree.

Under the Psarra's tree is scattered a medley of chairs and tables, bound in common only by their wobble. Most city tavernas have molded aluminum or plastic chairs, but the Psarra uses wooden tables and wooden chairs, and, like the country tavernas, paints them blue: teal, navy, dark, baby, light, or sea. Blue, one soon realizes, is the national hobby. (Another day, in a bright midday June sun, a woman of perhaps eighty-six, in widow's weeds, slowly repaints ten of Psarra's wooden chairs; she uses a two-inch brush and a half-pint can of blue enamel, no drop cloth, merely semi-careful strokes, and a tolerance she shares with her culture for the splatters of color that land on floors and stucco walls. Boats and chairs, windows, walls, and the hook-necked gourds hung to decorate the undersides of arbors are some of the things painted annually in Greece; the painting places are easily found, marked by layers of polychrome speckles.)

For dinner for four at Psarra, Kostas orders the following: fried squid; gopas, a large bony fish from the sardine family that is easily filleted, leaving a limber Fritz-the-Cat cartoon skeleton; greens similar to the collards of Alabama; thick ovals of fried potatoes; Greek salads; plates of steamed zucchini; bread; wine; and a plate of cut lemons. Twelve plates are crowded onto the table and, while small individual plates are handed to each diner, it is clear that to use them as more than a staging or boning platform is gratuitous, even rude. Over a long, courtly, and warm evening Kostas and Anne demonstrate that the host/guest tradition celebrated in the *Odyssey* has endured. And they show us how to eat in a taverna, that is, they initiate us into the foods, the manners, and, without speaking of it directly, point us toward the secret of the village taverna.

Three weeks later, by the time Peter and Tony have arrived and we have all come upon the remote fishing village of Skala Sikiminias, on the northern coast of Lesvos one mile from Turkey, we have learned just enough to enter into the communion that occurs throughout Greece in the great ritual of the village taverna. The conditions of the communion are not inevitable, nor spontaneously or easily achieved, nor, once found, enduring, nor even, I should think, apparent and meaningful to all participants, native or foreign. The intricacy and fragility of the conditions belie the notion that a spontaneous harmony is the natural estate of our species. For this particular communion to arise, Skala Sikiminias must have a climate and soil for vegetables and melons, and a fertile patch of the sea; it must be remote enough so cruise ships don't swarm, and close enough so that a few will come to be harvested like sardines. It must have an enormous boulder just offshore that provides the anchor for a harbor wall, a broad enclosure and promenade which snugs the fleet of fishing boats and accepts the wheel of infant prams, gangly courtship, working nets, and the labored climb of the old to the minute chapel perched on the rock. It must have a family-run taverna that serves, from dawn until early in the dark new morning, as the public living room of the village. The village must have inhabitants who are both ingenious and willing to mix their ingenuity into one soil; a people who may moon for faraway lands, but who come home after Athens, after life on the cruise ships, to tend *this* olive grove, *this* chapel by the sea—*Panayia Gorgona* it is called, the chapel of the mermaid.

Should these conditions—unique to this one village on Lesvos, different in every other place—be achieved and re-achieved by each generation, the taverna is a clock where the very rich hours turn their rounds. Throughout the long Mediterranean day, foods stream into the living room in baskets, sacks, plastic containers, and shopping bags. A back door exists in the taverna building and is used for taking out garbage, but suppliers to the communion make their deliveries by crossing the shaded front apron of the taverna among the tables and chairs and diners, entering the wide front doors. A typical early morning delivery begins when a Dutch couple place an order for yogurt with honey; minutes later a woman brings four containers of fresh-made yogurt from her neighboring house. A wiry farmer lugs in a lumpish burlap bag of onions; the taverna owner strolls up from the shore with a round basket brimful of glinting sardines. By ten o'clock, the first of a daylong procession of six-year-old boys scampers in with a limp octopus and an eel held by the gills. The baker sends his assistant down the small hill with a shopping bag of hot, fresh, mediocre rolls. Not only suppliers to the feast, but diners also are expected to come into the kitchen; one orders by repeatedly admiring and pointing to the array of hot dishes and chilled fishes. Next to the food cases, on a shelf amidst a stack of ripe red tomatoes, sits the village radio-telephone. The one telephone of the village sits in the tomato harvest like a tiny, perhaps friendly, alien craft landed in an Iowa cornfield, and its light-emitting diode pulses out resonant tomato-red numerals. Overhead, the wall is crusted with snapshots, all curling, of the owner's family linking arms with tourists, cousins, and returnees from Athens and Kos.

Sitting is a constant and important activity in the taverna communion. Early morning sitting is done by fishermen returned from lamp-fishing at night; after unloading the catch, they sit astraddle baskets three feet in diameter, each of which holds one taxi-cab-yellow nylon or pale yellow rope net. The nets are laced with corks and hooks and after each use the men rearrange them, smoothing all the hooks in one direction. Even earlier morning sitting is done by clusters of women at the work tables in the taverna: peeling skins from braised tomatoes, chopping garlics and onions into rolling foothills, turning the mounds with their shiny, flavored hands. Even earlier morning sitting is done by dozens of cats, motionless meditators before the bows of unloading fishing boats until a silver fish comes flying from the deck to land on the dock, compelling them into a flurry of fur and claws.

Greeks cats are thin, foxlike affairs, with ears large in proportion to delicate heads and jaws. The cats are not pets but hard-working members of the chain of being that involves legumes, olives, kelp, clams, fishes, rats, cats, amphibious children, fishermen, crones, tourists, the evil eye, and saints. The cat population is very large and fends for itself. When a fish-delivery truck pulls away one early morning from the dock of Skala Sikiminias and runs squarely over the legs of a young marmalade dozing under its axles, neither the driver nor any of the nearby fishermen, nor shopkeepers setting up postcard racks, nor backgammon players, nor kitchen workers, nor children even faintly move to tend it. Nor had the villagers stirred to shoo the cat from under the wheels as it became clear to all within eyeshot that it would likely be squashed. Only three American tourists having tea and breakfast rolls at the far end of the square leap up and start toward the unfolding accident. Too late; and the wounded cat itself seems to expect neither warning nor first aid, but soundlessly drags itself into a nearby shed.

No miserable sitting still is done by children in or near the taverna; they play under and between the table legs, chase cats, jump stone walls, squash plants, prance by with aquatic things. Mid-afternoon sitting is done by the old men, who emerge in their places at the old men's tables much the way mushrooms arrive on the lawn, soundlessly, without any apparent motion. Wonderfully, the word for "occupied" in Greek, as in "I am occupied just now," includes the meaning "I am sitting." The old men have reached this purest meaning, for although they can be drawn into political talk and sliding checkers across a checkerboard, most often the sitting of the old men appears to be entirely unsullied by any motion, *telos*, or worldly distraction. Late-night sitting is done by the oldest women in the village, who sit flat on the floors of their porches and courtyards, in gangs of six or more, their black-stockinged legs straight out, crocheting curtains and napkins on the round shelves of their stomachs, eating massive bowls of popcorn and, it must be said, cackling, until two o'clock in the morning. Just before the old women emerge for night sitting, and periodically during their tenure, the smell of hot oil and corn rises, and the street smells like a disembodied Bijoux movie theatre.

Some sitting is episodic: an old pedlar with watery eyes appears in town, lays out tin plates, nicked Swiss army knives, keychains, cigarette lighters, and pictures of the Madonna on a stone wall, and sits for one week, drinking coffee in a chair under a nearby awning. Some sitting is hard-won: in an ongoing pas de deux, waiters vigorously shoo gypsies away from the taverna with roughly the same success one meets when shooing away a housefly, and then, once or twice during the hottest swath of the day, relent, allowing three chubby gypsy women peddling bundles of one-dollar table-cloths to settle on a shady bench and slowly drink glasses of water. Tourist sitting is more desultory, done at all times of the day. A German woman sits for hours reading Kierkegard. Alone. At noon, a cruise ship drops anchor beyond the harbor and by launch brings four hundred traveling souls to the taverna. To one side of the taverna there is a huge, unshaded side terrace created for just this purpose. Normally this terrace is empty, even ignored as though it were a non-terrace; during the hour-long swarm, its chairs are briefly occupied to bursting.

At nine-thirty or ten o'clock on weekend nights, beautifully dressed clusters of former native sitters and relatives of native sitters arrive in the taverna from their homes in the city. After the Second World War, the horrendous civil war in Greece continued, with much bloodshed in the countryside. The prevailing regime found ways to round up villagers and persuade them into Athens. The city was swollen within a few years to four times its former population, and many villages shriveled. The migration into Athens continues, and among the professional and working classes of Greece are many city dwellers who have left their childhood villages. They often drive back on Friday and Saturday nights: they come in couples, in groups of six or eight, and cluster around one long table, perhaps visiting with a fisherman brother who stayed, ordering the catch of the day and, in mid-June, *kolokithia lololuthia*—the small folded squash-blossom pockets of rice, rosemary, onions, and cheese that taste like chlorophyll and color. After eating, the fisherman brother, who lamp-fishes during much of the night, leaves the others at the table and motors his boat out of the harbor to work. In a while you will see his lamps set out in a string, like Christmas tree lights, bobbing on the surface of the sea. The others linger: one young man has brought his guitar, and one of the women, who is plump and pretty in a tight red dress, gets him to play it and stirs her friends into singing Greek folk songs. Some in the group are embarrassed, some not at all. The scene appears to be the equivalent of young American financial consultants sitting around a Vermont inn wearing new Bean boots and ironed chamois shirts, singing "Green Grow the Rushes Ho." After the singing starts in earnest, the taverna owner's flushed, handsome son, Nikos—who manages the table service and talks exuberant if not smooth English with the customers—lowers the taped Theodorakis that comes from a walnut-veneer speaker wired in the tree, and the returnees have the floor to harmonize for the night.

In June, at the harbor taverna of Skala Sikiminias the evening air is reliably balmy, breezy. Each night, we gather during the early evening hour that bathes boats, cats, trees, faces, and stones in an intense coral light. We sit at a blue table on blue chairs and tell of divergent field trips. Peter, who spends his day in a mask and flippers underwater, draws a detailed picture of a fish who flies along the bottom with blue wings and eight legs. After the orange-red sun grows too heavy for the sky and slides behind Turkey, the lights strung through the trees come on. Humans and leaves collaborate in darkening patterns; speech emerges from the tables on a murmuring continuum with sounds from the sea. We order food in the manner of Kostas: marrow lolls in a shallow pond of lemon juice, the greens wade in greens liquor, and fishes yield their flesh from supple bones like fossils. Now and then our forks, approaching the same potato oval, clink in midair. Of the Penan Urun tribe's wild boar feasts in East Malaysia, the poet Carol Rubenstein has written that the sharing of their hunt meat "unites the group and binds it in communion with the forest animal whose life force and flesh they have ingested."[6] Surely the people of Skala Sikiminias are bound with the zucchini blossoms and gopa fish of their biome; even we brief visitors can feel the molecular tug, and our conversion, if allowed to continue, would require no ideology other than greens and things with blue wings. The communion occurs not only among different species along the fluent chain, but among the several layers of the human brain; particularly, the old reptilian brain of instinct courts, and is well received by, the outer rind, the big frontal cortex full of ideas. One afternoon I watch two tiny, slippery-wet boys splash in the water near a manta ray that their father has caught and put in a shallow box for safekeeping. The boys are so nearly aquatic that they easily recall the evolution of the human brain—that onion at the top of the spinal cord—from origins in the salty sea.

The ongoing ordinary communion of the rural Greek taverna is, after all, a form of travel in which individual boundaries become transluscent, allowing for an expansion of the self into a larger gyre of being. As the expansion of the narrow into the great occurs, I wonder if we can also follow Blake's maxim to infuse the great with the particularity of the small. Can we take love of the particular place with us to the foreign regions where our bodies and spirits must go? I suppose this is to ask, Can we expand the notion of what *home* is? As we understand through our knowledge of global warming et al., the village of Skala Sikiminias and a Kentucky farm community are one geography. Moreover, the landscapes that matter most to us occur in patches all over the planet: a wooden porch in Tuscaloosa, Alabama, with sulphur winds blowing in from the paper mills; a cement terrace on Lesvos ringed with gardenia bushes. . . . On our earthly travels, we encounter a being whose diversity and vastness challenge our emotional and intellectual assumptions about both self and home.

For the cautious, there can be no better place to begin to take the pleasures of ecological communion than in a Greek village taverna. Here, the tender fish taken into one's body is an enactment of the process by which any individual enters into a larger whole. In the case of the fish dinner, one welcomes with gratitude the end of the fish as fish, the beginning of fish as oneself. Moreover, by the immediate communion with other humans, sea creatures, trees, and time—the knowledge that this experience has occurred and reoccurred, here, over a great round of years—one may experience the analogous motion: in ritual time, one may take one's place in the full circle of life and sense less with dread than with calm that other passage that leads into the Earth. These yieldings occur lightly—as a story is told, a plate passed. The secret of the taverna is to make one a conscious member of a being of complexity and beauty. This ongoing naturally erotic encounter with our world, with our species and the creatures with whom we participate in a being called Earth, is our common wealth. In whose interest is it that wealth has been defined otherwise?

A circle of stones in the water

The small cement terrace of the *pensione* where we are staying is lined with gardenias growing from olive oil cans and crisscrossed by a clothesline hung with black brassieres, black slips, and black panties. Alternating with the lingerie are pale blue paper lanterns that recently held candles for the feast of "Ag-*yee*-a *Mar*-tha," Saint Martha's Day. It is after dark and already, just outside the terrace walls, a line of crones has begun droning in a music that bores through the walls of Afrodite's Rooms-to-Let. Afrodite's daughters, a coltish twelve-year-old named Nikki and a dreamy eleven-year-old named Tula, sit with us at a picnic table on the terrace, where their mother has put two reading lanterns and a plate of honey-dripped sweets. To the table the girls bring lined composition books in which they have written stories, for us, in the rudimentary English they have learned in school. To practice, the girls want to read their stories aloud. Nikki has enough English to make infant sentences, Tula less, and we have no Greek of which to speak. In the traditional manner, we all make up for these lapses with smiles and pantomime.

In Nikki's story, called "My Friend," she goes to the beach with Evgania, a girl just her age who lives in the one grand house in Skala Sikiminias for four months each year and goes away to school in Paris for the other eight months. The story is about what they do during a summer day and how much they miss each other during the winter. When Nikki gets to the part about the beach, she pauses and asks me the English word for something the girls are making at the water's edge. She repeatedly describes the activity, giving me the Greek word for it over and over, but I cannot make out what she is talking about, and Nikki decides to draw a picture. It is of a circle of stones in the off-shore shallows. Nikki's stones are wobbly ovals, carefully shaded on one side. Next she draws something inside the stones. It looks like a net that the rocks hold down in the water, keeping it fixed in the sweeping tides. And then she draws some fruits in the net. It is a moment of rapport when my face finally lights up with understanding: she is describing a circle of stones in the water to hold fruits and keep them cool in the sea, something for which there is one word in Greek. Now Nikki's face turns to me excited and eager for the equivalent English word.

There are other things that resist translation. Skala Sikiminias is tended by a circuit doctor—usually a young woman—who comes to the northern coast of Mytilini for a year or two to serve her residency after medical school. Dr. Anna was the circuit doctor for Skala Sikiminias several years back, and she has the easy authority of a crackerjack physician. She is here now to visit a tall, slim man who meets her each night at the taverna for dinner where the two of them exchange silent, smoldering looks. I meet Dr. Anna when she overhears me asking the woman who runs the crafts store if there are herbalists in the village. Suddenly, a nearby woman, speaking perfect English, is in the conversation. "Yes," she says taking over for the shopkeeper, "there are herbal healers in the village." Has she ever spoken with them about their remedies? "No." Would she like to go with us to talk with them, and translate for us? "Yes, very much." And then a pause: "But not today, maybe tomorrow." Another pause. And it would be better if she was not the one to approach them. Maybe Nikos, the taverna owner's son, would make the introductions.

Dr. Anna is always very friendly when we see her reading in the late afternoon, or with her silent paramour at night, but day by day her demurral becomes a bit more complex and firm. Gradually, I see that she has thought better of her spontaneous enthusiasm, and that between a medical doctor and the village herbalist the translation between Greek and English would not be the difficult one. Until the present century there was no rift; botanical healing was a scientific pursuit. The most prominent botanical scientist of the ancient world came from a small village thirty miles to the east. There, in Skala Eressou, Theophrastus—successor of Aristotle as director of the peripatetic school of philosophy—kept his garden and wrote the *Historia Plantarum*, a treatise in ten books, in which he distinguishes the habitats of plants.[7] As it turns out, the herbal healers of Skala Sikiminias are closer at hand than I imagine. One night during the English lesson, I ask Nikki if her mother makes any medicines from plants. Yes, of course she does. Nikki is so charming and eager to practice her English that she will talk about any subject, but I see from a lightly masked, perplexed film over her eyes that she considers the subject of how to make cough syrup from olive trees too obvious a body of fact to support any interest. It is as though I have asked her to tell me about the fascinating local custom of hanging clothes on clothes hangers.

Poems in
situ

Like plants, poems grow from particular habitats and have healing properties, and for a long while I have nursed the notion that poems are somewhat analogous to the organic simples and compounds made from plants. How pleased I was when reading one day in the taverna to come upon the following passage from the *Open Book* of Odysséas Elytes:

> Primitive peoples, poets before the age of poems . . . overcame evil by reciting frightful and incomprehensible words. In the same fashion, until a few years ago our island nurses, with utter seriousness, chased evil spirits from above our cradles by uttering words without meaning, holding a tiny leaf of a modest herb which received God knows what strange powers exclusively from the innocence of its own nature. Poetry is precisely this tiny leaf with the unknown powers of innocence and the strange words which accompany it.[8]

Lesvos, as everyone knows, is the soil of the poet Sappho (*Sapfo* in the Greek pronunciation). Less well known is a contemporary master who also traces his heritage to this coastline. A few miles to the west of Skala Sikiminias, on an unmarked country road, stands the Alepoudhelis family house. Both the mother and father of Odysséas Elytes (née Alepoudhelis) were from old families of Lesvos, and it was boyhood summers on Aegean islands that saturated this poet's language in luminous light. Elytes writes a poetry that comes, as he says, from an alphabet of the Aegean: the garden of the sea, olive trees, above all, the light, transmuted into a human script. Often described as surreal, in situ the poems prove to be a clear portrait of reality. About these matters, Elytes has said that he and his generation

> have attempted to find the true face of Greece. This was necessary because until then the true face of Greece was presented as Europeans saw Greece. . . . [W]e had to destroy the tradition of rationalism which lay heavily on the Western world. . . . Many facets of surrealism I

cannot accept . . . but after all, it was the only school of poetry . . . which aimed at spiritual health. . . . [I]t had cleared the ground in front of us, enabling us to link ourselves physiologically with our soil.[9]

To be linked physiologically with one's soil—this must also be what Conrad Aiken means when he says that "the landscape and the language are the same, / And we ourselves are language and are the land."

Renewing the sun

Near dusk one night on Lesvos I am heading back to Afrodite's Rooms-to-Let through a small woods. Rounding a bend in the path, I come upon a group of women and children lighting three large brush bonfires on a scruff of beach at the outer edge of the village. As the women touch matches to the three piles of brush, the sun is just setting, and for half an hour—until the bonfires somewhat burn down—four orange-red shapes flare against the evening sky. As the sun slips into the sea and the flames diminish, the women and their children turn into silhouettes against the sky and sea. One skinny boy, about nine, suddenly bolts from the cluster and leaps over all the fires, one after another, whooping. His small, wiry boy-body, at apogee over the low flames, looks like a twisting shape the fire has thrown up. Now a girl runs forward and jumps over the fires, and then all the children do, sometimes several times, like kids shooting down slides then running around to do it again. The mothers stand talking along the seawall, their plump bodies, black skirts, and olive skins glowing in the heat. When the fires burn still lower, the children gather stones from the beach and begin hurling them into the embers. It is the twenty-first of June, Saint John's Eve on the Christian calendar, a quasi-advent that foreshadows the winter arrival of the Savior. And on the pagan calendar tonight is the summer solstice, one of the two great turning points in the year. These hours exactly mark the time that shorter, colder days begin. In the old culture, tonight was the night of bonfires, lit all over Europe to signal, or perhaps ritually renew, the sun's waning energy.

Along the wall, one of the mothers recognizes me from the English lessons; she waves and I join her near the fires, which are still giving off a great wall of heat. She says that the girls and boys are jumping over the fires so that they will be fertile, and she encourages me to jump too. The children are excited that an adult might join them. The fires are mostly crackling-hot stones by now, with only low flames and rogue licks leaping up; still, there is a moment of thrilled fear, sailing over the heat. Afterwards, a boy named Alekos gives me two stones and tells me to throw them in the fire. When I do, he shrieks the Greek child's unparalleled shriek. The matronly women (who are probably ten years younger than I) giggle and look pleased with themselves. We stay until the stones grow cold and the light fails, and the women, who leapt over fires themselves not so long ago, round up their happy, spent children and go home. Unaware of their beauty, the uncountable leaves of the surrounding olive trees darken into the concentrate of all color.

Across the Gulf While I have been reading Elytes and settling into village time, Peter and Katherine have been falling for Turkey, visible from the harbor of Skala Sikiminias as an undulating ribbon of land, the westmost prong of Turkey that shimmers a scant nine miles northwest, across the Gulf of Eddremit. On even a large, detailed map, the gulf between Lesvos and Turkey is so slight that a thin red line demarcating the border almost entirely fills the channel. The East (here a bit to the west of us) is tantalizingly close, and each night the sun (and according to Katherine, the truth) slides behind Turkey, further suggesting to my companions that the ribbon on the horizon is a gateway to another reality. This time, the sirens do not sing for me. Peter and Katherine try to coax me to come with them, but this village persuades me that, for once, merely being is enough. From here, minds can sail across the sea, bones can wend through crooked streets, quiet as cats.

Passage to Turkey is booked in Mytilini, in the office of Spyros, a handsome man who wears a soiled yellow silk shirt in his dim rooms that face the slatternly harbor. From these rooms, with floors covered in rugs three layers deep, Spyros rents things: motorcycles, cars and houses and who knows what. He exchanges money, and he can sell tickets for boats to Turkey—which he calls "*Tour*—keees." He says to my friends, "I know you are wanting, since before three days, to take the boat to Tourkeees." How does he know? Spyros is a big man on the Mytilini waterfront, a suave braggart with a deskful of telephones. While we wait, any number of gamey men slip in through the open front door and are waved by Spyros into another room, behind a cloth hanging. In addition to vehicles and exchange rates, he knows people; it was Spyros who, after talking with us for ten minutes some weeks back, told us to take our books and sketchpads into little, off-the-path Skala Sikiminias. Now it is only because of a boat-scheduling dilemma, one even Spyros cannot outmaneuver, that my companions remain with me on the very rim of the Western world.

Spyros wants us to like him and is a little despondent to have failed in the matter of Turkey. Some days later, when Tony and Peter must fly to Athens overnight and Katherine and I are hanging around Mytilini city, waiting for them to return and staying in a sleazy harbor hotel, Spyros invites the two of us to something he calls his "hchauuummn." This version of an English word is said very fast and decisively, and sounds as though you are first clearing your throat, then humming, then quickly clamping down your mouth. To duplicate the word, the whole back of my upper palette must vibrate. When at last we understand the nature of the invitation, we are half honored, half wary. In all his dealings with us Spyros has been honest and insightful, but he does not cultivate the impression of a gentleman, rather the sense that all hell could break loose any minute. He is disappointed when we say we will follow him in our car rather than squeeze onto his motorcycle, but it all works out for the best when, ten miles out of town, we come upon a young American nurse whose motorcycle—rented from Spyros—is stranded with a dead engine. The young woman blithely joins Spyros on his bike and we all continue toward the hchauuummn in a twisting byzantium of dusty roads.

An hour later, as we thread through olive groves on yet another sinuous path, it finally dawns on Katherine and me that Spyros has arranged for a fishing boat at the end of this road, and that we are heading into white slavery via Tourkeees. Mercifully, what awaits us at the end of the road is merely a somnolent village and the home that Spyros is building on several overgrown acres of bearing trees. We tour the tangled orchards first, groves of olives, mulberries, jujubes, and citrons, and take the armfuls of lemons that Spyros presses on us, saying that otherwise the fruit will only fall to the ground and rot. Near the center of the orchard is a stand of carobs, a bushy evergreen whose bean-shaped fruits are ripening into chocolate-brown pods. Inside the pods will form the seed that medieval goldsmiths used to establish the carat measure, and that can be ground and used as a flavoring in lieu of chocolate. Around the carobs is a ring of cultivated almonds, whose nutmeats are sweetening inside pale green oval drupes. The velvety cases hold the hard, flat kernels that protect the edible nut. Come into Greece from Asia, the almond also thrives in barren country as a wild variety with a small and bitter nut. His enclave is, Spyros says, a paradise.

Paradise is a word first used in Greek by Xenophon, and it comes from the Old Persian word for an enclosed pleasure ground, a place wonderful not only because of what it contains, but because of what it excludes. In calling his orchard retreat a paradise, Spyros continues a tradition—at once Greek, Christian, and Oriental—in which the garden is considered a graceful mingling of human and more-than-human nature, a place of balance and spiritual repose. Even in prelapsarian Eden, gardening was the one labor required of Adam and Eve, who were instructed to "dress and keep" paradise, and early modern English gardening books such as *Paradise Regained* and *Paradisus in Sole* perpetuated the idea that cultivating the Earth is a way to grace.[10]

Walking among the shining leaves, as late sun spills through chinks in the green thickets, Spyros slips through several of his many orbits, gradually settling into the countryman speaking of how the trees will be mature when his son is, how he hopes the son will come here to stay summers with his grandmother. The child, whom Spyros refers to with proud formality as "my bastard son," lives in France with his mother and visits but rarely. The mother never visits; she is still angry about the other women. Spyros begins to allude to his trials and triumphs with women, glances at us, thinks better of it, and smiles wanly. The house is two stories, the bottom one of which—still open to the weather, with bags of cement stacked in towering piles—will one day be the apartment for the mother of Spyros. The second level, already finished, has an ice-skating rink of marble stretching away over the floors, and large sliding glass doors hung with heavy curtains that make the rooms dark and cool as a cellar. As he talks about the fine building materials, the trees and breezes, Spyros grows sadder and sadder, and finally his voice shrinks into a bewildered bleat as he wonders out loud, Why cannot the bastard son come this summer? Why cannot he Spyros ever find time to be here? Why does only marriage please a woman? Why cannot paradise be inhabited?

Why indeed. With Spyros, a come-on is never far from the surface, but this last question, ancient and as yet unanswered, is surely genuine. He has asked two middle-aged, foreign, bookish women here to show us his idea of paradise and to talk about the ideal home—what it may be, how elusive it is. The questions are so large and poignant that no response could be adequate. I am tempted to tell Spyros about the solution devised by wealthy souls in Victorian England. Also unable or unwilling to spend proper time in their garden worlds, they would retain a hermit to live amongst the flowers and trees as a spiritual proxy. Instead, Katherine and I veer into the objective correlative of trees, talking again about who tends and harvests them—the sadness of uneaten fruits, the inevitability of waste, the virtue of the wild almond. Here is the landscape in which Elytes writes: "And yet if you move from what is to what may be, you pass over a bridge which takes you from Hell to Paradise. And the strangest thing: a Paradise made of precisely the same material of which Hell is made. It is only the perception of order of the materials that differs . . . [a] perception . . . sufficient to determine the immeasurable difference."[11]

It does not diminish Spyros's queries to say that, as time went on, it was not lost on him that angst-ridden musings would strike another kind of woman as romantic. When we leave, we offer the nurse a ride back to town, but she declines, and later we hear that she had taken up living with Spyros, for a couple of weeks, in his apartment on the Mytilini harbor.

Fresh from a fishing village on Lesvos where old women are permanently bent from stooping over fields and firewood, we meet Elisabet Sahtouris in the cool, marbled and glass splendour of an Athenian hotel near the Euginedes Planetarium. Here, there are deep, soft leather lounge chairs, waterfalls spilling from every nook, a shimmering rooftop pool where bronze bodies worthy of travel posters disport themselves. Here are glossy banks of telephones and whirring fax machines, the seamless transfers of international business, a corridor of ease, life wheeled to and fro, at one's beck. In a room whose tables are covered in bright pink tablecloths, creative minds of the world's great planetaria are convened to plan their response to the disappearance of the night sky: save for the most remote regions, the electric grid of civilization has finally illuminated the whole planet. Elisabet, an expatriate American science writer, has been asked to speak to the planetarium directors on a recent geophysical theory about the Earth.

In the hotel enclave, we are a scant mile or so from the outdoor rooms at the base of the Acropolis, where questions about the nature of nature were first launched in earnest in the West, starting the trajectory that has brought us air-conditioned palaces in which to ponder present-day ecological conundrums. You wouldn't know it from the foul, scorching air outside these cool rooms, but Earth's atmosphere has the property of *homeostasis*, a word that refers to an organism's ability to keep its temperature constant regardless of surrounding fluctuations. Elisabet calls this a "wisdom of the body," and presents the view that the planet itself is a living organism able to regulate the temperature and the composition of its surface. This is the Gaia theory, developed by geophysiologist James Lovelock and microbial biologist Lynn Margulis—a theory that is, as Lovelock sanguinely admits, "at the outer bounds of scientific credibility."[12] The idea is that "the atmosphere, the oceans, the climate, and the crust of the Earth are regulated at a state comfortable for life *because of* the behavior of living organisms [italics mine]." Gaia theory builds on the theory of natural selection, introducing the idea that organisms not only adapt to their environments, but profoundly change them. In this theory, life and its environments are so "tightly coupled" as to be a single evolving system. Critics have seen Gaia as a teleological theory that imputes purpose to the planet and an absurd sentience to the biota. To reply, Lovelock created a modeling program that shows how global temperature is regulated "over a wide range of solar luminosity, by an imaginary planetary biota without invoking foresight or planning." Pressed about spiritual implications of the theory, Lovelock sidesteps the dreary division between science and religion. "Individuals," he says, "interact with Gaia in the cycling of the elements and in the control of the climate, just like a cell does in the body. You also interact . . . through a sense of wonder." After Elisabet's talk, a fleshy astronomer at my table puts down his pink napkin and mildly asks her, "Why do you find it *less* interesting to consider the Earth as dead matter?"

Katherine and I travel with Elisabet aboard a Russian-made hydrofoil called *Flying Dolphin*, to Angistri, a small island about forty minutes from the Athenian port at Pireas. The islands we pass on the way are characteristic Greek island moonscapes, the barren mounds produced by overgrazing and overlogging that people have come to find starkly beautiful in the harsh sun. Angistri Island has retained its lush pine forests, and Elisabet lives here with her husband, Arghiri, in a two-room, white-washed house near the forest, high in the steep hills of Metochi above the port town. Inside the house is a small room with a couch, two chairs, a tiny bottled-gas stove, and a minute sink, and another small room with a bed, a rocker, a writing desk, and a window with a long view down to the sea. On one side of the deep casement, Elisabet has mounted a small antler from whose prongs hang thirty dried seahorses. The horses are all different sizes, some with long elegant tails, some shriveled, some tiny, some black, some a sepia or taffy color. The wind is good on the hill; it makes the single lace curtain wave and the seahorses swish their tails. On our first visit up the hill, we bring a fish, a cake, and a ripe melon. Arghiri takes the melon and begins cutting it into slices. He uses a knife bigger than a pocket knife, smaller than a fish-cleaning knife. The melon is the color of a cantaloupe and veined on the outside like a cantaloupe, but bigger and sweeter. The Greek way to cut a melon is to divide it into about eight slices, separate the meat from the rind in one curved cut, and then, leaving the long scimitar of melon in the rind boat, to cut the fruit into chunks. Arghiri cuts each slice away from the melon body very slowly, gracefully, and one could not say that he *scrapes* the seeds out of the fruit, but rather that he strokes the seeds off the melon, just kissing it with his knife, letting what of the seeds and strings will fall of their own weight slip onto the plate. Then he takes a bite, and says something very firm, though humorously. Elisabet translates: "Arghiri says the melon should be fried." By usual standards, it is a perfectly ripe melon, but we are in a land where degrees of ripeness can be scrutinized like particles in an electron microscope. Smiling, Arghiri produces a melon that melts not in the mouth, but in the air near the mouth, so that one's lips encounter only a cool froth.

Later, Elisabet leads us to a secluded sea-grotto, following trails that wind along high bluffs; far below in the azure sea, two swimmers move slowly across the cove, nets of light flickering over their pale backs. The white sand floor is clearly visible, the sea a glass of water tinted with Carter's fine drawing ink. Strewn along the path are long, fragrant pine needles, dried to red-brown, and a stream of plastic cups, candy wrappers, ice cream cartons, and soda bottles. Everywhere, people still follow the old custom of disposing of garbage by throwing it in a gully, though the gully is now in a village or a city, and the garbage does not decompose, and it arrives on a massive scale. At the grotto, Elisabet laments her travel schedule and the grueling conference politics that take her away from this island. As she talks, the sea laps the rocks and washes into tidal pools thronged with mustard-green plants whose arms—neither spinning nor toiling—pulse over colonies of shining periwinkles.

Along the road The drive from Athens to the healing center of Epidauros is hot, through mile after patchwork mile of olive, lemon, and artichoke crops. Walking into one artichoke field, I am dwarfed by the giant, sculptural stalks, and wander among their shade like a field mouse through grasses. Most of the green globes (*anginara* in Greek) have already been picked and delivered to market, and the few remaining swell from their stems like fat candles on an ornate candelabra. It is the soft, inner core and the bracts of this spiny perennial that are eaten in their immature stage. At just about the same stage, the green closed flowerheads—the globes—along with the stem leaves, may be collected for medicinal use. Since the time of Theophrastus, herbalists have known that the flowerheads and leaves, boiled for twenty minutes into a decoction, may be drunk to reduce fever and stiff joints, and that a crushed poultice of the leaves is soothing to tonsillitis. These lingering, unpicked artichokes have been let go too long for either food or medicine; the globes have begun to splay into huge, soft, tufty, bright purple platters whose beauty is entirely sufficient.

Near sundown, we reach the outskirts of Nauplion, where a large gypsy encampment is sprawled in a dry riverbed wash. The road that runs alongside is under construction and as yet unpaved; passing vehicles stir up voluminous clouds of a pale grey dust that swirls through the camp. A rusting bulldozer and large barrels of chemicals are heaped at one end of the wash. When construction causes us to slow almost to a stop, three gypsy girls, perhaps six years old, race toward the car, smiling, all brown eyes, dusty legs, cotton dresses, leather sandals. The children reach out eagerly, confidently as morning glory vines into the abyss. Past their tangled hair is the city of canvas tents, big heavily roped rooms of ancient construction, surrounded outside by erratic patterns of bundles, jalopies, carts, and mules. The open fires for dinner are blazing up in the late heat of the day, making a shimmering heat-distortion band through which the scene wavers: women moving among the tents with children dangling on their hips, men sitting in the open doorways of the tents, everyone dressed in startling clothes over which has settled the grey road dust. Seldom have I felt more keenly how strong are the delicate membranes that keep one culture from another. The car window might as well be the glass wall of an aquarium: the gypsy girls and I gazing at each other from worlds with different specific gravities, requiring different methods of breathing.

Early the next morning we drive to the citadel of Mycenae, *The house* where reality refuses to stay in the tidy compartments con- *of Atreus* trived for it. The palace crowns an acropolis high in hills that overlook a valley of the Argolid plain, a long fertile avenue to the gulf. The approach is by a good wide road cut sensibly into the foothills. There is an ample parking lot, a cedarwood toilet hut, an enamel sign warning against starting forest fires with cigarettes.

Past the chainlink and the water fountains, one climbs to the entrance with its gate of keystone lions—the gate where Clytemnestra welcomed Agamemnon home into the net. What is left of the palace structure is low rubble, clinging to the shape of the hills. As we arrive, a party of tourists with cerebral palsy are slowly descending the wide rock steps from the palace toward their bus below. The bus is already revving its engines, filling the air with the sour mélange of bus smells. One man stops to tell me that he has lost his sunglasses; in difficult speech, he explains that he dropped them near the circle grave. Behind us, the horned peaks of the mountains Marta and Zara are rising two thousand six hundred feet on either side of the citadel.

At Mycenae, by 1500 B.C. the northern sky gods ruled; Zeus was supreme. His priests were the *wa-na-ka,* whose rule extended throughout the Aegean, a wise dominion it seems, founded on knowledge of natural cycles: the palace that worshipped Zeus is sited in the shadow of mountains that, according to Vincent Scully, form the upraised arms of the Earth Mother, a shape echoed in Mycenaean terracotta sculptures. We approach the Lion Gate. Wildflowers pry out of the dry stone walls and rock fissures, small plants who favor bare places and meadow-blanketing varieties that spill away and down the hillside. Past the lions, inside the palace walls, the grave circles—deep, straight-sided wells of stone and grass—are baking in the sun. There are moments when the world is suddenly more fluid. As we stand on the rim, looking into the graves, time arrives in its complexity: the sunglasses are nowhere in sight; it is July 1989; the shaft tombs are from the Middle Helladic period; nearby, Clytemnestra stabs her child-murdering husband to death in a bloody bathtub. Here we walk on stone, on theatre, on myth, on history; the present, past, and future. As I put on some sun-block, the Queen has come outside the Lion Gate to justify her revenge to the stunned Chorus.

> You see truth in the future at last. Yet I wish to seal my oath with the Spirit in the house: I will endure all things as they stand now, hard though it be. Hereafter let him go forth to make bleed with death and guilt the houses of others. I will take some small measure of our riches, and be content that I swept from these halls the murder, the sin, and the fury.[13]

The thick, old walls of her house stand on the Argolid plain as rocky testimony to these events, and the scrubby wildflowers, delicate little things of no long lives, soothe the painful walls.

You recall the story. For seducing his brother Atreus's wife, Thyestes is exiled from the Argolid lands. Later, Atreus invites his brother to a banquet of reconciliation where he serves up the children of Thyestes in a stew. Thyestes curses the house of Atreus and leaves again, his one surviving child in tow. The two sons of Atreus are Menelaos and Agamemnon. Agamemnon marries Clytemnestra and has three children: Iphigenia, Electra, and Orestes. Menelaos marries the incomparable Helen, and when she is seduced by Paris, the brothers mount a campaign to repossess her from Troy. The Argolid warships are ready to sail but becalmed in the harbor, and the asssembled warriors grow unbearably restless. Desperate for wind, Agamemnon agrees to the terms of Artemis: she will send wind for war if Agamemnon sacrifices his youngest daughter. The King agrees, slaughters Iphigenia, sails to Troy, and returns ten years later, victorious and with his mistress. During the absence of the King, Clytemnestra has mourned her daughter, taken as a lover the surviving son of Thyestes, and burned with rage. Alerted to the return of her husband by a series of signal fires, the Queen welcomes Agamemnon home, draws him a soothing bath, and when he is at ease and turning to her, stabs him to death. Orestes feels compelled to avenge his father's death, and with the blessing of Apollo, murders his mother.

Thus closes the second of the three plays that make up the grievous *Oresteia* of Aeschylus, a story over whose territory we presently walk in the rubble of Mycenae. Here, as time advances in its undifferentiated swirl, we pick our way over the palace ruins to the Cistern. This is a deep reservoir dug down into the hill to the level of an underground spring, creating a secret cache that supplied the palace with water during long sieges. The water filled an almost vertical cave that goes down ninety stone steps carved into a worn, narrow-walled passage. The entrance itself is through a corbel-vaulted arch, the kind that forms a pointed top without a keystone. In the fierce sunlight and from a distance of twenty feet, the opening is a pitch-black triangle into the underworld. Chiseled and placed in a limestone retaining wall of a nearby palace storeroom is a small marble sign: *The Cistern*, it simply reads. The overall effect should satisfy horror-movie fans. Henry Miller, who was not known to shy away from experience, once visited Mycenae just before World War II and went down a few slippery steps of the Cistern with his friend Katsimbalis. Later he wrote, "We have not descended it, only peered down with lighted matches. The heavy roof is buckling with the weight of time. To breathe too heavily is enough to pull the world down over our ears. . . . I refuse to go back down into that slimy well of horrors. Not if there were a pot of gold to filch would I make the descent."[14]

Before I set out to Greece, a philosopher had pressed a two-inch flashlight into my hand. It works by no moving parts; rather, squeezing the case activates a chemical battery and a minute, bright beam. "Good for alleys and theatres," the philosopher said. Digging the gift out of a pocket, I step just inside the cool lip of the Cistern. Everyone except the congenitally claustrophobic can probably descend some few steps. Daylight dwindles gradually, then on the sixteenth tred, the stairs turn left and the passageway goes utterly dark. Pressed into action, the philosopher's light illuminates a very small spot on the wall, and, as one, our party of three mature adults has strong stirrings in mid-chest and at the throat, and we wordlessly flee upwards towards daylight.

At the top, just inside the shady overhang of the cave entrance, we take stock. There are three fears: of closed-in, tight spaces; that at the bottom there is only emptiness; of fanged snakes. Peter has returned to America, and we can only wonder what this optimistic soul would find ominous. In the *via negativa*, Tony, Katherine, and I find that any two of us can counsel the third, presenting clear, obvious reasons why that friend's fear can be waved away with the kind hand of reason. The passage has plenty of air; there will be a bottom, likely a slimy pool of water; and lastly, my friends want to believe that no fanged things dwell on the walls, lying in wait. But apparently they have forgotten that the cave belongs to the House of Atreus. What is at hand if not a descent into the airless, empty, poisonous beings we can be? "How about a soda from the snack shop?" suggests Tony, but for women who have read Melville and too much Henry James, the symbolic descent is irresistible. As Katherine and I agree that we must try again but that we need a stronger light, a lone tourist approaches unsheathing a spelunker's light. Hermes has many disguises, but we have no trouble recognizing him this time. Mutely, we follow him into the Cistern, down and around the bend into complete darkness, past the twentieth step, down and down, and into a passage where the stairs are narrow as snake's hips. At bottom, the guide stops and shines his light, and we silently stare at a dry rock slab, dusted with crinkled leaves. Halfway back up the stairwell, pitch-black becomes merely ink-black, and here the mercurial guide speeds his steps and disappears. Above ground, we get to test the fibre of our renewed selves straight away, on the mountain roads of the eastern prong of the Peloponnese.

T raveling south along the eastern edge of Arkadia from My- *Under* cenae through the Parnon Oros, mountains which shelter *plane trees* brown bears, wolves, and wild boars, we teeter on thin veins of asphalt, roadbeds skimming gorges in hairpin turns and winding, sickening curves. No guardrails or roadside boulders offer protection against the sudden spin into the chasm. Instead, every few miles there is an elaborate roadside shrine, and gradually we surmise that roadside shrines *are* the Greek guardrail program. What these installations lack in continuous physical protection, they make up for with other powers. The shrines are boxes bolted onto a post or a rock, but in particulars each is an original: some are stucco boxes painted white, some are wood, others nearly all glass, edged in tin like a Greek lantern; there are elegant cages, diminutive model churches, and rough lemon crates. Always the side facing the road has a glass door or an opening into which the cautious traveler places votive candles, flowers, garlics, and personal icons. The candles are lit, the flames wavering over small, damp pools of wax, and at the base of each shrine is often a small, desultory cairn topped with drying flowers.

As the altitude increases so does the water supply. The subalpine meadows are much greener than the plains below; the air is cool and refreshing. This is the region of Greece traditionally associated with Artemis, said to be especially beloved of her. It is also prime beehive country, where steep and gradual hillsides alike are dotted in cities of hives, hundreds of hives carefully spaced over the land, and painted, not white but blue, for Greek bees. At the timberline, the flora shrinks into the dainty, miniature plants of alpine meadows. Here can be found wormwood, the *Artemisia* plant whose dried flowers and stems we bought in the Athens βοτανα as "mountain tea," and which, in distillate form, becomes absinthe. It has long been a symbol of all that is bitter and troubling to the soul: once a "furious star named Wormwood . . . fell from heaven across the darkened sky of the Book of Revelation and made bitter one third of the waters of the earth"; "Wormwood, wormwood," mutters Hamlet, listening to the Queen's protests.[15] Overhead, two falcons ride the windrafts on canyons of air. At noon, we safely arrive at Kosmos, a tiny village at the crest of the Parnon range.

The plaza of Kosmos is entirely defined by seven Oriental plane trees planted in an arc, and it is worth driving the harrowing chasms merely to drink a lemonade under these trees. All of the village shops and parking spaces, a town hall, three cafés, and a large Orthodox church fit themselves under the shady boughs of the planes. The crowns spread twenty meters or more in the air; the great trunks are dappled and multicoloured where old bark has flaked off, revealing white wood that has here turned green, there brown, in staggered phases. Judging from their girths, the trees are easily two centuries old. At this time of the year hundreds of round, green-headed bobbles dangle from the branches, inviting pollination. Since the time of Ecclesiastes, the Greeks have loved and planted plane trees, and have considered them wise. It could be because of the great age they attain, or the way their skin slowly peels revealing the inner life, or maybe just because they invite humans to sit under them and contemplate a cat snoozing on the sill across the street. They do especially bring to mind Willa Cather's remark: "I like trees," she said, "because they seem more resigned to the way they have to live than other things do." Just beyond the shade of the last tree, the big wooden doors of the village church open onto a quiet back street, and there, sprawled in the sun to dry, are a hundred glinting brass things: brass music stands and candleholders, collection trays, cups, chalices, communion trays, snuffers, brass bells and horns. The street around the polished objects is soaked dark with wash water. En masse, the panoply of liturgical brass is a blinding concentrate of solar shine, like armor, and it burns into the unsuspecting eye just emerging from the shade. Stopping so briefly, all we know of Kosmos is shade and brass. Such places come fleet across the mind like haiku, everything parsed to a handful of syllables: a dappled understory of Oriental planes, burning brass beyond.

B y evening we are halfway down the prong in Arkadia, on the coast, and as the sun slips away we make our way on foot down a sandy hillside to a speck on the map called Porto Sambatiki. Here a dashing man named Yorgas Lysikatos, come home worldly after twenty years on cruise ships, has built a small taverna and guest house that looks as much like a ship as anything on land can: here are mahogany rails and doors, polished brass fittings, ropes swagging the perimeters of decks and rooms. An actual vessel, a dinghy, rests on the sand in front of the taverna, and before dinner Tony and I row the blue boat out into the harbor, rowing in the Greek way, facing ahead, pushing rather than pulling the thin oars. For dinner Yorgas cooks fish stew, and later that night, upon seeing me sweeping sand from the porch in front of my room, proposes marriage. This night I have a hard time sleeping. It is not only that Yorgas prowls around his garden, unreconciled to my reply. We are in the land of Artemis tonight, and it is her unsettling role in the old play of Aeschylus that keeps me awake.

"Night, hear me, o Night, mother"

Several hundred miles north of this seaside taverna, the denoument of the *Oresteia* unfolds: Orestes has just killed his mother, and now the Furies appear to the boy, hounding him, eager to tear him limb from limb. Only in Apollo's new temple at Delphi can a matricidal child find even partial sanctuary, and as the Furies recognize neither Apollo's young logic nor his purification rites, they relentlessly torment Orestes, at last pinioning him on the rock of Athens. All the aggrieved appeal to Athena, soul of Athenian society. The goddess appoints a court of citizens to judge the case, and when the jury is deadlocked casts the tie-breaking vote on the side of Orestes, affirming the new patriarchal code, saying, ". . . I am always for the male / with all my heart, and strongly on my father's side. / So, in a case where the wife has killed a husband, lord / of the house, her death shall not mean most to me."[16]

Even so, Athena knows that the old order of the Furies must be propitiated. Says Athena, "I promise you a place of your own, deep hidden under ground that is yours by right." Not easily removed from their original, central place, the Furies groaningly reply, "Earth, ah, Earth / what is this agony that crawls under my ribs? Night, hear me, o Night, / mother. They have wiped me out and the hard hands of the gods / and their treacheries have taken my old rights away."[17]

But as the play occurs in fifth-century Athens at a time when Olympian divinities and city-state laws have long triumphed over the old goddess culture, inevitably Apollo and Athena prevail. Gradually, the Furies are made to soften and to forego bringing blight on the land. They even accept the name Eumenides, "the Gentle Ones," and allow themselves to be buried under the law court on the Areopagos, the hill of *arai* and *dike*—curses and justice. Until the recent theory that the subjugation of women and the degradation of the Earth are related phenomena, generations of scholars have found this a fine and believable ending, one that resolves tensions between the culture in which the most sacred thing is the Earth itself—figured as female, immanent, life-giving, and death-dealing—and the culture in which the dominant forces are transcendent male gods who sanction legal and warrior codes. By the great tensions in his play, the poet Aeschylus shows the older lifeworld undergoing an imperfect, painful subordination to the values of the patriarchal city-state, and poses a question: What ethics best align the human house with the preexistent Earth forces? Lately, some readers (reading as the rainforests burn) have begun to notice how fragile is the play's official happy ending that buries the elemental forces. Donald Carne-Ross finds the play so laced with oppositional values as to fundamentally resist reconciliation: on one hand, tribal bonds, fertility, immanent deities, the cyclical renewal of life within a numinous landscape; on the other, hierarchical power, linear time, allegiance to law and transcendent gods. Adding weight to the view that the situation remains unstable is the peculiar role of Artemis. Why should the protective, life-loving goddess demand the death of an innocent girl? Why does she vanish, never to reappear?

Surely, when Atreus slaughters all but one of his nieces and nephews and feeds their bodies to their father it is clear that even as the women in the *Oresteia* are reduced from sacred beings to property, the children are no longer understood by the Atreid fathers as beloved young life, but rather as markers in a political struggle. These values are anathema to Artemis, the otherness in nature, the I-Thou distance between intimates. Although her wilderness is inherently unlike patriarchal society, Artemis does not represent a rejection of the masculine, nor an upholding of the feminine, but a choice for inviolable being.[18] As the goddess unto herself, she cannot put much stock in marriage, and her primordial duty is to protect the wild, generative world; by her standards, the seduction of one man's wife by another man, however vexing, is not grounds for the slaughter of the next generation of children. Moreover, included in the green wilderness of Artemis is not only biologically young life, but the potential for renewal within human beings of any age. She is offended not only by children served up in a stew, but by all the carnage to be set in motion by the sailing to Troy. Artemis is angry because for generations the house of Atreus has responded to relatively insignificant wrongs with acts that are transgressions against life. When Artemis gives Agamemnon the choice of his daughter's life or a wind for war, she hardly extracts a sacrifice that pleases her. Rather, she sends her arrows straight and deep, revealing starkly that his mission and values entail the routine sacrifice of youth and of the nurturing quick of the soul.

Other observers have viewed the *Oresteia* optimistically, as a work that envisions a new morality, achieved in tragic but warranted tension between primitive powers and the new codes of justice. Certainly the *Oresteia* is concerned with ending the cycle of sorrows caused by the custom of revenge. But this concern is woven with others: What happens to the human moral order when "female"—the whole constellation of human mother and Earth—is no longer an inviolable, numinous being? For the sake of humans and the Earth alike, we may very well want to shed the idea that nature is female, but the old questions of Aeschylus remain. Carne-Ross finds that the basic assumption that Aeschylus makes about the relationship of the human to the natural worlds is that "disorder in one realm" can spill "over into the other."[19] What Aeschylus evidently knows is that by dishonoring the green, protective wilderness within our own specifically human nature, we invite the anger of Artemis. His play is not a historical exercise. By the fifth century B.C., the Greek conception of nature has evolved from chthonic force to an "infinite abundance" that is the context for civilization.[20] However, the old Earth divinities, and the old-culture values they embody, are more than a memory. They remain powerful for many citizens for hundreds of years, even into Hellenistic Alexandria, where Philo writes:

> The Earth . . . as we all know, is a mother, for which reason the earliest men thought fit to call her "Demeter," combining the name of "mother" with that of "Earth" for, as Plato (*Menexenus* 238A) says, Earth does not imitate woman, but woman Earth. Poets quite rightly are in the habit of calling earth "All-mother" and "Fruit-bearer" and "Pandora" or "Give-all," inasmuch as she is the originating cause of existence and continuance in existence to all animals and plants alike.[21]

At nearly the same time that Aeschylus wrote his play, Sophocles wrote a passage of the play *Antigone*; known to us as "The Ode to Man," it is also the work of a mind lamenting the human will to overreach: "Many things are *deinos*. Nothing / stranger than human kind. This being / overpasses the grey sea, blown / by southerlies under the arching swell / that chasms to the depths all round; / wears at the eldest of the gods, / Earth . . . / year in, year out, as the plough wheels to and fro."[22] (*Deinos*, which does not come into English, means at once terrible, wonderful, strange, and uncanny.)

To appreciate the prescience of these poets, consider that the word *oekologie* was first coined in 1868, and that for decades early ecologists noticed only interactions among non-human life. When, in 1864, Charles Perkins March wrote a book called *Man and Nature* that detailed human degradation of environments, his book was politely ignored as pessimistic. Only after World War II did the perceptive begin to recognize the degrading human impact on the planet.[23] In their writings, Aeschylus and Sophocles, who already saw, are not forecasting the future misadventures of humankind, rather they are witnessing the troubled relations that our species has had, from early on, with the rest of nature. As their plays predate all that we recognize as technology and pollution, the startling thing they tell us is that our problems of habitation are an accelerating, but not new, condition. In the last two decades, a new branch of philosophy has emerged; this is how K. S. Schrader-Frechette opens her book on environmental ethics:

> If environmental degradation were purely, or even primarily, a problem demanding scientific or technological solutions, then its resolution would probably have been accomplished by now. As it is, however, our crises of pollution and resource depletion reflect profound difficulties with some of the most basic principles in our accepted systems of values. They challenge us to assess the adequacy of those principles and, if need be, to discover a new framework for describing what it means to behave ethically or to be a "moral" person.[24]

The shaping powers of *techne* and reason have emerged from the Earth, and it would be unnatural if we did not use them in creating our habitation.[25] Yet we also contain what lies beyond the likes of Apollo and Athena. Once upon a time in the heyday of determinism and logical positivism, the French physicist Laplace thought that with sufficient data and computing power we would predict every event. Both Heisenberg's uncertainty principle, "the first crack in the crystalline structure of determinism," and chaos theory tell us that a fundamental wildness saturates the universe.[26] Wonderfully, the evolving planet is more complex than our minds can ever encompass, and a choice for wilderness is not only placing vast geographical acreage beyond human influence—indeed, doing so is to *exert* human influence. The wild asks us to accept mystery, to temper the authentic planning, questing vein, and when we agree to do so, curiously, wilderness cultivates in us the light touch of the truly civilized.

The secluded hotel on the delightful island of Lemnos comprises a hundred and twenty-five charming stone-built cottages, each with its own walled garden. A superb buffet is served at the open-air beach restaurant. The hotel is situated on its own fine golden sand beach and offers excellent windsurfing, pedaloes, sailing boats, canoes, sun shades, and easy chairs. Myrina, the island capital, is a pleasant ten-minute stroll from the hotel and has a colorful port where one can watch fishermen mending their nets.

—from the advertisement for the Akti Myrina

Problems outside the hotel

I came upon this description of paradise and a photograph of a family reading in their walled garden—vines spilling over the stones, a lamp glowing—while staying on Angistri Island, living in Studio Vassilari, a motel-like row affair entered by means of a concrete bridge that spanned a gully full of garbage and year-old construction trash: conduit tailings, fiberglass insulation sheets, paint cans. Studio Vassilari is a housekeeping arrangement, which means that for twice the cost of an ordinary *pensione* one can exchange maid service (of which there was none) for a hotplate. This deal seems to strike a large number of travelers as a good idea, for the Vassilari is full; indeed all of the *pensiones* on the island are full, and we consider ourselves lucky to have found the last room at the Vassilari.

The rooms are not simple dull rectangles, but hybrids of parallelogram and rhomboid; arranging ordinary furniture within this geometry has defeated the best efforts of the management, and the standard large Greek hunks of bed, chair, and chest are left dangling at odd angles, touching walls here and there as if to steady themselves with fingertips. A great deal has been done on balconies and walkways with decorative cement blocks. The plumbing is plastic and important pieces of it move alarmingly when touched. The electrical work, other than the major conduit cables, took place after the walls were completed, requiring the electricians to puncture the surfaces in spontaneous, abstract patterns in order to thread wiring through to outlets. Sometime later, the holes were covered by round plastic discs screwed into the walls. But since the holes themselves are not round, but square, the disc covers leave intriguing triangles of dark space revealed. Lightbulbs hang bare off electrical fixtures that spring from the wall with alacrity. Cabinets and fixtures are made of wood-grained plastics and hold their shapes with the tenuous integrity of cold jello. Entrance doors and balcony doors have been laid out to thwart any cross-draft that the island winds and breezes should attempt. Curtains and shades have been considered unnecessary, and large glass sliding doors (to the concrete balcony) are sited so that maximum sun streams in throughout the day, making interiors hot as a top.

The manager (if that is the word) of Studio Vassilari is Mary, owner Vassily's fiercely overworked daughter-in-law, a woman who also serves as head waitress at the family's seaside taverna. To the extent that Mary manages to serve in both jobs, it is because she effectively shuts the idea of the existence of Studio Vassilari out of her mind. Sympathetic, we nevertheless gird ourselves, after a week, to ask Mary for clean sheets—an act made possible only by having once read *Oliver Twist*. Upon receiving the request, Mary delivers an impromptu and imperious lecture the chief point of which is that she has been to hotel school and we have not, and thus clean sheets are not necessary for another two days—at the very earliest. The full-stature fury with which this corrective is delivered would be cited as *vant le voyage*. A quickly summoned, earnest piece of diplomacy, stressing Mary's absolute right to run her lovely hotel in whatever way she deems best, followed by a delicate plea for help since the sheets in question have already been lugged to the laundry room, yields the win: Greeks honor the pride-saving gesture followed by the humbled request.

Life in a blazing hot rhomboid/parallelogram does to the mind what walking all day in ill-fitting shoes will do to the body; one is off-balance from the foundation up. And I have a fever, a residue from the toxins of Athenian air. It is in the sourest mood that I allow myself as a traveler that I look out on Angistri Port from a comely inn and taverna up the hill from the rhomboid chamber, and observe the slow progress of six more motel-studios like the Vassilari going up. It is two o'clock in the afternoon and there will be no customers until six because everyone is sleeping off the heat. The owner of this coolest interior in town, Dmitri, generously agrees to my lying on a bench near a window which occasionally admits a shimmer of air. His interior courtyard is planted with flowering vines and bushes, and the taverna has curving stucco benches that appear to grow out of the floor and wind through space in graceful arcs.

"He had a German architect do it," says Joe. "The architect said to use old beams in the ceiling, but Dmitri did not want old wood; why use second-hand when he could afford new wood beams?" Somehow the architect won that point, because the beams are old, as are the tall shutters in the thick white walls, and there are old ceiling fans rotating slowly. Joe lives in Pittsburgh now and returns to his family's island home for two months each summer, frequently visiting at his friend's inn. He is a mechanic, thin, wearing Hush Puppies and a short-sleeved plaid shirt, and his wavy thinning hair is brushed straight back just like Richard Nixon's. He has lived in America for six years and he tells his two brothers to forget about America, but they are saving for the plane ticket. Joe makes much more money than they do; he has a car, a television, an apartment near the plant; he gets a week's paid vacation and he can drive to Florida. Joe tells his brothers that he has gotten a nervous stomach in America, that everything is fast: "Fastfastfast." He says it as one word. But, he laments, "you cannot tell them." The brothers like the sound of work and money. "It is more relaxed here," Joe says. "The food is good. I take out my boat. At night we hear the sound of our voices. This year, I don't make so much money because I am here, but in America it is fastfastfast."

Out the window, things are not quite the way Joe remembers. Down the hillside, the concrete floor slabs and verticals are poured for the new motels: electrical cables pop like bugs' antennae from each floor, the surrounding earth is hard-packed, a dull red color. What is the fatal thing that happens in the shift from the traditional affordable way of building to the new practices? The modest houses in Metochi Village, uphill from the port, have a bedrock integrity: the windows are not precisely, merely beautifully, located, making striking graphic designs of each wall. The proportions of windows to rooms are unfailingly pleasing. Casement depths are just right to invite one to lean and look out the windows. Breezes are caught; coolness is captured. White, terracotta, brown, and blue cooperate. Materials, forms, and colors have come to understand each other; tile yields to wood, wood to stucco, stucco to white, white to cracks and splatters—old hands at the marriage of function and beauty.

I suppose the reasons for the disastrous change must be complex, involving industrial production methods, new economies, bureaucracies of building codes. The result is easier to depict, and it is more than shoddy, grotesque buildings which are built only because someone has decided that a cheap hotel is a way to make money. In the series of calculations that go into these decisions, somewhere along the line, perhaps at the outset, the host/guest tradition is ended in favor of the entrepreneur/consumer tradition, a different ritual altogether—one not without its own points of honor, but a practice that fundamentally changes the way value is measured. Now each member of the encounter, and the encounter itself, is allotted worth on a solely economic scale. The hideous buildings in Angistri's port town violate not only aesthetic but moral principles and demonstrate again how these are irreducibly twined. The rampant building on Angistri Island is increasingly typical of Greek villages and islands where tourists can be easily harvested. The next step is inevitable: huge increases in raw sewage which is still dumped directly into the waters off the village, resulting in water too foul for fish or human swimming. The clear, brilliant sea-blues of travel posters notwithstanding, in all of Greece only seven beaches have recently been found clean and safe by the Greek National Tourism Organization: three on Rhodes, two on Crete, one on Chios, and one in central Greece.

Faced with this and other devastating interactions between tourists and Greek life and ecosystems, one traveler wrote *The Athenian:*

Dear editors,

My husband and I . . . would very much like to re-visit Greece but, in view of the damage which tourism is doing to the natural heritage, we are loathe to support the tourist trade and thereby hasten the destruction. I cannot think that my husband and I are alone in being . . . satisfied with simple facilities in private homes, instead of large tourist hotels. . . . I feel confident that eco-holidays may well be the answer—the local people would still enjoy extra income from tourists and tourists themselves would enjoy . . . the proper Greece, with its cultural and natural heritage intact. . . .

Sincerely,

Delia Burt, Old Storridge, Alfrick, Worcestershire

Two new concepts in tourism are being floated by the travel industry these days. One is what Mrs. Burt refers to, and is generally called eco-tourism. Offered by various enlightened agencies and the travel wings of conservation groups, eco-tourism stresses benign observation. Another kettle of fish altogether is something being called "quality tourism." Business writer Nigel Lowry follows the tourist industry and noted recently that "not only Greece, but all those countries which on the strength of their sunny climates have been favored travel destinations for many years are facing the same challenge. Many feel they have reached, or are approaching the saturation point in terms of numbers of foreign holidaymakers, and are now seeking ways to attract better quality tourists with a higher level of purchasing power."[27] Mr. Lowry notes two areas that may affect quality tourism; he calls them "marketing" and "reality." Marketing is first and foremost, but Mr. Lowry adds, in an afterthought worthy of Monty Python, that "changes in reality must not lag too far behind." In Lowry's analysis, the improved marketing effort for Greece must generally consist of spending much more money on advertising and of devising a better slogan than the one Greece pitched in 1989 to Scandinavia: "You are at the right time-distance for vacations." (The world will be poorer deprived of this hint that Scandinavians plan holidays with the calculus and relativity theory.)

Now for reality. The opinion of the tourist industry is that pollution, "the toilet problem," and unsafe traffic conditions cannot easily be changed, if they can be changed at all. Thus the industry recommends that more self-contained luxury hotel compounds be built to attract what it calls "higher quality tourists." A model compound is The Cretan Village, a resort owned by Mr. Angelopoulos—the savant who sums up Greece saying, "There are problems which exist outside the confines of the hotel." In addition to the luxury fortresses, more conference centers, yachting marinas, and luxury spas should be developed to make Greece a "more varied holiday destination," an increasingly important plan so the industry is not dependent on what it calls "the sundrenched scenery, *which in any case is gradually being spoiled* [italics mine]." Having defined higher quality as synonymous with more purchasing power, while at the same time having written off the natural world and the insoluble problems outside the hotel, the Greek tourist industry (and no doubt many others) imagines that it will be left with a myriad of small paradisical compounds that will insure its financial security during the next decades of planetary devastation. Multiply this kind of logic several billion times and you have the plight of Hotel Earth, degraded by a swollen human guest list, each room and wing within the whole believing that it may pollute with impunity, then wall itself off and arrange not to be affected by the problems outside the hotel.

The deep appeal of the impulse to retreat into small personal solutions is clear to me the day I lie feverish, unable to avoid the view of Angistri Port being degraded. I gaze upon the color photograph of the walled village of Atiki Marini with unabashed longing: the little walled garden, old stones over which the bougainvillea drapes in bloom. My fervid wish is to be transported into the walled garden, the scent of flowers, the lap of water. . . . Another day, that wish is granted as wishes ever are—sort of. Far from little Angistri, near the tip of the eastern finger of the Peloponnese, is the offshore island of Monemvassia, a castle and fortress town that has been exquisitely restored by a consortium of bankers and architects. It is a town in which the basil plants that rise to giant heights in clay amphora are perfectly formed globes, the tips of the leaf-whorls plucked each morning to thwart the plants' impulse to go to seed. The stone streets are among the only streets in Greece entirely free of crushed cans, plastic straws, and paper trash. At every window hangs an elegant crocheted curtain, the lacy pattern opening near the hem into a cat or a moon. The wood frames on all the windows are sanded and refitted; the signs are regulated by codes—handmade, wooden. Even the one trouble in paradise is elegantly presented. In the castle where we have rooms, a calligraphed sign hangs on a polished brass fixture: "There is problem in Castle," it reads in English, "Please use water carefully." No motor vehicles come inside the walls. I put down my camera after ten minutes;

taking pictures would be like fishing for trout in an overstocked trout pond.

This crafted, walled garden is a place well beyond our means and dauntingly ordered, so we will stay but one night, entering the undeniable beauty as a meditation chamber. The moon grows full on our night in Monemvassia. The castle's windows have deep ledges and the view is over red-tile roofs down to a slate-blue sea over whose undulating surface the moon hangs round, paving a broad gold road from the horizon to the beach, or from the beach to the horizon—in any case, a passable road through a night far too luminous to spend in sleep. By eleven o'clock the only sound is a mouse nibbling on the roof. On a broad stone ledge I set out the last of the bay leaf and wormwood bundles, which promptly begin to shed their light powdery scents into the night air. The moon comes further into the room, glazing a pool on the polished floorplanks and on the intricate layers of rugs, and causing bits of metal sewn into the Turkish pillows to wink.

THE VERY
RICH HOURS

*. . . for every hour and change corresponds
to and authorizes a different state of mind.*
—Ralph Waldo Emerson

The sound of a delicate drum surrounds the boat. It is a houseboat anchored in a mangrove swamp, glazed with a sheet of dew. By dawn, the fruit of condensation is spilling over the roof in a bead curtain of rain around the cabin, each string glistening, plashing the deck. Clouds recede in the deep perspective of dioramas. The world is withheld, the blast of sun cushioned by the million miles, creatures just rustling awake. Out of the hush, a flurry of fish cracks the water-mirror, a surface suddenly ruffled with choppy, wedge-shaped patches. The green-striped fish are jumping to an urgent rhythm, each one wriggling in the large wedge that shifts like a gust over the cove and on out into the channel. At cove's edge, a snaky cormorant neck pops up near a dark shape floating under a fingery branch of the sort that canoeists call a strainer. Upon scrutiny, this shape looks to be a rotting log, possibly a winkling reflection of the root tangle growing into the water.

The cormorant is motionless as by imperceptible degrees the shape emerges from the strainer, evolving from winkle to wood to reptile: gliding, now gathering speed, swishing its tail in an elegant, horrifying motion, a long S-shaped movement that powers the animal effortlessly through the water. The creature swims in a beeline for the boat, head slightly elevated, snout skimming the surface, gliding closer, stopping five feet from the pontoon hulls. The houseboat is incomparably bigger than the creature; just how at home and fearless is this being can be known from the long, even, unblinking, unworried glare it gives the boat. For ten minutes, it looks headlong into our pod of civilization, never flinching. The eyes do not shine with our kind of intelligence; they are merely as old and wise as the hills: bottomless, brown-black marbles. From behind an apron rail of metal, we can choose to return the gaze of this confident emissary.

The animal opens its mouth. You'll want the word *primal* even before alligators open their mouths. When they do, the word describes one's involuntary recoil, and the unspeakable innards of the sawtoothed jaw whose butter-yellow gums resemble molded extrusions of industrial waste. One yellow tooth is longer than the others, not sharp but rounded from age and use. That would be the fourth, enlarged tooth of the underjaw, the one that fits into a pit formed for it within the upper jaw. When the jaw snaps shut, one sees the wry line of mouth. The sinuous slit that dips and rises and extends well past the wrinkled eye coaxes us to see a boundless smile, the unmediated joy of old men and babies. "See him sweating o'er his bread before he eats it.—'Tis the primal curse, but soften'd into mercy." So says Cowper about the origins of the likes of us. Among its virtues, including scrupulous keeping of the glades, the alligator gives us a chance to grow in mercy: the old monster's good works, while not performed by our terms of altruism, have a most benevolent effect on the chain of being.

In the marshy grasslands of the everglades proper, alligators use their feet and snouts to clear away vegetation from the largest water holes to make more comfortable, commodious pools for themselves. During dry spells these pocket lagoons are oases for a toothsome concentrate—sunfish, gambusia, snails, soft-shelled turtles, and Spider Lilies—all water-dependents who cohabit with alligators in their holes until the rains return.[1] Some of these creatures become the alligator's winter food, but in the glades, lack of water is more deadly than the happy jaw, and enough survive to renew their kind when the rains return. In the weeded holes, fish can freely swim and grow, and the discarded, decaying flora flung up by the alligator surrounds the hole with mucky land ideal for emergent cattails and arrowleafs. In time, these plants combine with marl to form a soil that can support ferns and tree seedlings;

when the latter appear, the gator hole is well on the way to becoming a tree island—one of the willow heads, cypress heads and bay heads that rise up from the sawgrass marshes. Taken together, the luxuriant worlds framed by wax myrtle, cocoplum, gumbo limbo, swamp holly, slash pine, cypress, saw palmetto, and willow trees succor a wealth of life: frogs, lizards, otters, and spiders; the *Liguus* tree snails that breed in fifty-two colors and resemble turbans wrapped to the pointiest logical extreme; the rare and more rare Florida panther; the soaring Everglade kite and its only food, the pinkish pomacea snail. From the sides of many trees grow the air plants from whose tips are squeezed the last word in hothouse blooms, the orchids. Evenings in the tree islands are heady with the scent of the night-blooming epidendrum, whose sweetness radiates from a spidery white flower, yielded by the plant but one at a time. In a very real sense, the formula for this perfume includes the mucking-out labours of a reptile species, a member of which now stares at our boat.

It is January, just after the new year, the season when the gladekeepers are in their winter torpor, eating but rarely. After long assessment, the enormous tail muscle ripples, the waffle-iron-plated body slides underwater in one of its fluid, immensely graceful motions. Instantly the water ruffles again into wedge-shaped patterns as a froth of fish commence leaping out of harm's way. To riverboat pilots and wading birds it will not be news that water shows tracks, if fleetingly: this patchy wedge is *feeding-alligator-water*. Seconds later, traces of the hunt have disappeared.

O ur houseboat is a modest, rectangular hat that sits atop a *A floating* double-pontoon hull. It is named the *Cobia* after a good- *house* tasting Florida fish and rented from the Flamingo Marina, located on the Bay of Florida at Buttonwood Canal. Houseboat *Cobia* is forty feet long, with a narrow walkway around the cabin, and is said to sleep eight. This floating house, the most perfectly compact house since the microcosms made in cardboard boxes at five, has a tiny sink, a tiny shower, and a tiny cooking range. It has cups and saucers, a drawerful of linens, and three dinged and dented cooking pots. My notion had been that Peter and I would board this idyll with rice and beans, our field glasses and books, and commence bucolic drifting through the mangrove waterways. Only after Peter had spent some weeks studying a bulky blue book titled *Chapman's Piloting* and insisted that we purchase a marine chart detailing the bays and rivers over which we proposed to float, did I grasp that we would need to navigate—that we would be doing such things as weighing and setting anchor, signalling other human craft with a certain number of toots to mean "trouble around the bend" and a different number of toots to mean "passing on your left." I mean *port*, for on the boat there was to be no left and right. Many things had new names: a map would be a *chart*, closet *stowage*, dashboard *helm*; front would be *fore*, and back *aft*. In fact, we had new names too. At the same marine supply store where we bought the waterproof chart for Lostman's River to Whitewater Bay, I found Peter shyly fondling a dark blue cotton hat with a brim. Its appeal lies in the fact that it is a Chinese Mao cap, retrofitted for the capitalist yacht trade with a chintzy gold and blue patch on the front that reads CAPTAIN. It gives Peter an insurgent air and, come the revolution, the patch can easily be removed.

The Maoist workers' cap, the waterproof chart, and Peter's few weeks of studying *Chapman's* completed our nautical lore, and we wondered at the judgement of a marina that would rent a forty-foot houseboat to the likes of us and release us into the mangrove wilderness. But the sheaf of rental and insurance documents at the marina clearly said, "Prior boating experience useful, but not required," and the marina is run by the National Park Service. That's our government. Surely Sam wouldn't rent hundred-thousand-dollar boats and send them into the wilds if citizens routinely destroyed the boats on submerged rocks or disappeared without a trace. And, too, the young ranger at the marina promised "a thorough orientation." During the thorough orientation, we were shown the location of skillets and spatulas, how to relight the water heater if it blew out in a stiff wind, and how to use the marine radio.

When the ranger said to us casually, while reviewing the instrument panel at the helm, "As for the throttle, you just throttle her like you would your own powerboat," we exchanged the look for *We won't say anything now*, and realized that we would be picking up a few more nautical tips on our own, such as how to actually make the boat go forwards and backwards. As to how the *Cobia* was powered out of the marina slip in view of rangers and a crowd of tourists waiting for the noon tour boat, one can only report that it— that is, she—*was* backed out and turned around in the slim channel between rows of pricey boats, and that she missed ramming two pylons and a sailboat by inches when the Captain practiced a maneuver he had read about in *Chapman's Piloting*, which was to swivel the stern smartly around by throttling forward very fast. At that, the waters churned, and blessedly the marina, the waving ranger, and the flocks of tourists and turkey vultures on the dock grew small and faded away as we entered the calm, green waters of Buttonwood Canal. Signs flanking the canal instruct craft to creep along at no-wake speed so as not to harm, or even disturb, the slow-moving manatees who browse and graze on the underwater vegetation. Creeping is also the proper speed for catching one's breath and entering the swamp.

T here are no other Everglades in the world." Since the late nineteen-forties, when Marjory Stoneman Douglas began her praise-poem and political drumbeat on behalf of the glades with a simple declarative sentence, this watery plot of the Earth has been named a bioregion of international significance. Its existence arises not least from the fact that the lower Florida penin-sula—likened to spoon, paw, and penis—slopes south at an incline of two to three inches a mile. Beginning along the southern rim of Lake Okeechobee, the everglades are a lazy, shimmering sheet of water—fifty miles wide, inches deep—trickling down the impercep-tible tilt of the peninsula through a time-worn longitudinal valley. The film creeps for one hundred miles through knife-edged saw-grass and sloughs, slowly nosing south-southeast over peat and muck to the Florida Bay. Grasping its nature precisely, the native turtle islanders named the great watery plain *Pa-hay-okee*, which translates into English as "Grassy Water" or "River of Grass."

Not fully explored

It is a first-rate act of the imagination to have seen the unifying topographical logic of this vast alliance of water and land. Radically diverging from the shapes of conventional rivers, this one forms itself from an expanse of freshwater marsh woven with mangrove islands, pine hammocks, marl prairies, and salt-invaded marshes. It is safe to say that the everglades will never be fully charted. Near

Florida Bay, the southward-creeping *Pa-hay-okee* meets the tidal estuaries and, mingling there with salty waters, gives rise to a swamp. This is a region laden with quasi-solid islands of salt-tolerant, water-loving trees all loosely, collectively called mangrove. Mangrove swamp rims the point of the peninsula and sways up its western coast, a swath commonly said to be impenetrable save by boat. In truth, there exist innumerable other time-honored ways to enter this world, among them: on heron wing, by gator tail, via shrimp larvae. It is into this southern-most feature of the peninsula that we are headed, lacking wings or tails, on the pontoons of the *Cobia.*

Close by the helm, the big waterproof chart is unfurled on a table and weighted against the wind with field guides and a pocket knife. The chart is peppered with tiny black soundings (in feet) and puns such as Snake Bight and First National Bank. (So rare to find play in officialdom.) It is a beautiful map, water-coloured in pale green for mangroves, periwinkle for shoals, paler blues and whites for deeper waters, sand and mustard tones for marshes—all tinctures that blend with the swamp that the map tries to picture. Save for the flanking glamours of sunrise and sunset, the palette of the southern glades is muted: greens, greys, blues and browns and silvers in endless combinations. Here and there are large, unmarked areas in whose expanses antlines of typography read "not fully explored." Printed about the perimeter are firm caveats concerning shifting realities of the shores. The line where land and water meet is a lace of form, each element reaching toward the other in a complex filigree. Through these rococco shapes, for five hundred map miles through the pale and numbered expanse—through bays and a maze of creeks, snaking north through The Nightmare into the Broad River—runs one thin red line: the Wilderness Waterway, winding from Flamingo north to Everglades City. In the way of worlds and maps, the idea of the line exists continuously on paper and in the swamp not at all—an inevitable discrepancy, like the lacunae of gender and desire, that opens the space for creativity and disaster. To respond to this discrepancy, the idea of line is imported to the waterways and noted on a series of numbered posts topped with Christmas-green squares and cherry-red triangles—shapes and colors like nothing else in the swamp.

Within the hour, Whitewater Bay appears: a brillig expanse of water surrounded and studded with shiny green mangrove thickets, each oily, oblong leaf of which shines separately—a glinting green tribe with pocket mirrors, signalling intelligent life. Upon entering the shining bay, our common thought is to swerve off the platonic line that leads dully through the center of the chart and cruise instead up the winding Joe River to the west. We speculate that the channel through mangrove and marsh will be a congenial home for wading waterbirds and silurian monsters. Planning for the journey, it had occurred to me that alligators or crocodiles might clamber aboard the houseboat at night while we slept and . . . The qualm, rooted no doubt in a fine archetype, was interrupted by an account of Mary Kingsley, "naturalist, ethnologist, sailor, scholar, guest of cannibals and champion of lost causes. Or, as she refers to herself: 'the voyager.'" In *A Long Desire*, Evan Connell reports that Mary, who left England for Africa in a gloom following her parents' deaths, "liked mangrove swamps. She would paddle around for hours examining everything, stung by flies and threatened by crocodiles." Reflecting on her outings, Mary left this note in her journal: "On one occasion, a mighty Silurian, as the *Daily Telegraph* would call him, chose to get his front paws over the stern of my canoe and endeavoured to improve our acquaintance. I had to retire to the bows to keep the balance upright, and fetch him a clip on the snout with a paddle." Well. The voyager's field notes had put things in perspective. Lacking a paddle, we stock a longish maglight, but, predictably, it is now we who need to be fetched a clip on the snout.

We marvel at the silence. Over this first day we have seen *A night for* one canoe tied to the stilts of a camping platform, a thin *hunting* plume from the fire of two souls in red bandanas. By dusk one kingfisher has shown itself, a small flock of storks, a lone ibis. Otherwise we seem to be alone inside three simple bands of color over which plays a net of constantly changing light. The temperature drops at sunset and a mass of mackerel clouds materializes. We tuck for the night into a small divet on the map, a protected cove nipped into the north shore of the river. What little wind there has been dies down, and by dark the houseboat rides at anchor on a sheet of black glass. So smooth and dark is the glass that it sparkles with Orion's belt, the Dippers, and Columba the Dove. In the cove's fluid skymap, clear as a planetarium, even the faint sword of the hunter is clear, the little blade that holds Nebula M42. Shining in the pool of anchor light is a swirl of water bugs; skimming the surface of the reflected winter stars, they might as well be the Pleiades.

Stargazing the double heaven, we come upon the spiders weaving in a space between the cosmos and the cove. In the brief hour between sundown and the ink-dark night, a coven of shaggy night-hunters have set up shop and now, under each corner of the roof eave, they are loosening large, dense webs from their unerring bellies of design, each web attached to railings and struts by long silken lines. The spiders are allies; though diminished in winter, the museless mosquitos are an ever-present whine. Given time, spiders will make the whole houseboat into a hunting platform; one of them has an enormous belly, promising a mass of minute and perfect young. The stars and spiders spin; from the mangrove comes a chirrup of insects; a pontoon creaks. Far off, to the south, off the bow and just grazing the hulking silhouette of trees, a tiny red light pulses on and off. That would be the light atop the ranger station tower miles to the south, a weak, immensely comforting signal. At two o'clock in the morning, an orange-gold boat of a moon lifts from the swamp, spawning its perfect duplicate in the cove as the white-bellied spiders quickstep across their webs.

"The Spider has a bad name," says Jean Henri Fabre, the great French entomologist.[2] Heretofore, the only good ones of which I have knowledge are Charlotte, the writer, and the very French spider who descended nights from the ceiling of Colette's mother's bedroom to sip from the chocolate bowl that simmered on the bedside lamp. By night watching the swamp spiders spin and stalk, by day consulting field guides, I glean the most basic facts about these homely, patient creatures. By their large roundish webs, we know that the spiders aboard our houseboat are aerial orb-weavers (rather than funnel-weavers, cobweb-weavers, or wolf, crab, or jumping spiders), which puts them in the family *Araneidae*. The white abdomens suggest that they are an ubiquitous American spider named *Araniella displicata*. But so voluminous are the number of spider species (upwards of thirty thousand) that biologists make a habit of proposing new classification systems, and, as Fabre sensibly says, "A fig for systems. It is immaterial to the student of instinct whether the animal have eight legs instead of six or pulmonary sacs instead of air tubes." In any case, our two-inch spiders are handsome ones, with chalk-white bellies, brown carapaces, and medium-long black legs. Smart and dapper they are, like a man wearing spats, or a woman in a polka-dotted dress and white pumps. By night they step out to hunt, each wrapping the hapless moth or insect that bumbles onto its web in bands of silk before stunning the creature with a toxic bite, then releasing a powerful digestive juice over its body, liquifying it so that the spider can easily suck the food into its small mouth. Some spiders slurp only the soft innards of their prey, which explains some of the light carapaces of grasshoppers that lie about summers, apparently unharmed but utterly empty. Our spiders like to eat the whole thing, and in the morning, all that is left are tiny, indigestible shards of insect matter that dangle on the sticky webs.

The spiders spend their sated daylight hours in a little spun nest, at a remove from the web, deep under the eaves. The nest is called a retreat and it is connected to the hunting web with a signal line that allows the spider to know in a flash if anything is stirring on its threads. The web is essentially "an extension of the spider's sensorium."[3] By keeping the tip of one leg on the signal thread, the spider in the retreat perceives the least vibration of the web, and can distinguish between the struggles of prey, the ruffle of wind, and the touch of a courting male, who gingerly taps the edge of the web—to tell the female that he is not prey. But night-hunting is so good in the mangrove swamp that we never once see our spiders until the hour before sundown, when they emerge to repair their lines.

Mornings are a prolonged upwelling of color and light: from the earliest cool blue-greys, through infant pinks, until the sky/water/mangrove triptych flares red for a quarter-hour, and the vault of clouds recedes as into the Pleistocene. When the sun ebbs into a yellow-white ball, the trance of sunrise breaks; the working day begins with the romance of weighing anchor. It is a delicate operation. One person stands on the bow

No more than a hint

runner, a little galvanized platform inches above the water, and slowly drags the clanking anchor chain aboard; the other inches the boat toward the set anchor. When the bow is directly over anchor, the helmsmate brings the boat to a smooth stop, and the bowmate heaves the plough anchor aboard. The houseboat throttle has proven to be a sticky, clumsy affair, with a gaping six-inch segment in the middle of its arc where nothing much happens and a one-half-inch zone at either end of the arc where each millimeter of movement hurtles the boat forward or backwards. Fixed for cruising, the throttle is harmless, but for weighing anchor one wants a precise and fluid action. A sudden jolt telegraphs to the boat, and promptly to one's companion, who—holding taut the anchor chain, poised on the tip of the bow—would tumble into the water, properly regarded as alligator-infested. Peter has the muscle to pull the plough anchor from mud-bottoms and heave it on board, so it has been my task to gain a light touch at the throttle; it is a pleasing pas de deux.

Upriver into Oyster Bay, distinctive shapes appear in the water, circular patches smoother than the lightly ruffled surround. Something, not an alligator, is underwater. A hummock swells, then subsides. In time, ahead of the boat, the life reveals itself, leaping just off the bow, its slick grey skin tinged yellow-brown by the leaf-soaked water. This animal is sleek and fast, much faster than a squat cabin on pontoons. When we throttle back to better admire grace, it arrows toward the bay, circles back, races ahead, repeating the gesture until we get the message. At the *Cobia*'s full forward speed, the creature stays with us, contentedly diving alongside. With each submersion, the smooth circle reappears: the surface track of a diving dolphin. As we slow down to enter a manatee zone, the dolphin glides on the wide pressure wake of the bow, swivels the unfused vertebrae of its neck and makes fleeting eye contact. Elsewhere, we have come face to face underwater with these beings. They like to look directly into human eyes, mammal to mammal. Their large eyes are full of sensuality and intellectual scrutiny, windows into a soulful brain with considerably more computing power than ours. A moaning sound from their nose (properly, the rostrum) is the scanning signal of echo-location, a neurological ability by which they "see" three-dimensional patterns of marine doings. So precise and acute is this ability that dolphins can perceive the fetus inside a pregnant woman. So lovely is their character, they will surround the woman gently, competing with each other for the pleasure of protecting her. These beings are a most compelling example of complex consciousness; this one evolved into an utterly sensual, generous being. As the *Cobia* leaves the river, the brainy, playful, peaceful one veers away. We last see its dorsal fin cresting in the shallows.

As we can never know when some other face—flushed out, drawn or repelled by the boat—will rise up to meet us in the coincidence of being, the unpredictable rhythms school us in a quiet watchfulness. As the days pass, our senses are tuned to splash of fish, settling of wing—a world of nuance that refines the human notion of plot and drama. The mind evoked by such a place is the one described by the Lakota shaman Lame Deer, who says: "We Sioux spend a lot of time thinking about everyday things, which in our minds are mixed up with the spiritual. . . . even little insects like ants and grasshoppers. We try to understand them . . . and we need no more than a hint."[4] In one of the conflations of landscape and mindscape that regularly occur, the estuary, a cleansing for the peninsula ecosystem, yields a cleansing for our kind of consciousness, too. Our preoccupations are filtered in the play of light and the timing of dolphins, the constancy of mangrove, the solacing turn and return of the sun. The change occurs so lightly that we do not know that it has happened until much later, upon emerging into the fried and batter-dipped premium octanes of the strips of southern Florida where we drive like stunned Okies in Times Square. It is not so much the bray of traffic, the scream of primary color—things astonishing in their own way—it is that each pancake house, rib joint, and fossil-fuel way station makes a kind of sense on its own, but not in aggregate. The strip is visually and logically complicated, but not complex. In the swamp, we are immersed in something whole, a being that comprehends in its compass a plenitude of parts, an interweaving of elements not simply coordinated, but moving in cycles of subordination.

As we well know, the whole of the everglades is grappling with a recent insubordination—the unbalancing of the water membrane which, along with the sun, supports the ecosystem. Throughout the peninsula now, the everglades wetlands are battered in a harsh ecological see-saw. Sometimes they have too little water because rivers have been diverted to supply water for the balmy cities and citrus groves, or because the glades have been drained to reclaim land for same: one thousand four hundred miles of canals cleave the limestone and marl of the everglades, changing the historic drainage pattern. From the point of view of agriculture and amusement parks, these operations have been successful; at this time of year, trucks migrate daylong out of southern Florida, their beds carrying half the winter vegetables marketed in the country. But the river of grass itself, at the bottom of a watershed turned Rube Goldberg apparatus, is last in line for water. Then, in a perverse irony, a wall of fresh water is occasionally released—for agricultural irrigation—from Lake Okeechobee in the north, where it rushes into the slow-moving sloughs, brusquely mangling the balance of salt and sweet in which the marshes flourish. Often water that reaches the everglades is a too-rich toxin because big sugar interests release phosphorous run-off from four hundred thirty-three thousand acres of fields south of Okeechobee into adjacent glades, starting explosive algae and cattail blooms that suffocate the ecosystem; at the height of the hot, fertile growing season, they choke four acres a day.

At another magnification, the unbalancing of the everglades is the same story that Miss Coffee told our seventh-grade class about genetic mutations. Miss Coffee said that, while offering a source of novelty and change to an organism, virtually all mutations will prove harmful to it. This is so, she explained—her short-cropped hair a Viking helmet over her head—because any lifeform existing today has taken millions of years to arrange itself in a genetic configuration that serves it well. She said this theory applied to us, too. In Miss Coffee's view, it was highly unlikely that any fundamental change in the basic organization of a being would prove useful. I could see that what she said was true: the attempts Ellen Jane Warne and I made that year to mutate ourselves with orange-juice-can hair rollers and pancake makeup were failures. Darwin's children, we persisted, evolving through waterproof mascara and curling irons, emerging decades later with the discovery of a good night's sleep.

The problem can be deciphered. Earlier human cultures, including peoples with benign and worshipful Earth philosophies, occasionally degraded their waters and lands, but not with industrial and radioactive toxins, and not with the bulky wastes of a population spawning like an overfertilized algae bloom. We could probably have it one of two ways: either a polluting industrial culture made by a microscopic population, or a technologically benign culture made by a large population. For the moment, the intersection of toxins and scale has unravelled such Earth wisdom as our species achieved in earlier dwellings, and the new circumstances are analogous to a massive mutation, wrought by the Earth itself, through its cleverest species suddenly rendered an ecological teenager. If the analogy holds, there is hope: from a later vantage, the skewed logic by which adolescents endure pain for bouffantry collapses in relief.

S ome of the silence of the mangrove swamp is simply the relative quiet away from nature's noise-filled human hubs. Compared to the gleeful and preening sounds generated by a city, the swamp has always been hushed. But accounts of the nineteenth-century swamp reliably mention a sound now entirely missing—the throaty hissing and bellowing that arose from congregations of alligators when a bull issued a challenge and one after another alligator answered, their clamor resounding for miles. "Roiling" is the word settlers often chose to describe the animals' abundant, thrashing presence in the waterways. By the late nineteenth century, alligator hides were fetching a nice price; Marjory Douglas tells that all the young boys along the mangrove rivers knew how to "grunt-up" an alligator, imitating its sound by making a "quick squeal deep in the throat with the mouth closed." At the turn of the century, it was possible for a certain young boy named Lopez to "take ten thousand alligators in one month of night fire-hunting from a lake near Shark River and sell the skins for fifty cents apiece."[5] For most of the nineteenth century, this hushed swamp also rang with the chuckling calls of egrets, the whooping

*Hissings
and
nuptial
feathers*

trumpet notes of cranes. Before the Victorian plume craze, two and a half million wading birds lived on the southern Florida peninsula. When a flock took to the air, the sky could grow suddenly dark, and when at sunset the flocks returned to their rookeries, they poured from the sky like a rustling river of wings. "Clothe yourself in them: they are your riches . . . / your treasury of birds' plumes black and yellow, / the red feathers of the macaw / beat your drums about the world: / deck yourself out in them: they are your riches."[6] That is William Carlos Williams's working of a song of feather-loving people to the south, the Náhuatl Aztec, who made not only hats and headdresses but whole ceremonial cloaks from feathers. As their example shows, it was not feather-gathering *per se*, but lack of moderation that unhinged an old and pleasurable liaison between the human body and the outrageous ones.

The most ravishing plumes, the lovely white nuptial feathers of the American egret and the snowy egret, came from the Florida rookeries. These "aigrettes" brought seventy-five cents each in the millinery center of Paris, and during the height of the frenzy one New York wholesaler bought two hundred thousand dollars' worth of aigrettes. Such markets made for unbearable temptations in the peninsula; each night a few men in canoes could kill hundreds of birds. In four years the rookeries of Okeechobee had vanished, and as ladies were now wearing whole dead birds on their heads, hunters followed the escaping flocks into the southern reaches of the glades. The first bird warden, sponsored in 1910 by the Audubon Society in an attempt to stop the slaughter, was found, a bullet down his spine, drifting in blood among the mangroves.[7] Ravaged by fashion, the birds suffer even more from the remote engineering of modern water managers. The best guess: that a whispery population of two hundred fifty thousand remains, a line of decline that continues inverse to the swell of washing machines, irrigation pipes, tumblers of ice, and amusement parks—the human artifacts that have brought the everglades to what park superintendent Robert Chandler simply, starkly names "biological collapse."[8] Without the storks and spoonbills and the gregarious ibis (whose gently curving beaks explain ancient Egyptian aesthetics), the swamp is now a tumulus hush. We encountered this same eerie silence once before, when—a week before we boarded the houseboat *Cobia*—we hiked through a swath of the forest that bounds the northwest side of the everglades proper, the Big Cypress Swamp of Collier County.

Spinoza in cypress

I n winter, a cypress swamp is silvery with sunlight through the scrim of canopy: the bald cypress called bald for the deciduous habit of dropping needles. Thirteen years ago, just at this time of year, my mother first traveled to Big Cypress Swamp. She says that she will never forget the sight and sound of the wood storks, our only native stork, nesting in the tall cypress stands. She heard them first, deep in the forest, raising a din as loud, she said, as the steel mills of Birmingham when she was a girl. When the flock came into view, it was raucous, smelly, and jubilant, a colony of thousands flapping huge wings, gliding on thermals over the swamp, mingling in air with swarms of roseate spoonbills—an empyrean of pink wings and stork anvils. Following her footsteps, we arrived in the cypress swamp this year at fledging time, approaching the forest across a prairie of sawgrass and maiden cane, bleached tawny and dry from drought. As we entered the forest and came under the canopy, the air grew suddenly cool, dropping perhaps eight degrees in seconds. Dark high-water stains ring each trunk some twenty inches above the ground, a dipstick of the drought. It was so quiet that a rustle startled us: a dark rope oozing around the base of a trunk, a black racer in the dry brush. So as not to overwhelm the delicate sounds, we whispered. What nesting pairs of storks survive have gone north near Lake Okeechobee, where water is marginally more reliable. The surdity left in their wake is analogous to the hush over peoples whose rituals, once perfectly engraved in the memories of shamans, have ceased to sound as initiates have died without successors.

Still, the cypress swamp is rich with life: red-shouldered hawks, strangler figs, luminous lizards, bright green-legged spiders dancing across four-foot webs, and herons who stalk for crayfish near torporous dark reptiles. The life that is left is powerful enough to alter our consciousness during hours hiking through the dappled light. With all that remains and only a story to go on, what is the loss of the wood storks to us? Finding the wood where one played as a child turned into split-levels with aluminum siding is eviction from the Garden. Yet to those who come after, the tidy bluegrass, a hydrant, and the two sumac trees must be the incomparable place, and out of these limbs and town plumbing may be formed perfect happiness and poetry. Does the end of an animal leave a wooly ache and sag in the idea of the Earth, or does a hole in memory open and lightly abandon a particular, raucous, winged manifestation?

There are many sound arguments for preserving birds and beasts—some based on anthropocentric utilitarian principles, some on the ecological catechism that each thing serves the web. But the human notion of *useful* fluctuates greatly and the web itself embodies change, making itself up as it goes. Our Earth is a radically creative being, and creativity relies on risky companions: uncertainty, destruction, and flux. In truth, the Earth offers no proving ground, no ecological bottom line or script that we must, or may, follow faithfully, no absolute argument in favor of "saving" wood storks, or manatees, or ice ages, or any of us. Where is the place of fixity, a time when the Earth was more or less authentic than now, when it should or could have been cast in ecological amber?

How similar we are to our source: containing in spades its impulse for novelty, for destruction, its whirl of polarities and harmonies, its search for form and tolerance of formlessness. How like meteor bombardments and volcanic eruptions—other strong forces that have provoked new forms of Earth—we have proved to be. We seem distinctive only for the riddle of conscious choice: the change-force unleashed, by the Earth itself, from the temperance of time and instinctual bone-knowledge. Some limits—the sun's heat—profoundly define our choices, but we live within a being, are *part of* a being, who has produced hundreds of versions of itself, some boiling hot, some cold and white, of late one green and blue with oxygenated life. That nature would risk something as creative and destructive as humankind merely confirms what a daring being Earth is. A venturing, Hölderlin said.

This is also Spinoza's view of nature—*natura naturans*—an open-ended process neither rule-bound nor chaotic, but creative within evolving forms. To rely on the Earth's principles as a guide for human morality, technology, and aesthetics is to reference an open-ended and constantly evolving ground of being. This is different from the vision of an harmonious Earth, which when taken as a model for humankind, implies a corresponding quietism. In a creative Earth, human artifacts—jetports, say—are as *natural* as bobcats and snail kites, which leads one straight to the age-old rub: in the special case of humans, natural is not the same as good. Goodness and authenticity arrive, in human artifacts, in alliances between the human and the more-than-human elements of the Earth: of Spinoza's idea of *natura naturans*, Ernst Bloch says that it "presupposes . . . a notion from the Cabala, of *natura abscondita*, a nature pressing for its own revelation. Thus 'nature in its final manifestation' lies within the horizon of the future of those alliances mediated through humanity and [the rest of] nature."[9]

It may be, as microbiologist Lynn Margulis has said (not, I take it, in jest) that the human species' primary contribution to the planet is voluminous amounts of methane gas. Another possibility: that Earth is evolving—via the vehicle of conscious ethical choice—towards a sustainable planetary community (heaven expressed in an ecological vocabulary). The gas theory is perhaps more sensible, or at least a sensible hedge. As we know, to be capable of ethical choice does not guarantee that a culture or individual will achieve the strong, and always aesthetic, pleasure that characterizes genuine morality. To define and choose the sustaining alliances, we can neither turn to the pre-human Earth for a precise script, nor sanction all possible human activities: the interplay is neither rule-bound nor chaotic. *Natura naturans* resembles the creative discipline of an artist as well described by Coleridge: "If the artist copies the mere nature, the *natura naturata*, what idle rivalry! . . . Believe me, you must master the essence, the *natura naturans*, which presupposes a bond between nature in the highest sense and the soul of [a human being]."

At the root of elephants, physics, *chiaroscuro*, and carbon molecules—every formed thing—lies an immensely fragile reality, both arbitrary and inevitable: call it a moment when some grain of sand or understanding clusters in the leeward side of a shell, when one of the world's infinite logics slants across a room like a light. It is such a delicate base for the sandy premises on which we make long solitary walks, tempt babies into the swim, put stones in pockets, instruct the young in the eloquence of geometry and tidal pools.

En route from the cypress swamp to our houseboat in the

mangrove waterway, Peter and I pass a single wood stork wading in a roadside culvert. Squatting on a nearby knoll, we sit for a while, watching the mute bird splash in the puddle.

Gnarls and webs After a week floating in the mangrove swamp, hoping all the while that dark forms in the water and trees will prove to be reptiles and astonishing birds rather than old sticks, my preference for the flashy animal genus begins to seem crude. Mangroves are handsome trees that come in three varieties: red, black or honey, and white—the buttonwood. All three share a similar structure: as their trunks near the water, they splay (much as the heron's foot splays in stalking) into a swirling tangle, indeed a labyrinthine maze, gnarl and thicket of roots and shadowy interstices that invite one to contemplate an impossible, Gordian knot, a Rubic's cube or snarl, a task of unravelling set for the heroine of a myth. The swirl is visually akin to the convoluted foundation on which the mangrove islands rest. The limestone, awash with holes and eroded hollows, presents a surface much like that of the roots: a boggle of ceaseless change, unrepeating shapes that record the transformations of an undulating reality. The roots, stained dark with water, present a daunting shoreline, and walking over the mad jungle-gym of roots looks impossible: a trespasser would lurch into one hole after another. Only the tiny-footed birds and otters are fitted by nature to scamper over the thicket. With field glasses we can peer behind the curtain of leaves: here and there, a bit of pine trunk, a sliver of light, a patch of weathered grey. The inaccessible is, as ever, slightly repellent, mostly irresistible.

Each night in the hour before sundown, our snappy spiders dart from their retreats and survey their hunting webs. Always the webs are mildly to horribly torn from the struggles of the previous night's prey, and each spider spends time repairing its net. Twice a spider reweaves its web entirely and, with nothing better to do, I watch the entire process unfold. Of this activity Fabre has rightly said: "To appoint one's self, in this way, an inspector of Spider's webs . . . means joining a not overcrowded profession. . . . No matter: the meditative mind returns from that school fully satisfied."[10]

First the spider delineates the area for her web by framing it with several silken moorings, foundation lines attached in this case to the houseboat eave, the rope from the sun tarp, and the metal deck railings. These form a three-dimensional, asymmetrical triangle in space. One of these foundations is the bridge-line, on which the whole web will rest.[11] In about the middle of the bridge-line is a thick white point that marks the core of the web. From this center, the spider begins to spin the radial threads, the spokes of the web—first one on the left sector of the web, then one on the right sector, one on the bottom and one on the top, alternating the way a painter does when stretching a canvas. Her web follows the plane of the bridge-line, not precisely vertical, but cast on a slight angle. After some twenty radii are spun into place, the spider goes to the center and spins a mesh of lines called the hub. Next she moves outward from the hub, laying down a spiral thread that will hold the radial lines in place temporarily. It is like a basting stitch in sewing that holds a seam together until the finish stitch is made, and although it is called a scaffolding spiral, nothing in the spider's repertoire is curved; only straight lines and combinations of these are employed. The web now consists of the framework, and it has taken some five minutes of spider time to spin, the creature darting in a fast, jerky fashion. Up to this point, all the threads have been dry. Now the spider begins to lay down the viscid spirals over the framework. The viscid spirals are the short, sticky, catching lines that connect the radial threads and make the web into a trap. These appear to be much harder for the spider to spin. Slowly and deliberately, over some twenty minutes, she lays them down, moving from the periphery of the web inwards toward her hub in a to and fro course. Simultaneously, the spider is eating away her temporary spiral scaffolding thread. Just before she reaches the center, she stops spinning, leaving an unwebbed area called the free zone. Lastly, she strengthens the hub area with a mass of lines called the stabilimento. The web has taken just under a half hour to weave, and when it is completed, near sundown, the spider takes up her hunting stance in the hub, on the underside of her web, head down toward the deck. Her weaving has been done entirely with her sense of touch; even in pitch-black night, or if she was blinded, her web would be perfect.

Wondrous material, spider's silk. In the biologist's vocabulary, it is an albuminoid protein. At its finest, it is spun from the spider's silk glands at 0.03 microns wide, one millionth of an inch, the width of a single molecule and a measurement that causes Peter to whistle between his teeth. It is a high compliment from a man who writes, among other things, about wafer-steppers, the ultra-precise machines that make the silicon chips that make our electronic culture go. At one time, this thinnest spider's silk was itself a feature in high-tech instrumentation, used for sighting marks and in laboratory instruments, in levels and astronomical telescopes. Its other properties are equally impressive: enormously elastic, the material would have to be nearly fifty miles long before it would break under its own weight; its tensile strength is second only to that of fused quartz fibers.

For its entire life, a spider is connected to its silk thread, constantly playing out a "dragline" that can be used for a sudden drop to the ground, or climbed again to a bedroom ceiling in Saint-Sauveur. The dragline comes from silk glands inside the spider's abdomen and flows out any of eight flexible, fingerlike appendages along the lower belly, called spinnerets. For the spider, its silk is as all-functional as, say, caribou was for the old Netsilik Eskimo culture: not only is silk used for the dragline, but for hibernating chambers, egg sacs and nursery webs, sperm webs, courtship and mating bowers, and of course the hunting web and the bands with which larger prey are bound prior to dining.[12] And one more thing, most pleasing for a traveler to contemplate: it is likely our houseboat spiders were already lurking under the *Cobia*'s eaves when we plied Buttonwood Canal, but they might have boarded by air from one of the nearby mangrove thickets. By releasing a bit of silk, *gossamer* it is called, into the slightest wind, newborn spiderlings and smaller adults as well can be lifted up to fly on the wind, a form of travel called ballooning. By such ingenious and daring flight, spiders can migrate long distances on gossamer threads, and sometimes at very high altitudes, arriving in new geographies. No one believes that spiders can cross whole oceans on gossamer wings, but in *The Voyage of the Beagle* the reputable Darwin records that "some thousands" of tiny dusky-red spiders were blown, with their "flocculent" silk lines, into the rigging of the *Beagle* sixty miles off the coast of South America.[13] The gossamer threads themselves, released by the thousands as young spiders try and try again to fly away from their cannibalistic siblings to more promising lands, can sometimes, especially in autumn, fall to earth as a shower, draping meadows and marshes in a thick white mat of shed silk.

A t Ponce de Leon Bay we poke the houseboat into the Gulf, *Leached* rock a while on the rougher, saltier waters, and withdraw *from* to a sheltered part of the bay for the night. Thinking *memory* back, it's clear why the Fountain of Youth story (utterly false) persists in popular history, linked with the name of Juan Ponce, penniless grandee of Leon become Governor of Cuba. Perennial youth couples well with the story of an endless frontier supplanting the old world. The fountain pictured in my youthful, imaginative wilderness, circa 1956 history class, was Roman and rustic mingled: a spring burbling from a creek, with a sculpted basin encrusted with shells, a froth of elixir spraying from a crocodile mouth. I saw the lull of waves on hulls luring conquistadors to the fountain where, happy and young, they washed away memory and salt; saw them shed their silver armor . . . How we savored the sound: the exotic "cone," the bright "keest" and resonant "tador" that seemed in one roll of syllables to reenact the big-chested sallying forth. They were told as heroes, and we were each allowed to choose one to paint on the classroom mural.

From the houseboat deck, we watch the garish red spectacle of tropical sunset over Ponce de Leon Bay. It is a big bay, this name-sake. Save for the likes of Juan Ponce we would be in these waters, if at all, at the pleasure of the Calusas, a fishing people who were ritualists and canoe-borne traders. We call them Calusa after the Spanish corruption of the name they called themselves, a praise-name that has leached from memory. They moved by highways of canoe travel through coastal waters and savannahs, building cere-monial centers on likely keys. One of these, the settlement at San Marco Key just north of this bay, was typical. There a sea wall of shells was built to protect the central court where the temple, flanked by garden courts, was situated. Straight canals were built radiating from the temple to the sea, allowing canoes to travel freely into the central court. It was, I realize with a start, a kind of subtropical Venetian world. Like all other Amerindian habitations, the Calusa dwellings contradict the European notion that the continent was a wilderness. True, the land looked unexploited, the forests and streams were pristine. But as Peter writes in a song, "America was not a virgin; this land had a lover."[14] The forests were woodland parks used and tended for millennia and the grand ecological condition of Turtle Island was an artifact carefully produced by tribal philosophies and technologies. Perhaps Europeans, having nothing like this back home, simply "did not understand what they were seeing."[15]

The sophisticated Calusa artifacts point to artisan specialists in a culture with a highly developed ceremonial life, a culture based on leisure time made possible by an abundant food supply. Great shell piles and middens reveal that favored foods were roasted oysters and shellfish, turtles, birds, and root truffles. These were a superb fishing people whose tackle included hooks, harpoon points, and gourd floats for their nets. Clearly, the canoe was all; even the toys they made for their children were canoes, and many cooking bowls ended up carved with prow-like ends. Naturally, the canoes were cypress, probably fire-hollowed using pitch to facilitate burning, roughly shaped with conch chisels, finely shaped with sawfish-tooth adzes, pared on the sides to a uniform thickness with hafted barracuda jaws, and finished so smoothly by sand polishing that no trace of a tool remains. The tools themselves are clever things that use every possible jawbone and fibre; even the spine of a stingray could be an arrow point. From the metapodal bones of deer, they made pins, points, beads, and spatulas. From *Busycon perversa* shells they made dippers and spoons; from the Venus shell, anvils and hoes.[16] The Calusa community was a strong alliance of tribute-paying members who maintained exchange routes over which foods could be rapidly redistributed: should fishing be poor some week at one village, dried palm berries or a nice smoked fish would come via canoe from another settlement up the Caloosahatchee River.[17]

Trading still goes on in Ponce de Leon Bay, the southernmost bay up the western coast of Florida and the first sheltered place for deep-hulled boats to rendezvous. Around sundown, just inside the bay, a huge and elegant sailboat arrives at the end of the cove where we have dropped anchor for the night. Fifteen minutes later another huge and elegant sailboat arrives and sidles cheek-by-jowl with the first. Both vessels seem empty—no sign of sunburnt hands kicking back for a beer. Beyond a sensible glance, watching boats through field glasses seems quite rude in the privacy of the swamp. We are just putting down our glasses when a figure emerges from one boat and begins, ever so carefully, to pass identical bundles wrapped in black plastic to the other boat. We busy ourselves with rice and beans for dinner and hope like hell the runners are too smug to care that we have seen their deal go down. Chopping garlic in the galley, we affect enormous disinterest in any matter beyond papery, plump cloves, and by the time the warding power of garlic has permeated our fingers, the sailboats are slipping away. By this night there are more than ten large hunting webs slicing across the decks, filling the railings and corners of each roof and all the spaces between the tarp lines. It is impossible to walk the decks without passing through one, tangling our hair in the silk, shredding their work. We broom four of the webs most poorly located from our point of view. A few hours later, two of the shaken hunters have crept back up the metal railing and are clinging to the side of the boat, legs huddled-in tightly around their bodies.

Unable to change the map, we have entered this bay to remember the story America declines to tell. It was already well underway in the Easter season of 1513 when Juan Ponce, only thirty and not in want of youth, sailed to the land he named after *Pascua Florida*, flowery Easter. The Calusa arrow that ended his path likely arose from the news the peninsula tribes had learned from the south. The conquerors' idea for the Caribbean had been slaves for cattle operations, canefields, for gold and silver mines. But the peoples died rather too easily—collapsed from lashes and starvation, from toil, from new diseases. Resisters were wrapped in straw and set afire in the public markets or were dismembered by dogs.[18] Merely begun by the Spanish, the blunder continued, rendering an America lousy with ghosts. We might talk with them: the Calusa found that each person "has three souls; one is the pupil of the eye, another one the shadow that each one makes, and the other one is the image one sees in a mirror or in clear water, and when a person dies . . . two of the souls leave the body, and the third one, which is the pupil of the eye, always remains in the body; and thus [we] go to speak with the dead . . . and to ask them advice about things that have to be done."[19] They made an alliance with the land that endured ten thousand years. In our present circumstances it is only pragmatic to inquire into the vestigial remains of such success.

These are some of the actions that the Calusas found respectful: wear amulets incised with figures of wheeling dolphins; carve sun-circles; have buzzard cults; and cultivate the powers of turkey-vultures and rattlesnakes. Paint the woodpecker in beautiful colors with accomplished perspective. Show the bird to be a deity in command of its world—under its talons locate the raccoon of land, under its wing a paddle for dominion over the sea, and from its mouth leading toward its heart etch the four circling word-signs of the Earth. One precaution: when carving a six-inch wooden cat sitting in a dignified, heroic pose, be sure to cut off the paws so that panther god can be handled with some safety as it shows forth in ceremonies of incarnation. Through this night we remember them and wait on the spirits in the bay that had some other name. It may easily have been named Bay of Gold Crabs, Bay That Laughs Like Twenty Girls Bathing, or simply Sweet Marrying Salt.

> One by one I proclaim your songs;
> I bind them on gold crabs as if they were anklets;
> like emeralds I gather them.
> Clothe yourself in them: they are your riches . . .
> deck yourself out in them: they are your riches.[20]

Piloting Meticulously we plot our progress through the glades, monitoring the homogeneous mangrove shoreline, compass and clock, the tidal variations in the shallow waters; the ranger had said, "You can get turned around up there real fast." When passing a numbered marker or positively matching a patch of shoreline with its map image, we sing out "mark," remembering Twain. The chart is covered with penciled marks recording the times we made a positive identification entering some river or passing a distinctive island bend. The slow laze down the Little Shark River in late afternoon is one of the easy stretches, a time to watch anhingas spreading their wings to dry on crones of branches. Lacking oil glands with which to preen, the birds assume their characteristic motionless pose, three-foot wings stretched and bent like scarecrow arms at the elbows, the front feathers dangling down, exposing the soaked feathers to a warm afternoon sun. The male, whose back is black, white, and silver-grey and patterned like an Arabic scarf, shimmers in green iridescence. As we glide like Emerson's snakes—"not to eat, not for love, but only gliding"—the radio faintly crackles with a garbled question from some faraway boat: "*something something* oysters in the *something* river edible?" The marina's reply is also broken up: "*something something* if I was you *crackle* have heard *something* could *crackle*."

On this smooth passage, we only need find a junction with the channel that leads southeast to an evening anchorage in Cormorant Pass. At the junction we twist through a puzzle of islands and nose serenely down a narrowing channel towards the pass. The mud along the banks is still glistening in the day's last heat; the channel winds upon itself, threading the mangrove islands, lovely as anything in the swamp, overhung with trees, surrounded in bright greens of leaves and the ochre waters. We are lulled to the land of lotus eaters, where it is always mid-afternoon, before we realize that nothing on the map corresponds to such a long and sinuous passage to the bay. The channel has shrunk to little more than the width of the boat. Sure hands by now, we deftly swivel the boat 180 degrees in the slender creek. Peter calls out, "Well done!" I juice the engine forward to head back upcreek and run the *Cobia* hard into a deep shoal of silty marl. The pontoons slide some, like skis, across the shoal, nestle into the slurry, and the big boat comes to a sluggish halt, fast aground in marl. The outboard, still whirling and whining under the muck, churns up a pungent sulfurous geyser. The motor dies and will not restart. An eel slithers past the boat.

Marl is a deposit of carbonate of lime, limestone, and clay, and peat is a layer of partly decayed plant matter that accumulates in bogs and swamps to depths of seven to fourteen feet. In this little out-of-the-way creek, passable only by canoe, the peat and marl bottom has surely been undisturbed for decades, possibly for centuries. The putrid smell given off by the slurry plume—now tingeing the whole immobile situation—suggests why, since Milton, poets have turned to marl to symbolize the torments of hell. "It seems the unjoyous dissipation of demons, seeking diversion on the burning marl of perdition," said George Eliot. Before settling in to perdition, we assess the new state of reality. Evening is coming on quickly; the propellor is caked and clogged with decaying muck and grass; the tide table says high tide. We find that the hollow aluminum curtain rod lacks strength for pushing the boat, but proves to be ideal for sampling the tremulous marl. The pole slides down and down, fills up with a core of unjoyous dissipation, and never touches bottom. On the map, the creek is an obscure hairline that dwindles into nothing; the nearest camping platform is ten miles away through mangrove. Lacking jungle boots and gear, a trek through the mangrove labyrinth is futility defined, and intuition deters us from casting anchors off stern and bow and trying to haul the boat—from the boat—into the deeper side of the channel. If there was a reachable bottom, we could push the boat; but there isn't and we have both seen *The African Queen*.

Had we better remembered cub pilot Sam Clemens learning to read the Mississippi from Horace Bixby, the scroll up the creek should have been an italicized, capitalized passage "with a string of shouting exclamation points."[21] To our embarrassment, we must radio the rangers for advice. To our surprise, the rangers do not answer. After some forty-five minutes of hailings—followed by silences—we inch a few notches up the marine code of distress, making an All-Vessels call, then an Any-Channel hail, stopping well short of the call MAYDAY that *Chapman's* warns "should not be used for situations such as being out of fuel, running aground, or engine failure under conditions of no immediate danger." The hush of the radio, matched only by the shoal's, is itself a signal that we gradually decipher. Cruising the outer perimeter of the houseboat's territory, we have gone out of range of radio contact with the marina station and are now among low-lying thickets that deflect and trap our signal. The shoal, simply by being in place as our knowledge grew shallow, has altered our engagement with the surround. Another face of the swamp appears as unexpectedly as dolphins. The grand solitude hums. We are close by a marshy bank, a slew of rushes, flags, and vines draped with ball mosses; the root-tangle is caked with oysters, a scraggly limb overhangs the back of the boat. Mute as ever, the trees shimmer in the reddening sun. Months will pass before a canoe comes spontaneously up this hairline creek. Tilted up out of the shoal, the engine slowly drains a brown gruel; come morning, it may be dry enough to clean. Tonight we stare at the mud banks.

Along the shoal, an immature blue hunts hypnotically. Against the greens and ochres, these birds are surreal swatches of dazzling white: how does a creature remain immaculate plucking through a world of muck and decay? The heron's hunting dance is a hypnotic, snake-necked swaying after prey, then a lunge: crayfish in pincer bill, it crunches down and swallows whole, the telltale lump in its throat. The bird composes itself along the shore in the manner of a Hiroshige print, and each step is a slow-motion marvel: three finger-like toes slowly retract, pulling up and together; the leg bends; step; the toes spread over a mat of leaves stealthily as thieves caressing jade plates. In a brilliant green bush hard by the boat there sits a brilliant green anole with baby-soft, luminous skin. The little lizard straddles a limb and holds in its mouth the furry body of a large black moth, half swallowed, wings still feebly fluttering. With an elastic jaw, the skink clings to the body and every few moments, gulps a little more wing. The beautiful throat bulges with metamorphosis. At sundown, the creek is suffused with lusty, reverberating calls like raucous monkeys hooting and laughing; these are courtship calls of a pair of barred owls, whose romance sounds as full of mischief as of sexual mysteries. Overarching all other phenomena is the lingering, most foul smell of the marl in which we are lodged for the night.

Mired and settling in marl, the thing is to become light. Through a pungent night, we tell ourselves a story and in this familiar way, travel to a place we name Cobeloosa, known for souvenirs and songs.

The old place is entered through a fishing wier—the feeling being that visitors are a harvest as fine as fish. At the rickety stick-built pier, you will be pulled in by a welcoming net and expected to divulge news and pocket trinkets to the little crowd always meddling about the boats. Not that this is a trivial custom. The posts of Cobeloosa's structures are cabbage palm trunks and roofs are palmetto thatch, but walls and streets are built entirely from news and trinkets, the bits of news mostly yellowing and papery, the trinkets metallic and glinting. Here and there a working eggbeater or astrolabe is sandwiched among tin plates and carved shells, parking receipts and coconut lifesavers. Very occasion-

ally, half-hidden among fork tines and shards, a keen-eyed visitor can find the edge of an idea or, rarely, an entire idea splayed out on the surface of the wall. Beloved, but not fawned over by visitors to Cobeloosa, an idea might nest between a nicked pen-knife and an oyster shell, gaining a sheen from their presence. Four nights each year are street-commemoration nights, special not-to-be-missed nights when old-timers put on the cormorant and turtle masks to wander the barnacle-town, touching souvenirs of grandnieces and shell traders, making them softly or loudly sing their inner songs. The cormorant masks have noses longer than Cyrano de Bergerac's and carved oval mouths, surprised as the moon.

I say old-timer, but it is well known that there are no permanent inhabitants of Cobeloosa. There are shady markets with large woven baskets of surplus trading materials, and many well-built shelters, each with a household shrine—the favored talisman of worked bone. But each and every soul in town is a visitor, lingering at most a week or two to make the rounds, returning to scents and sounds and crusts of self and companions stored up in the settlement. Each traveler takes time to pluck the iridescent beetles off a patch of squash, the only cultivated food, or tend the smudge fires against the mosquitoes. The ones who can catch fish, others gather cocoplums and cabbage-palm hearts, this last a delicacy that draw many to the wier. Although there are no permanent residents, some travelers die in Cobeloosa, and there can be found bones and teeth in the steaming shoals along the edge of the settlement. It is curious, since the entire town is made of aggregate and memory, that the bones of the traveler are not placed in the singing walls, but they are not: they are taken out of the town, and placed in a marl, knees to breast and arms crossed, head bent, the position of utter weariness or an embryo in its mother's womb. The final and secret thing to know about Cobeloosa is that animals easily travel into the place. They arrive wearing stylized human masks, heads with moveable jaws and staring shell eyes. It is thought that they do this not only as a disguise, but as a courtesy, in response to the masks old-timers wear: the cormorant and turtle masks, sunfish and bat masks, wildcat and bear masks—fine likenesses carved from cypress, fitted with polished hollowed antlers. It can happen, and often does, that when old-timers wear the cormorant and turtle masks, a sunfish, eel, or wildcat arrives with a human face.

Bogie and Hepburn are awakened by salvation, torrential rains that lift their *Queen* from the mud into navigable channels. Our morning is dry and bright, the pontoons settled slightly deeper. Cleaning away the cake and goo from the Johnson SeaHorse, we ponder the logic of naming this mass of metal after that epitome of delicacy, a dark horse whose male number is the rarest sort of male, one who cradles the eggs. Under the cake of muck, the propellor blades look intact. At the turn of the key, a new plume bursts into the air, but the engine turns. Alternately gunning the throttle in reverse, then into neutral, Peter rocks the boat, transplanting to a subtropical shoal the northern trick of rocking a car out of icy snow. Big and sunken as she is, the boat pulls maybe a quarter-inch with each motion. A tormented eternity passes with acrid blue smoke gushing from a straining transmission; as it writhes in the marl, the engine churns up a steady geyser. After an eon, the *Cobia* has stirred an inch. Another age passes in metallic screams. I keep a close eye on the engine, ready to say when it explodes.

The ship's log reads: "7:45 the *Cobia* steered upstream toward the Little Shark River." With the joy of alligators we gingerly ply the stream back to the river, released to the hymn of ordinary motion.

A s days in the swamp go by, the suspicion forms that even in the time of the great flocks of birds and the roiling gangs of alligators—when the mangrove swamp and glades were thronged with living creatures—the greatest movement must always have been the literally overarching one, the circadian arc of the day, during which the water flickers with a braid of light and color, the air with a portmanteau of smell and temperature by which one feels the Earth revolve, calming and stimulating in equal measure. As the medievals observed, in a calibrated world each hour of the wheel is its own song. In my book of hours, the easy prayers have long been the aubades of hope, the shimmering mid-day verve, and the tender exhales of night that gather in kin. These blessings surround those haunted, round, unbounded late afternoons for whose duration life collapses into a marginal field. I speak of the yellow hours. Even afternoon tea, invented to stave off the haunt, to insist that the cozy combats the existential, is a precious inadequacy. The yellow hours routinely give lie to the

The yellow hours

notion that voids are countered one whit by the bric a brac of philosophy, petit fours, and love. In the wan hours, the atmosphere of earthly form grows thin, and through the transparent veneer, non-being easily seeps through window panes, suffusing the household, dissolving as fluff the shelves of books, family albums, the pins and stays. In the swamp as elsewhere, the oblique yellow hours come faithfully round. But perhaps being each day under the entire arc of the sun modulates the intimate dance with emptiness. In the swamp, it comes to me that these too are distinguished and necessary hours. The formerly desultory, concessional hours are a clearing between the fierce peak of sun and last light. It is these few hours when everything hangs in the balance. The emptiness is a conduit for those who would, like Hermes, move between worlds. The cleared space holds for an hour or so, then yields to the gaudy thrill of brilliance streaking water, the passage to twilight and dusk.

Evensong In the west, and perhaps in the east as well, a poet first named twilight, a creation like that of aborigines who sing their desert into existence. Twilight comes into being on Virgil's songline at the end of the first of the *Eclogues*, as Tityrus implores his neighbor Meliboeus to put aside his grief for a night: "For tonight," the shepherd murmurs, "you could take your rest with me couched on green leaves: There will be apples ripe, soft-roasted chestnuts, plenty of pressed cheese. Already rooftops in the distance smoke, and lofty hills let fall their lengthening shade."[22] It is a difficult invitation, one that encapsulates the whole stance of pastoral poetry—a modest poetry that claims no powers to reform. Old Meliboeus will be leaving in the morning for a permanent and hard exile, his family lands legally stolen by the emperor to pay the Roman legions. Mourning loss of place, Meliboeus is further anguished to know that loutish soldiers will run roughshod over the little farm. Is it kind, or grotesque, to urge the farmer to take comfort in the last sweet light of a world that slips more surely from him with each passing hour?

Either way, centuries have passed. Of nights, we sit on improved porches in our fine boots and stare across industrial valleys, still liking the shadowy rabbits, the rare movements of deer, and spontaneous cries. In our hands, we turn over and over scraps from the unretrievable book, something about fishheads and corn. Here in the mangrove swamp, during the turn to twilight, shadows comfort the land and a hundred shades of slate-blue grey gradate across the water. Flying inland from the Gulf comes a wedge of ducks, wings flapping in staggered rhythms. The chevron passes low overhead with a sharp rustling, a distinct duck-whir, louder and smoother than the rustling of palm fronds. As the sun enters the water, the surface is burned into glass. A last, thin grey light lingers over the mangroves, turned from green speckled with sun to a dark fringe. As it cools, the glass ripples again, alive, textured like a mackerel skin. A light rain begins to patter on the water and Peter steps out onto the deck to inquire after the spiders. In the beam from his light, the big weavers are back from their daytime hiding, each poised at the center of its world.

SOUTH OF THE
ULTIMA THULE

GLOSSARY

BAIRN   baby, child, heir.

BANNOCK   cake, like barleycake.

BERE   a primitive form of barley

CEUR   cure.

CINNO   (*c* hard) cannot.

CROFTER   a tenant, rather than an owner, of a landholding in Argyll, Inverness, Ross and Cromarty, Sutherland, Caithness, Orkney, or Zetland.

DEE   die.

DOO   thou.

FAE   from.

GLOY   the straw of oats.

HANDSHOUSE   gloves.

HUMEEN, HUMING   twilight.

KEN   knows.

PEEDIE   little.

RIVLINS   shoes of undressed hide.

SKELKIE   seal.

SWA   the low, prolonged note of waves heard at a distance.

n his early twenties, my father traveled greatly—to Iceland,
Scotland, Ireland, England, and on to Normandy, wading
ashore shortly after the invasion of Utah Red Beach in June,
1944. His tour of Europe continued into Luxembourg for the battle
of the Bulge, and into Germany during the crossing of the Rhine.
Near Frankfurt, he watched as General Patton, fulfilling a longtime
ambition, took a piss in the river. Ever since these travels, my father
has preferred to stay at home. His preference increased during a law
career that sent him on innumerable domestic trips, travels that
were, he insisted, glamorous only in the minds of his children. In
these minds (young, Southern, schooled in respect) the opinions of
elders had weight, but the glamorous view of travel prevailed,
supported by annual viewings of the mottled, shiny sealskin gloves
and lap robe that he had brought back for my mother from Iceland,
and by seeing our father disappear with a wave into the *Viscount*, an
early prop-jet plane with a distinctive, high-pitched engine whine.

All during those years, my mother was not traveling but was
making a home for our family. To this end, she often tromped into
the east Tennessee hills to gather ferns, columbines and lady slip-
pers, which she transplanted into our garden in Oak Ridge. My
mother's work was a rescue mission, as the Clinch River was soon
to be dammed for the TVA energy grid and the new lake would
drown whole forests. At the cocktail parties that adults had during
the fifties, my parents' guests made remarks about my mother's

"weed garden," and as far as I could tell, she was the only person in town who valued wildflowers. Sometimes she took me along on her field trips, and we ate sandwiches on a large rock in the sun before we commenced the delicate work of digging up forest flowers by the roots. We also went walking in the Smoky Mountains, to Gatlinburg and over the pass at Newfound Gap, where Clingman's Dome shimmered to the south. At Cades Cove, my mother bought cornmeal, a fine powder that came in cloth sacks with drawstrings and made a very sweet cornbread. After several trips in and out of the grist mill house, my brothers and I pieced together how the great wheels connected: how the paddle wheel in the stream transferred motion to the horizontal stone slabs that creaked over the fat corn kernels. The mill was grey stone, shaded by black locust and tulip trees, and there was a constant rushing sound of water and wind. Watching the wind, water, leaves, and wheel in a perpetual motion that could not be traced to a cord or plug, it seemed to me that this was something alive.

In the mountains we visited craft shops where the hill people made willow-twig baskets, homespun, and cotton coverlets named Young Man's Fancy, Lee's Surrender, and Blooming Leaf. Once a mountain blacksmith explained to me and my brothers, our faces gleaming from his oven's heat, that "red-hot" was not the hottest fire, and brought the tip of a "white-hot" poker close to our noses. The hill people were friendly to us, but we were, in their words, "fotched up"—which meant outsiders. From the insiders came "The Cas Walker Hour," a country music show on local television: the twangy accents, rhinestone jackets, straw hats, and above all the breakneck bluegrass, were like nothing in Oak Ridge, a town populated by nuclear physicists imported to the hills to distill not moonshine but uranium. For years it did not occur to me to wonder where the wonderful-talking mountaineers had come from; they seemed to have been in Tennessee as long as there had been coves, hollows, and hills. But of course, like every American, including the Amerindians who migrated across the Bering Straits, the Appalachian hillbillies came from somewhere else: these distinctive people brought their fondness for splendid, isolated mountain fastnesses, their genius for ballads and storytelling, and their recipes for clear grain whisky from the glens and vocabulary of Scotland. History books show the Scots-Irish pioneers streaming first as one large arrow from Scotland to Ulster, Ireland in the early seventeenth century, and then as many arrows sweeping from Ulster to America in the eighteenth century, and finally as two arrows flowing from Philadelphia and Charleston into the Smoky Mountains.

By the time my mother was in her mid-fifties, it was clear that she would love to travel to places like Kyoto, Leningrad, Florence, and Provence, and it was also clear that my father would not, could not, travel with her to those places because of things that he remembered, often at night in dreams, from when he had traveled before. For my father, travel has been warfare and the sublimated battles of economic conquest and it is no wonder that he no longer yearns to journey. With some reluctance, and a good deal of regard for my mother, he will travel with her to beach resorts where the beds are soft and the food good, and things seem safe, and, homeopathically, he will go anywhere his surviving Second Infantry buddies convene for their annual reunion, an event that once included retracing their wartime path through France with their wives, a tour that must have been a many-splendoured triumph for the old warriors. The trek through the onetime battlefields of Normandy came within one hundred yards of the Bayeux Tapestry (itself a chronicle of conquest), but as my mother delicately put it more in wonder than despair, "We did not stop to see it."

The remedy to my parents' distinctly different travel plans readily presented itself, and my mother and I traveled first to Italy, where we thrilled to Etruscan artifacts, the Blue Grotto in Capri, the Medici Palace of paintings, and in Venice stayed in the Hotel de Bain, where the film version of Thomas Mann's *Death in Venice* was shot. Thinking of Aschenbach at his taper-lit desk, we walked moodily through tall, quiet rooms, stared out dark, shuttered windows and ambled the Lido past rows of striped cabanas. Once we had a small tiff about how to buy stamps and perhaps it was because we were no longer sure who was leading whom or if anyone was leading anyone. Several years later, my mother suggested we travel again, this time to Scotland, the land of her Presbyterian faith—specifically to Orkney, a remote island group where an ardent birder like herself might add the fulmar and Arctic skua to her life list. I would have gone anywhere that my mother chose, but I was especially curious to explore the place that had generated the Tennessee hill people, who among many boons provided my favorite childhood stories, a collection of tales called *Which Witch Is Which?* In these stories devils were invited in to eat apple dumplings big as fists, women threw kettles of boiling water at hellcats, coal-black carts came down the road under their own steam, white chickens scratched at the doorstones, and a boy called the balsam tree a "she-balsam" for its milky sap. In the tale "Like Meat Loves Salt," a trio of daughters, called upon to say how they love their father, answer variously. Two offer flattering homages. The third says she loves her father "like meat loves salt." Banished for her homely, plain speaking, she is, of course, Cordelia to Lear.[1]

An ancient skin

A transatlantic crossing by air is a chamber of eschatological thought, this one tempered by the returning burrs that now and again hum through the cabin. Shortly after dawn, the in-flight movie screen lights up with aerobics instructors who settle with fierce brio into airplane seats, fasten their seat belts, and beckon us to "shimmy forward," to stretch and pull ourselves into other shapes. As the plane descends, masses of fog are opening over something soft and wrinkled like a skin over an old animal. What is this enormous animal whose radiant skin ripples from one shade of green to another, forests yielding to fields and fields turning back into forests?

Courtesies

The first sign of how Scotland works comes in the baggage claim area: expecting the standard grapple for scarce and wobbling carts to trundle belongings through customs, one is braced for minor public warfare, but scurrying and graceless lugging are merely unthinkable here where dozens of flawless carts are wheeled toward the weary by airline personnel. In a calm, even spirit that one soon recognizes as characteristic of the Scottish way, travelers glide toward their adventures. "Harry will help you with directions," says the hired-car agent. Harry is scrubbed, fair, freckled, smelling of lavender soap. His accent is burbling as he unfolds a city map. When he gets to the part about crossing the river, he pauses, looks up, and says with affection, "And here is the River

Clyde." "The Clyde," he repeats, and the word *Clyde* is lingered over, made into three syllables, crooned like the name of a favorite child. This tiny window onto a people who think of their rivers as beings is good, and so are the directions, but we go off course in Glasgow city centre. Righting our compass and homing in on the West End of the city takes three stops to ask directions of passersby. The first is a silver-haired gentleman wearing tweeds and carrying a dark, carved wood cane. His directions are clear, given in complete grammatical sentences, with a mid-course pause to recapitulate. At the end of our encounter, he tips his hat, faintly bows, and wishes us good day. A bit further on, we must ask again; a young businessman waiting for a bus delivers much the same performance. Finally, driving through a narrow back alley, we come upon a street punk in leather, chains, and dyed hair who is slouched against the back door of a pub. His flawless discourse, like that of the staid citizens, concludes with a tip of the head (all the more effective with bright red spiked hair) and "Good day, ladies."

Direction-giving is one of the great public courtesies of Scotland, a national art form whose elements are these: apparent delight to have been asked, precise knowledge of routes, directions tendered in well-wrought sentences with pauses to judge how much of the proposed route is sinking in, succinct and timely recap, and a final fare-thee-well with flourishes. We are in civilization. The happy fact is borne out day after day in courtly encounters with fruit stall vendors, motorcycle gangs, Presbyterian elders, hotel maids, and naturalist guides. Manners are, of course, not a petty husk but the core of a people. What is the secret of a society that in the late twentieth century has preserved public courtesies through all its classes? Scotland is an ideal country in which to test the premise that a people who cultivate civilities in public life also tend their lands and waters with care—that relations between human beings and those between humans and the rest of nature are mirror images.

I t is blistering hot in a bright, unusual August spell. Soon enough raw cold rain will return, weather so predictable that forecasting seems a gratuitous occupation. For now, the rare heat wave delights the Scots, and for their sake we try not to be *Nymphs, Lord Kelvin, et al.*

overtly dismayed by our woolens and waterproof gear. The heat merely accentuates the fact that all Scottish interior spaces are designed to be close and warm. Indeed, one detects the interior, insular constraint of Scotland most immediately in the physical spaces. This is a country assiduously arranged to conserve heat, to keep everything as cozy and firelit as possible, in all seasons. The Mediterranean concept of cool breezes, ventilation, and airiness is the enemy. Even during the heat wave, the faux fireplaces in our little West End hotel are blazing, the bathroom heat ring is wired permanently to ON, and in restaurants, piping hot food is served on warming trays that keep the dishes bubbling. From hurricane lamps placed on each close, hot table rise thin snakes of heat distortion and smoke.

In Glasgow for two days to collect maps and supplies for the drive through the Highlands to the North Sea ferry, we repair to the Botanic Gardens for relief from the steamy weather. The palm houses themselves, usually a reliable way to take off the chill, are suffocatingly hot and humid. Fifteen feet into the Kibble Palace palm house, my mother's asthma alerts her to a hostile environment; we go no farther than the Victorian marble of Eve amidst a bed of ivy. In the outside gardens, a BBC crew has arrived in the old oaks section to film a special program about the heat wave. To illustrate the temperature, the crew has arranged a bathing beauty on a pink towel set in the impeccable, clipped, apple-green grass. Off-camera, the crew has positioned two gardeners: middle-aged men wearing work coveralls and Wellington boots and holding one of the industrial-grade hoses used to irrigate the grounds. At a sign from the photographer, the gardeners' job is to spray the nymph with water. Holding a hose and watering, say, the Lapland rhododendron, would ordinarily be a one-man job, but in the case of nymphs apparently another hand is needed: the second gardener stands just behind his buddy, steadying hand on his shoulder. The girl poses in the manner of 1940s pinups, fluffing her long hair, arching her neck, eyes closed in mock, or perhaps quasi-, ecstasy for the television camera. Now and then one of the photographers comes from behind the camera rig to adjust a silver rectangle of light-bouncing material planted in the lawn just beyond the beach towel.

At the corner of a nearby palm house, a cluster of other gardeners has gathered to stare—some ogling, some horrified—at the spectacle growing on their grounds. In her bright yellow suit, the girl does resemble a flower they might tend, sprung improbably from the manicured lawn, a botanical assumed human flesh, riotously vulgar amongst the other parkgoers. These are chiefly old women in print dresses and pale cardigans, the less old helping the toothless ones dodder down paths, the whole assembly of age stopping to coo at pale, complacent babies. There is also a stout father and stout son exchanging a black and red soccer ball in the dappled green clearing of a grove. This close to the Arctic Circle, summer evening light lasts until ten o'clock. At eight, back in the hotel, murmuring voices rise into our window: a few families have entered the small neighborhood garden below. In the garden ring there is a cluster of prams, picnic baskets, fathers, mothers, three toddlers, and an infant who sits, wobbling, on the grass at the edge of the sand path, letting grains sift through its tiny hands.

The first hours in a new place are unique: with the advantage of total ignorance, unencumbered by the complexity that comprises every reality, one is free, as at no later time, to sound the place like a simple tuning fork. In Glasgow the atmospheric vibration is markedly calm. The serene tone must arise from many sources other than the wilting heat. Indeed, such heat regularly ignites simmering social tensions in Chicago and Detroit. One clue must be that this is a small country of a relatively homogeneous people with many shared traditions; moreover, the Scots have engineered a dose of socialism that secures certain basics: education, health insurance, child care, long vacations, paid parental leave, and old-age pensions. Whatever the ingredients, one quickly detects agreement about many values and how these are to be manifested in shopwindow displays, tones of voices, deferences in conversation. The general idea seems to be that life can be made plausible, that average desires can be fulfilled rather than teased along a miniature golf course of obstacles named society and possibly dashed in the mouth of a painted wooden clown.

It takes only a day to register the footfall of another note: the sweet, courtly, and decent ways of the country are entangled with a constrained, dour, and fiercely practical chord. This is the year for

Glasgow to be the European Capital of Culture, and the city has made a model of itself, much like the animated house within a house of Edward Albee's play *Tiny Alice*; this one is an exhibit titled *The City within the City*. It is a poorly designed show housed in a structure now called The Arches, an old transportation station whose high brick arches and cavernous vaulted ceilings are themselves the best exhibit. Sound from too many videos and audiotapes bounces indiscriminately through the grand underground cave, jumbling immigration, Singer sewing machines, James Watt's steam engine, optical devices, North Sea oil drilling, and fossil records. Something earnest and utterly empirical, a utilitarian genius, is revealed in the exhaustive displays of Scottish engineering feats and inventions, and in the stolid, didactic style of the presentations themselves.

Characteristically, Scottish scientist James Hutton is here, remembered as the father of geology and pictured in a cubicle of sedimentary rock, but there is no mention of his most visionary idea. In 1785, speaking at the Royal Society in Edinburgh, James Hutton said that the nutrient cycle of the Earth's soil and the cycle of water from oceans to land were analogous to the circulation of blood, and he proposed that the Earth is a "superorganism." This is the first known modern scientific statement of the ancient idea that the Earth is alive, and the thought had to incubate nearly two hundred years before it was taken seriously. James Lovelock, geophysicist and author of the Gaia theory, says that Hutton's "idea of a living Earth was forgotten, or denied, in the intense reductionism of the nineteenth century."[2] Here it is still forgotten. The bare and quantifiable fact is supreme, and it is not surprising to learn that the word *statistic* was invented by one John Sinclair of Ulster. (It was also Sinclair's idea to send a questionnaire of one hundred and sixty-six items to every minister in Scotland, and from their dutiful parish reports to compile the twenty-one volumes of the *Old Statistical Account of Scotland*, published 1791–1799.) The tone of the exhibit is perfectly expressed by the text of an exhibit panel accompanying a tabletop of scientific instruments from the Kelvin Laboratory. Said William Thomson, Lord Kelvin, Professor of Natural Philosophy at the University of Glasgow: "I never satisfy myself until I can make a mechanical model of a thing. If I can make a mechanical model of a thing I can understand it." Even the repetition, which admits the shift from satisfaction to understanding, seems part of the temperament for which Lord Kelvin might be speaking on behalf of a whole class of Scottish inventors, industrialists, engineers, and tinkerers. This climate surely culls ingenious and sensible characters from the stock of dreamers, who have, by now, all been swept overboard in rolling North Sea crossings, or have wandered off slippery seacliffs into oblivion, or Ireland. The selection process has left behind a national stock of practical modifiers, survivors who have lived another day to understand many mechanical models, to perfect the tight flue, sturdy table, fast door, and to make the deepset windowpane snug against rain, fog, and winds.

T he roads north up the eastern coast, past Loch Lomond and *Through* through Crianlarich and Glencoe, are mountainous and *the* narrow, winding through a landscape that is a changeling of *Highlands* continuously shifting character: dark, implacable foothills mutate into bucolic, sunlit pastures that give way to low heath barrens and moors followed by sublime gorges grown over in supernatural greens. Just past the dark purple moors of Rannoch, in the mist-birthing Grampian Mountains, lies Glencoe Pass, a place whose power compels humans to stop their cars, to stop talking, to stand in the cool mist, to walk over a nearby ridge and gape. Six tall mountain peaks of the Grampians recede in a perfect Lord Kelvin mechanical model of perspective, each receding hill more silvery green than the last, until the farthest faint peak is lost in an ever-shifting fog that dallies with the mountain tops and glides between the steep valleys—a suffused interplay of air and land. In a distant realm just past the mountains a radiant field of light glows between the receding ranges.

Past Invergarry, the road hugs the shore of Loch Ness, meadows spilling on the east toward the Highlands, on the west toward a bluff overlooking the long, narrow finger of water. At this time in August, the meadows are reaching their climax; vegetable abundance stretches away in tangles of wildflowers, vines, and berry bushes. Halfway up the loch, we walk into a flowery, wild world, and are encouraged by the land to amble on forever. The air is bracing, clean, packed with spicy late-summer smells; thistles are four feet high, bristling and purple-topped; these and the tall Queen Anne's laces with heads like umbrellas sway over mustards and musk mallows, clover, vetches, and the well-named self-heal plant. Like most meadows, this one is a pharmacopoeia. Here are the raw materials to prevent colds, bind wounds, balm bee stings, and soothe sore throats. There is tall St. John's–wort, source of anti-inflammatory oil for burns and sprains and also the drug hypericin, now used in AIDS therapy to block the virus from shedding its sugar-protein coat (preparing to mingle with DNA) after entering the cell. There is mullein, which makes an antibacterial remedy for earaches; red clover, the blood purifier; and the little, jug-eared leaves of sheep sorrell that, like most sour tasting things, ally with the stomach acids. There is comfrey, whose coarse leaves, bruised and applied, can draw splinters from the skin. And there is yarrow, the greatest healer, named *Achillea millefolium* after the wounded hero of the *Iliad.*

After a while, we come to a bluff overlooking the loch and rest under an evergreen where a small ring of stones has recently held a fire. Like the prolonged, flowery spring of eastern Tennessee, the summer Highlands suggest that plans be abandoned, that unwise love affairs be begun at once. It is a slow hike back to the car and our map; along the way we gingerly harvest spurs from two hardy thistles. On the dashboard of the car, the thistle tops are tight seed cases, just showing purple. Over the next weeks, the cases will imperceptibly begin to open, and one day on an Orkney peat moor will suddenly burst, strewing the interior of the car and the black hills with a scarf of airborne, downy seeds.

By late afternoon, we have been driving for hours through a continuous countryside, a landscape virtually empty of human artifacts. An occasional small stonewashed cottage pops up in this continuum of moor and meadow; otherwise sheep are the only visible actors. Never have I traveled through such a vast tract of unsullied landscape; how wonderful, I think, that somewhere a human culture has fitted itself so modestly into the Earth, if anything, underwhelming the carrying capacity of the land. The fields are a radiant green, the lochs clean; outside the rare cities the air is an edenic vapour. What virtues have allowed this light habitation to survive through the whole of the twentieth century? Have dourness, the impulse of making do, and the experience of limitation served to protect the landscape? In fact, the Scots do bring distinctive conserving values to the care of the Earth. However, as those whose European history is better than mine will already know, part of the secret of the Highland beauty is a sad and brutal episode called the clearances—a tragic lapse of good manners.

These lands are not without human influence; indeed, the stretches of seemingly untouched land are an artifact profoundly influenced by human economics. For centuries, the Highlands were dotted with the villages, houses, and fields of the clans—traditional crofters, Gaelic-speakers, and famous warriors. Then, throughout the nineteenth century, the clans were systematically destroyed. As usual, the story must start *in medias res*. As John Prebble tells it, few Highlanders participated in the Jacobite rebellion against the English, but after the battle of Culloden was lost in 1746, all the Highlanders suffered: they were forbidden to carry arms, to wear their traditional dress or play the bagpipes, and the chieftains were stripped of their hereditary jurisdictions. These diminishments, combined with suppression of their language, proved to be fatal. In addition to the Scots-Gaelic tongue, the clans were held together by a pyramidal hierarchy with a code of warrior allegiance to the chieftain-laird. In this system, the chieftains leased land at nominal rents, taking in return some crops, but above all warrior service.[3]

Once the lairds could no longer call regiments into battle, they found themselves leasing land and receiving nothing of equivalent value in return. In time, they began to envision themselves, not as warlords and custodians of their people, but as landlords who needed paying tenants rather than cash-poor, loyal soldiers. By the late eighteenth century, the whole clan system was crumbling: the chieftains and their heirs had largely migrated to southern cities where they needed money to conduct prosperous urban lives. The solution to their dilemma, and the final unravelling of the clans, came in the form of the hardy new Cheviot sheep. It was more lucrative to lease the Highlands to southern sheep graziers (who could pay in cash) than to subsistence crofters. The chieftains ceased to renew their kinsmen's leases, and the long eviction of the clans from their homes was underway. Even so, it did not occur to the Highlanders to protest; they were a people who revered tradition and maintained respect for the lairds even as they were being abandoned by them.

That sheep were the proximate cause of their undoing must have been an especially bewildering detail. Until this time, the Highland sheep, scarce and thin, were blessed animals, often named as lambs and carried inside on cold nights. But word of the clearances came to Highland clans via a seer who travelled through the villages calling, "*Mo thruaighe ort a thir, tha'n caoraich mhor a' teachd!*" "Woe to thee, oh land, the Great Sheep is coming!" In a report prepared for the Society for the Improvement of British Wool, Mr. John Maismyth described the animal as so uniformly bred that "a flock of some hundred ewes may be found, almost any two of which might pass for twin-sisters."[4] For uniform and hearty profits, ancient Highland villages were burned and whole communities evicted with no schemes for alternate shelter, food, or livelihood. The most "benign" of the landowners suggested to the farmers that they migrate to coastal areas and become a fishing people. Most painful are stories of families who lived entire winters in the lee of a gravestone; many others emigrated unwillingly to the New World. Those who remained were the subjects of intense anglicizing: by 1773, when the Scotsman James Boswell took his friend Samuel Johnson on a tour of Scotland, the distinctive sounds of the Highlands were fading. Said Johnson, "Their peculiarities wear away fast; their dialect is likely to become in half a century provincial and rustick, even to themselves."[5] Save for imports into standard English (among them the words *bog* and *inch*), Scots-Gaelic is a relic tongue, spoken only on some of the western islands. The vast, gorgeous, empty Highland acreage is yet owned by a handful of absentee landlords and, secondarily, by the Nature Conservancy Council and the National Trust for Scotland. Much of the land is designated as National Park Direction Areas, which prevents "undesirable landscape alterations."

This story would seem to be a serious challenge to the notion that inhumanity and the degradation of the Earth mirror one another. Judging from the rare beauty of the Highlands, one might say that the brutal clearances episode was good (if unintentionally) for the land itself, much like the bubonic plague outbreaks that reduced human population in Europe by nearly sixty percent and allowed depleted soils to recover fertility over the next century.[6] The conundrum of this rugged beauty achieved at an ugly cost calls for rugged mullings. The first question must be, Was there as much natural beauty when the Highlands were populated by the clans? No one doubts that the human presence creates conditions that test both the capacity of the land and of our humanity.[7] Still, it is easier to approach the question if one sheds the notion that humankind is distinct from something else called nature.

J ust north of Loch Lomond, on the north coast of the Gram-pian peninsula near Forres, there is a small fishing village that since 1962 has been the site of a new-age community known as Findhorn. At seven o'clock in the evening, as we pull onto the crunchy gravel and sand driveway of an inn near the community, there are hours left of a particularly clear, silvery light. Home this night is the house that whisky built, an elegant, pale-pink stucco villa constructed for the great distilling Glenlivet family, now owned and operated as an inn loosely affiliated with the Findhorn community. Renamed Minton House and described by its owner as "A Place of Rest and Inspiration for Leaders in Our New Emerging Culture," the villa nestles in a slight hollow on seven acres of estuarial beach and moors. It is a welcoming place even to those like ourselves, who come neither as leaders nor disciples, but only as travelers. The proportions are generous; tall windows open the house to the sea and moors on all sides and receive huge planes of the silver, astringent light that reflects off the bay and sky. There is calm and simplicity in the lines of the slowly curving staircase, the archway into the music room, the portico, and the potting shed linked to the main house by a garden of herbs. The windows of my room are hung with lengths of heavy peach velvet, and on the old oak dresser is a motley collection of bleached shells and sea glass, some nicked, some whole, a collection that a child leaves behind at the end of summer.

In silvery light

Surely when Minton House was Glenlivet House it was intended to be A Place of Rest and Inspiration for Leaders in Our Old, Entrenched Culture. Perhaps its current life is not so different from its original purpose as the words *whisky* and *new-age* suggest.

The blending of old and new (long admired by whisky makers and made possible by single-malt zealots such as the Glenlivets) is the guiding idea at the inn. Seldom does one find an inn brochure with social commentary; here, a pamphlet sweetly reasons that "'although there are numerous aspects of the past that are of value, we need to leave behind the rigidity and stagnation of many old ideas and structures. On the other hand, much of the new 'alternative' culture has a glamour and lack of realism which is irrelevant and simplistic. What is needed, we believe, is the birth of something new, resulting from a marriage of the saner elements of both." In the new age, where Tartuffes and their Orgons are ever present, here is Molière's Cléante, alive and well beyond the Sun King's Paris, speaking in a voice rare in any age.

Downstairs, young Dutch contemplatives serve a mushroom soup, then encourage us to have polarity massage and to join a morning meditation. No one mentions hydrotherapy, but the Minton House bathtubs are grand, six-foot-long, slender vessels that allow one to float fully extended, and the soaps are rose-scented, amber-colored rounds of glycerine, so fragrant that whenever a guest opens a room door a rose scent slips into the hall. The long, narrow shape of the bathtub is, I suddenly realize, something very characteristic of this country. I've seen it before in Glasgow, in furniture, in arches and doorways. As it turns out, we will see the proportion again and again. The long and narrow appears in the pinched, winding roads, in the traditional shape of the longhouses of Orkney, and in boats—the old Viking craft and the new fishing vessels alike. The shape of Scottish bathtubs, roads, and dwellings is only the most outward expression of an inner architecture of constraint, a distinctive Scottish pattern language that has also come into the symbolic shapes—the tall, narrow arches and vaults of cathedrals—and into the character of the people. Like the restraint of the natives, this form bespeaks something hemmed in, not meanly but in mild accommodation to the place.

A caravan park **D**uring the prolonged subarctic sundown, my mother and I slowly walk the village beach, talking along the Moray Firth, the large wedge of the North Sea that bites deeply into the northeastern edge of Great Britain. The approach to the beach is along a sandy plain of heather clumps, purple plants of two distinct hues—one dark and vivid, the other a light lavender Easter shade. Both are inflamed in the late sun. The beach is protected by massive boulders near a rise of dunes, and is swaddled in a trove of sea-smoothed stones: grey ones with white bands, salmon-colored and white ones, egg-shaped and flat ones. Near the top of the dunes, we come upon a large flat area, where we stop to rest. We have collected a small sackful of stones; aimlessly, while we talk into the gloaming, we arrange the stones in a spiral and in the opening of the whorl place a spear of beachgrass, grain end toward our destination, due north. Coming through the Highlands, I had begun to hear the rocky meditation of this land. Now from these sea-cast boulders comes one of the bass notes of the Earth, the old chord of rocks, a prelude for the igneous choir that booms on the sandstone cliffs and in the menhir rings to the north.

Inland from the meandering dunes of Findhorn beach, the sand slopes down into a protected hollow; squatting in the hollow, shielded slightly from the sea and wind, is a middling-big trailer park ("caravan park" in the Scottish vocabulary) of some fifty rounded metal shelters. Each caravan has a propane gas hookup, and here and there a picket fence surrounds a tiny notion of a sand yard. At ten o'clock last light begins to elide into night. As we watch, the park recedes into grey-blue shadow, and from inside the small metal huts, yellow lights begin to glow, filling windows and open doors. A few boys dart between the caravans, scuffing up sand and dust. It looks to be an ancient city seen from a distance and, far from bleak, the encampment is cheerful with nomadic lightness. So close to the wind and sea, the park has accepted the ephemeral, tinsel-and-tin nature of settlements. This being so, the city and its shadowy inhabitants sit easily on the sandy moor, and such coziness as comes inside the shelters is all the more legitimate for being so delicately invoked. The night has turned blue-black; on the way back to the inn along a sand road, we catch the quick movements of brown hares scurrying across the plain—dark, blurred forms racing against the nocturnal sand.

By morning, the gardens of Findhorn are speckled with the heavy dew of saltwater farms. Everywhere there are gardens: vegetable gardens that once, so the story goes, grew cabbages five feet around; pocket gardens of water lilies; flowering vines overhanging paths that wind through clustered houses, trailers, print shops, and organic food stores. In early summer, when the gardens were being planted and new brochures were wet on the press, the world was still dazed by the fall of the Berlin Wall; a Findhorn brochure exults, "Humankind is breaking new ground . . . Those we were told were our enemies are becoming our friends."

Sitting among the orange, brown-speckled daylilies of early August, we don't know it yet, but on the morning we prowl through Findhorn's flowers and wells of idealism an army has invaded Kuwait.

North   **I**f we were to stay at Findhorn we could refine our composting techniques and study the light that glances off the bay, but we have a ferry to catch and the Pentland Firth to cross. The road north toward Scrabster is along the coast, then through high, wild mountains with gorges falling away from thin roads glazed by changeable weathers: rain, hard rain, mist, brief sun, followed by rain, hard rain, mist, and brief sun—a repeating round like a sea chanty. At the ferry town of Scrabster, near Thurso, Orkney-bound hardies are gathered at the ferry dock, vehicles bristling with outdoor gear. One sedan holds three Brittany spaniels, whose muzzles, aligned in a sleepy row along the back seat, point delicately toward the islands; a jeep is laden with lacquered wicker creels and a quiver of long plastic tubes filled with fishing rods. When the rainstorm lets up for a brief interval of sun, the sportsmen and women unfold from their cramped seats and lean against their cars; in high-tech hiking shoes and rain parkas, they are unmistakable among the oily, navy blue coveralls and short-sleeved flannel shirts of the ferry yard hands and boatmen who run the P & O ferries: seven ships whose names are saints, among them *St. Ola, St. Ninian, St. Rognvald*, and *St. Magnus*, all household words in the island world to the north.

The Scrabster-to-Stromness ferry trip is a two-hour sail on the MV *St. Ola* north across the Pentland Firth, a route that hugs the western side of the island of Hoy, then turns east and tucks between Hoy and Mainland islands into the protected inland sea of Scapa Flow, landing at the port of Stromness. The northern tip of the Caithness peninsula is remote, yet it is Scotland proper; the crossing to Orkney is a sea change to another inheritance and habitat. The islands that make up the Orkney cluster lie at 59° N, the same latitude as Fond du Lac in northernmost Saskatchewan and Kuskokwim Bay in Alaska, closer to the Arctic Circle than to London. On the ancient Roman map, Orkney lies just south of the *ultima thule*, the end of the world.[8] Due east is Norway, and Orkney is awash in vestiges of the seafaring Norsefolk: they left a distinctive cadence in the Orcadian accent, free fishing and unique landholding systems in the legal code, faint scratches of walruses and sea serpents on the tomb walls of Maeshowe. For five hundred years, the people of Orkney spoke the Norn, a now extinct variant of Old Norse; modern speech is standard English, with a Scottish accent layered with Old Norse overtones.

Edwin Muir, son and poet of Orkney, recalls that when he was growing up on the farming island of Wyre, "the men spoke for the most part in a slow, deliberate voice, but some of the women could rattle on at a great rate in the soft sing-song lilt of the islands, which has remained unchanged for over a thousand years. . . . It is a soft and musical inflection, slightly melancholy, but companionable, the voice of people who are accustomed to hours of talking in the long winter evenings and do not feel they need to hurry: a splendid voice for telling stories in."[9] Not only the inflection, but almost every ancient place-name in the islands is Norse, and the lattice of names for bays, villages, hills, and rocky ledges comprise a continuous topographical poem and a bonanza for the native tongue: from Deerness come Tammy Tiffy, Skaill Skerries, Creya, White Fowl Nevi, Swin Ber, Scarva Taing, Iron Heelia, Braebuster Ness, Muckle, and Peerie Castle; from Holm come Mirth Hilly, Point of the Liddie, Scare Gun, Cockmurra, and Haddieweel; from Orphir and Stenness are Smoogro Skerry, Scorra Dale, Mid Moss, Button, and Biggings; from the northwestern and middle regions come Glebe, Skorn, Tunga, Quoyloo, Nether Linklater, Fibla Fiold, Little Brillia Fiold, The Hog, Nisthouse, and Winksetter.

Before the Vikings of the wondrous syllables, there were Celts and Picts, and before them, the first human colonists, Neolithic farmers who, judging from the kinds of beehive tombs they built, came from the Mediterranean. Of these southern peoples' settlement in the northern isles of Scotland, archaeologist Gordon

Childe has wryly commented, "The reasons which might have induced anyone to travel the treacherous roads of the sea from the sunbathed coasts of the south to our fog-enshrouded shores have been the subject of intensive speculation."[10] At least part of the answer is that Neolithic Orkney was neither fog-enshrouded nor cold. By 7500 B.C., the frigid glacial climate had warmed up and the balmy Boreal Phase was underway. Summers in Scotland were warmer and there was far less rain and wind than at present. Even with good weather, it was an adventurous tribe who sailed their lamb- and seed-laden boats up the coast from the Mediterranean, coming ashore as far north as Shetland. The warm climate continued, with fluctuations and increasing rain, until about 700 B.C., when startlingly cooler weather arrived, and a southern people found themselves stationed in a cold land that had become home. From the very beginning, the whole long line of Orcadians has been made of people who came from somewhere else: immigrants and invaders who have raided, settled, and populated the remote islands, producing what Orkney writer George Mackay Brown calls (in his poem "What is an Orcadian") "a fine mixter-maxter."

> First the aborigines
> That houked Skara Brae from the sand.
> Then the Picts,
> Those small dark cunning men
> Who scrawled their history in stone
> . . . .
> And then the tigers from east over sea,
> The blond butchering Vikings,
> Whose last worry on sea or land
> Was purity of race, as they staggered couchwards
> After a fill of ale.
> Finally, to make the mixture thick and slab,
> The off-scourings of Scotland
> . . . .
> But that's not all.
> For many a hundred ships have ripped their flanks
> On Rora Head, or the Noup,
> And Basque sailor lads and bearded skippers from Brittany
> Left off their briny ways to cleave a furrow
> Through Orkney crofts and lasses.

There were also the Amerindian wives who came with Orkney husbands returned from working in what we call Hudson Bay. Appropriately, a good etymological guess is that the name *Orkney* is a multicultural sound whose first syllable is the Celtic *orc* for wild boar, and the second is the Old Norse *ey*, meaning "the islands"— plural. Thus, both *Orkney Islands* and *the Orkneys* are redundancies; the correct usage is just plain *Orkney*, which must mean something close to "Islands of the Wild Boar People."[11] Possibly there was a Neolithic people for whom the orc was the totem animal. This is plausible because in the prehistoric culture that prevailed in Orkney, as elsewhere in Europe, the boar was an important animal, the primary emblem of death and renewal. As early as 60,000 B.C., it was the custom to place the jawbone of a wild boar in a grave, and the magical death-boar continues to appear in bristling, Iron Age sculptures and in the legends of western literature: you will recall the one that gores a young boy's thigh, leaving a brush-with-death scar that will reveal him to his baby-nurse as not a stranger, but the returned Odysseus. If Orkney is named for the Old European divinity in her aspect of wild boar, it would have presented no difficulty for the later Norse invaders, in whose mythology the goddess of death and regeneration was Freya, nicknamed *Syr*, or "sow."[12] But, like much information relating to prehistoric Orkney, there are other reasonable ideas. Another best guess comes from George Mackay Brown, whose word must always be respected. In the foreword of *A Time To Keep*, he writes, "The stories in this book are nearly all set in a little group of islands off the north coast of Scotland, called Orkney—'the islands of the whale.'" Whether you lean toward whales or wild boars, you get the general idea that the name holds a powerful animal.

Only eight miles separate Orkney from Caithness, but at *Cliffs* flood tide, waters race through the Pentland Firth at nine knots. In a hard wind and slanting rain the crossing is very rough, the huge ferry rolling back and forth, rising up and down in enormous ocean swells that are dark at the base and grade to a pale flute of foam-green seen against the sky. While my mother happily identifies skuas and shags through her field glasses, I grow green at the gills and must stagger to the topmost deck to ward off sickness by the whirling dancer's trick of staring fixedly at one point on the horizon. For two hours I follow the discipline precisely, steadied by a rail, standing under a dripping canvas tarp, never lifting my gaze from the massive, brooding cliffs of the island of Hoy. The time amounts to a tutorial in the slabby strata of sandstone palisades that rise, in places, one thousand feet perpendicularly from the sea— striated structures pocked with fissures and facets, weathered into fantastic geos, gloups, arches, and sea-stacks, the massive palisades crested on top with green and gold fields. Only surrounded by the tumult of the Atlantic could such an architecture seem calm, and perhaps it is more the idea of something so long firm that braces. Underneath my feet the ship lurches and rolls, but for my mind the world is a relatively steady rockface whose colors and weathered shapes seep into my eyes.

Relatively is the key word. The foundation of rock is stable only in our slender grasp of time; rocks are vigorous participants in evolutionary change. Indeed, by Scottish standards, these cliffs are not very old; perhaps four hundred million years ago the Orcadian foundation rocks (now deep below the visible cliffs) were folded into the Caledonian mountains.[13] As these foundation granites and schists eroded and washed into the sea, a sediment was formed; by three hundred fifty million years ago, just about the time that fish were becoming common, the layers had compacted into the famous rocks that comprise these cliffs and much of northwest Scotland, the Old Red Sandstones. The phrase is technical—the description by which geologists identify this kind of rock—but coming from the British the term sounds very like the "Old Egg" and "Old Thing" by which a P. G. Wodehouse character expresses affection. As a result, I can never read "Old Red Sandstones" without having an image of the author looking on the rocks fondly, as on a school chum with whom one has survived many scrapes. Elsewhere in Scotland, the Old Reds are brownish, greyish, and ochre reds, but the striated Orcadian cliffs are unlike any others. The timepiece of the eroding, water-worn rockface passes the ship imperceptibly in veins of rose and wine-red stones, in melting sea-soaked russets, oranges, and magnificent plums: the source of the luminous walls of St. Magnus Cathedral on Mainland Island.

After an hour of my intense staring, the shapes of animals and baroque forms emerge in the craggy surface patterns of the rocks. Then recognizable forms subside into nothing but shapes, fissures running the whole vertical length of the cliff into the sea, ending in deep black holes that recede into sea caves. Now and then a mighty sun splits the heavy clouds and illuminates one great section of the colored sandstone face, throwing another into dark shadow, casting a frail rainbow over the cliff. The stark light and dark of this sea-and-rock world opens one's mind to the stark notion of sin and redemption. Still the colors come, the bright ones sometimes muting into nearly colorless browns and greys. Finally, in a body too precarious to entertain the dizzying rhythms of rational thought, my mind abandons analogy, interpretation, references: now in the blow-holes, striations, surface inlets, and undulating facets of the cliffs, I see only *thereness*, and to such existence one cannot apply the story of geology with its comforting names and eras and methods of layering time, nor the story of aesthetics, with forms judged beautiful, moving, and moody, nor the story of morality, with analogies from a rock world to human affairs.

With knowledge held at bay, one can only see and keep seeing; it is very hard work, staying just there, in the openness prior to resolutions. But here at sea, the lenses of science, art, religion, and philosophy all make me queasy. If I allow, even for a moment, any one of these filters to slip over the uninflected looking, my body immediately threatens to betray me, as have the bodies of several young children along this deck rail. ("Careful," says a passing burr to a companion, "it's a sick.") And since the very idea of looking down to find the zipper on my red windbreaker is dangerous, my head stays high, the jacket open, and both hands firm on the polished wood rail. After an hour both hands are bone-cold, rigidly curled around the rail. Sprays of salt water fly across the deck, coating my face with a thin white crust.

It doesn't matter; this body and the slow-moving, slowly eroding rock formations on the distant shore are by now nearly the same; the fine distinction between "rock" and "self" blurred into time washing into forms, carving sea-caves and dark hollows out of the flatness. All the while, the fierce Atlantic crashes into the cliff wall, searching out weaknesses, laving the rocks with a glistening film of salt and water. The handsomest results of this ceaseless engagement are the long-fingered inlets (called geos) that reach back into the cliff, the rock arches that spring like rough Arc de Triomphes from the cliff, and the towering sea-stacks, each one the lingering leg of an arch, worn freestanding by the fluid sea-chisel. Two miles south of St. John's Head on the island of Hoy, in the lee of a protective jutting ledge, stands a pillar four hundred and fifty feet tall, this one named the Old Man of Hoy. Over all the fabulous formations wander great masses of life: green patches and dripping veins of vegetation, swirls of wings, herring gulls, shags and fulmars, cries in the wind, and on sunny rock ledges and stacks high above the smack of the sea, soft bowers where speckled eggs are hatched. Who can say what this really is. Looked at intently, the reality only becomes more and more unknown, accepting then sliding from each net of knowledge, even as the sea squid emits a black image of itself, then disappears behind the ink, leaving a camouflage of ink tentacles waving, curling, dissolving gradually into the water until nothing can be seen.

Arrival on
Mainland
Island

There are some sixty islands in the Orkney archipelago, although many of these are best described as *skerries*, large rocks that are overwashed at high tide. In 1933, twenty-eight islands were inhabited, but the more marginal human habitations have gradually faded and the primary island communities now number sixteen: Mainland, Rousay, Egilsay, Wyre, Gairsay, Shapinsay, Westray, Papa Westray, Sanday, North Ronaldsay, Stronsay, and Eday are the North Isles; Hoy, Burray, South Ronaldsay, Flotta, and a scatter of tiny others are the South Isles. Mainland is so much larger than the others that it makes up nearly one third of the total land area of the chain. The startling first impression of the big island is of a treeless, unsheltered landscape that stretches away to the sea in wide plains and gentle hills. In the Scandinavian way, farmhouses are widely dispersed across the land, creating a sparse terrain. With no imposing hills and no forests, and few villages to act as a break, a strong southwesterly wind is always blowing, singing, howling, or whistling over the island, carrying in its teeth a saline tincture that saturates even the most inland areas. Gale winds blow for twenty-four days a year on average, and the combination of caustic salt and wind is so potent that it has long been considered an eccentricity to attempt to grow a tree on Orkney. Planted in the lee of a house or barn, a sapling will begin to grow, but no sooner has it outgrown its protector than the trunk begins to bend in the wind, eventually keeling over nearly ninety degrees toward Norway. The southeastern prong of Mainland is articulated by a thin neck of land, an isthmus shaped as though an oceanic thumb and finger had slightly squeezed a warm hunk of dough, leaving two fat bays on either side of a narrow land bridge. This strand corresponds with the crossing point of two huge geological rifts: the North Scapa and Brims-Risa faults. Kirkwall town is nestled on the isthmus along the northern bay, perhaps a half mile from the intersection of the faults. Rising up from a plateau in town, halfway up a slight slope from the sea, is St. Magnus Cathedral. "Kip carrrrryin' doone, Leddies, kip carrrrrryin' doone," are the melodic, accurate directions we receive from two little lads playing on the hill above the kirk.

The flanking sandstone columns of the entrance are worn and pocked in places, and they lead inward in rows toward a dark vaulted recess where a door is hidden in shadow—a dark sea-cave shape into the sanctuary. The cathedral is small, only one hundred feet long; its power comes entirely from color, proportion, and a material bond with the native palisades. The surfaces inside and out are polychromed marvels: red stones from the nearby Head of Holland and yellow-tinged ones from the island of Eday, the tones alternately patterned throughout the kirk so subtly as to be found the finest medieval example of woven architectural colour in Britain. Building began in 1137, under the watch of Norse chieftains and master masons with names like Rognvald and Kol. We enter the high, narrow nave on a morning made of rain and mist as the bells of St. Magnus sound over the square and all of the town, carrying down onto the pier over the heavy slate-grey stones of the streets. The three big bells are turned but not tuned; that is, not altered in pitch. The clappers beating against cast-iron crownsta-ples release the same sound, rung in the same way, that the islanders have heard for five hundred years—ringing in the old Norse way known as clocking.

Inside, we join a sea of the faithful who wear stout tweeds, good

Let your fears go, fly away in the wind

wool suits, and burnished leather shoes. Oiled raincapes and black umbrellas are neatly arranged over their arms. The pews smell of waxed wood and damp wool, and the faint scent of lavender soap rises from the neck of a man directly in front of us. It is a special Sunday morning: Reverend H. W. M. Cant and the Kirk Session are welcoming their former minister and his wife back to the island. The Reverend R. S. Whiteford is to speak on Christ as Victor. Whiteford is in his early sixties, tall, commanding, handsome with gleaming white hair, and he wears the ingenious vestments of this theatre: ink-black robe and a dazzling white collar that splays like a forked tongue in two brilliant short ribbons over his chest. Against the soft, worn terracotta of the choir and pulpit, his black and white dress cracks and leaps across our vision, stark as an absolute line between good and evil.

Whiteford speaks English with only a rare *glisk* and *sough* from the old regional variation of English called Scots. This is the way it has been from the pulpit since the early seventeenth century, when James I ordered the Kirk to conduct services in standard English. Even today, no complete Scots Bible is available, but William Lorimer's long-awaited 1983 translation of the *New Testament* is embraced in households that keep lowland Scots alive as a language of identity. In this translation, there is a delicious bit of poetic justice; the only voice in standard English is the Devil's.[14] In the cathedral this morning, Whiteford's accent alone makes me glad for the Scots language, and his *Christ* is a word made for the intricacies of Scots-accented English, the rolled *rrrrrrrr* caressed with each sounding. In this tongue, the story of forgiveness and spiritual victory comes in sprung rhythms and taut pronunciation, a rigorous music of tension and release.

The same stark rhythm wells from the island itself, the alternately fierce and bucolic sky and sea, the bleak grey, then lustrous green fields. Here, too, the imagery of fish and boats and Isaiah's vision of a holy union with the land are not archaic pastoral, but the ordinary pictures of daily existence seen from farmhouse, kirk, and pier. Over the whole scene comes the wind, scything through towns and farms, shearing across the open headlands. All the leaves and stalks, the stiff shrubs, grasses, and loose gates of the island are sounding daylong and through the night: wind plays the island like an instrument. Outside the small villages there are no other sounds. In the barley fields of August, the grainheads, still green, rustle in the continuous wind as light and shadow play over the long waves and shifting runnels of the half-pliant, half-resistant stalks. Always the wind comes against the skin, the body—a constant force, wearing, drying, lowing. After a day the face is windburned, ruddy. After a lifetime, the farmers' faces are brilliant red and rough-lined, their eyes sunk far back under brows like beetled cliffs. When Whiteford croons to his flock in a deep oratorical burr, "Let your fears go, fly away in the wind. Let your fears go, fly away in the wind," the sounds marry belief to the air.

In her evolution from southern Baptist to Presbyterian, then away from and back to her chosen church via Buddhist study, my mother has given her children a steady example of questing and permission to travel. With that visa, I lament the ambivalence in Christianity toward the Earth, and have come to admire an open-ended song of praise, grappling with form and formlessness, gravity and light, in the mysteries of phosphorus and poems. As for the Fall, surely Shinto believers and the Hopi have it right: being in balance or out of balance with the cosmos is a fruitful way to describe the great human choice, with the pain of imbalance ample reason to seek another path. But, as this morning reminds me, all this floats over the rhythms laid down in my childhood, just as they were in my mother's, sounds that are not lightly shed.

What is being worshipped here includes the irresistible music of a unique English sound, the accretions of a particular local vocabulary, and acrobatics of the tongue curated not only by the Scottish Church and its groomed men with the gift of beautiful speech, but by the population as a whole. When the people of Kirkwall rise to sing "Lord for thy tender mercies' sake, / Lay not our sins to our charge," the male and female voices buzz through the chamber in harmonies, the texture of gender playing with the notion of transcending itself. Outside, the skies have opened in deluge, and after the service, clumps of worshippers duck back into the kirk, gathering under the rose window to have what they really do call "a wee spot of tea" until the storm abates. Over a strong cup of tea, a Mrs. Skea offers us a booklet about the saint, a work that opens with a photograph of Kirkwall's prize relic: Magnus' skull split open by an axe.

Grey In a world of grey flagstones, grey seals; fences, buildings, and streets made of grey stone; and a rhapsody of grey skies dripping over a grey sea, the peoples of Orkney have responded not by a stubborn resistance, not with intrusions of gaudy paint and bright cloth, but by melding themselves and their artifacts into the landscape. The palette of earth, sky, and sea has sufficed and has schooled the local eye in subtlety and proportion. Out in the countryside, over the course of a day one might see three splashes of vivid human colour: a purple door in a grey farmhouse facade, a hunter-green painted gate in a grey stone wall, one outlandish pink house by the bay in St. Margaret's Hope, leaping from the grey continuum of the village. Departures from the grey-scale are prominent events and they pose a question: what danger would be courted by a more lavish deviancy, by a rash of magentas and pinks, yellows, cerulean blues, carmine reds? Would some fibre be weakened, leaving the community more vulnerable to the careless accident that comes of a momentary distraction, the frayed rope that leads to the splintered wreck on the shoals? The embrace of grey must arise from an old calculation in which morals and aesthetics have merged to mirror the palette of the surround. The colors that do appear—the green gate, the purple door, even the vibrant pink house—all arise from the colors of heather, grass, and petals. Even the ratio of painted door to grey stone facade follows that of tussocky heather to vast black moor, primrose petal to salt-lashed cliff. Very like the strategy of those animals who assume the protective coloration of their habitat, this human aesthetic has grown from and is semaphore to the surround.

Tuesday comes up wet, cold, raining, and grey. Drizzles probe into showers then recede to drizzles throughout the day. We make a trip to the post office in Kirkwall town. By chance, we are here during the culmination of celebrations for the birthday of Her Majesty the Queen Mother. As one might expect, a celebration of things English and royal does not especially stir the Scottish spirit, but this Elizabeth is from the Highlands, so shops offer a great line of souvenirs with her portrait applied woozily, slightly out-of-register to plates and ashtrays banded with gold. Best of all, the Philatelic Office has issued a stamp series in her honor: four stamps showing four stages of life. The first is a sepia-tone picture of a young wild-haired girl that at first glance seems an ethnographer's photograph of a half-feral child. Then comes a pale blue stamp: Elizabeth as Duchess of York, in her twenties, in ropes of pearls, a regal set of head already established, just beginning to contend with Wallis Simpson. The third is a stamp of a woman encrusted in a crown and massive necklace, her mild face firmset with concern. The last stamp is a release into vivid turquoise and fuchsia pastels: a blousey, calm old woman, wafting in her signature costume, a floral suit and a sort of floating, gossamer garland of flowers emanating from her broad-brimmed hat.

In the post office, as in banks and city halls, there are prominent spindle racks holding brochures about family programs, health care services, and how to get your old-age pension. Just as the Glasgow vibration hinted, in Scottish island society there is everywhere the surprising message that life will be a possible proceeding. In the America I know, the sensibilities of even optimistic souls are tinged with a competitive, anxious edge that hovers like a cautionary tale: very little about our society suggests that the average person can raise a family or grow old gracefully. Even the rich live with a grave wound: the knowledge that the economy that yields their material affluence dooms many others to misery. This short spell in Orkney invites a vicarious entrance into a slightly more secure world. The society cannot be all satisfactory, for I see in the paper that the youth are bored with farming jobs and are beginning to drink alcohol in public. It is a greyer society; it does not lightly tolerate the outlandish and speculative; yet there are many signs that islanders have a kind of inherent well-being lost even to the materially affluent in my country.

After the post office, we wander up to the main market street to buy scones, fruit, and local Orkney cheese for the next day's field trip. The streets are narrow, made of blue-grey flagstone slabs, crowded with shoppers and tiny cars that weave slowly through the pedestrians. Women push their round-headed babies in prams that are uniformly fitted over with clear plastic rain jackets that can be opened or zipped up in a trice. When the rains begin, as they do at some point nearly every day, mothers and fathers all up and down the street are suddenly bending, zipping up the hoods of prams. The babies process placidly through the wet streets with splots of rain bouncing and beading on their plastic ceilings. When the sun comes out again and the hoods are unzipped, the babies must experience a miniature version of what is happening over the whole landscape: the abrupt parting of a blanket of clouds that renders the island a sudden bright, wet jewel, all the more astonishing for its rarity. On a sunny day along these streets, one commonly sees a practice that in most other cities could only be found today in a book of old statistics: in front of meat shops and tea rooms and bakeries, there are parked pramfuls of babies, wee ones left outside near the warm stone walls, safe and unattended save by the passing people of Kirkwall. From one blanketfold comes a peedie, tiny hand, stretching out to the sparkles in the grey stone wall. Well underway are the countless perceptions and sensory minutiae that will cause this baby to relish greys. Orcadians are said to be wary towards outsiders, and one can easily imagine that the climate engenders a stoic and braced psyche. Yet a community that can leave its tenderest members unattended for a spell, on its busiest street, during market hours, has preserved a kind of trust that is elsewhere only a memory. Perhaps it is not too much to say that such a trust and the National Trust that tends the landscape of Scotland are two faces of one virtue.

Whispering
at the hide

In late afternoon we arrive at the bird hide of Birsay, a small wooden shack on a preserve called The Loons, located on the northwest side of the island. The hide squats on the edge of a large, reedy, marsh pond favored by wading birds and waterfowl. On three sides, wooden horizontal shutters can be latched open, making the hide into a concealed viewing stand. Inside, sitting on the wooden benches under the windows, our elbows on the window sills, we are cold and damp but as close to duckdom as one can get in clothes. Over the next hours we adjust our clocks to the cadences of little grebes, wigeons, mallards, a goldeneye, a pack of coots, a raggedy flight of lapwings, and whimbrels. Here my mother is in one of her elements, geared with lightweight, powerful binoculars, a many-pocketed waterproof jacket, decades of birding experience, slender field guides, and the birders' secret code. At bird identification I am an inadvertent apostate, always ambling off, in my mind's eye, from Linnaean schemes, but the names of the birds and their parts are like a song to my ear: the sounds stumbled onto the human tongue full of confidence in categories, full of the wandering syllable of life.

And then, they are the vehicle of delicious dialogue. When an Orcadian naturalist and his nine-year-old son arrive, they and my mother nod gravely to each other the secret birder's nod; then, after some thirty obligatory minutes of deep silence, my mother whispers to her clansmen. It sounds like "Pardon me, I wonder if you think the bird to the left of the reeds" (she indicates) "is a Snouted Scoter or a Mauve-Bellied Thwerp?" The man and his son lean toward her slightly, and reply in fervent, barely audible whispers, "Surely the pintail feathers suggest the Mauve-Bellied Striped Thwerp, but the overall shape indicates the juvenile Grimp." "Yes," my mother considers, "that is quite right, it could be the juvenile Grimp"—a long, pregnant pause—"except for the tail spread." "Too spade-shaped for the young Grimp," chimes in the lad. "Could it be the Mauve-Bellied Thwerp?"

The child is already a dazzling birder, and both the adults of the species beam on him with affection and pride. For another hour the three of them carry on in a deep, contented silence, punctuated lightly with occasional hushed exchanges. Even in whispers, the Scots accent is a feast. I'll venture that the *main* point of this tongue is to produce the most extraordinary sound from each sentence. Here at the hide, observing various species, I ken that the language itself is the secret transport from the dour, constrained temperament of the land. All day long, in ordinary speech, these people are entering one portal of liberation. Elsewhere during our journey, we stop along a country road to ask directions to a hamlet called the Bridge of Eirn; the farmer who tells us how to get there makes the place-name into a small, impromptu song—"tha' Buurrrrrriddjjje 'a Ayyrrr-rrruunn"—nine syllables lilted with as much syncopation as you could hope for in Gershwin. Since it is such a nice sound, he says the name some five times while telling us how to get there. (It's right down the road.)

Another night, on Scottish television I come across a program that consists of eight people sitting in a semicircle speaking what I soon realize is to me an entirely unintelligible language. I have never before heard, in the West, a language whose every syllable is foreign, a flow of sound that is a fast-rushing river with no branch or twig onto which one can grasp. The group of speakers is discoursing with a verve that elides into near hilarity, but subtitles indicate that nothing especially funny is being said. Gradually it dawns on me; these are revivalists, people who have learned to speak fluent Old Scots–Gaelic, and they are simply delirious to be speaking it together. It is a melodic, muscular stream of sound ("Cha chuir, cha chuir, arsa bean an tuathaniach; cha'n 'eil an creutair bochd ach a' magaran mu 'n cuairt a' trusadh a cuid mar tha sinn fein. Agus leigeadh air falbh a' mhuile-mhag le a beatha") and after a while I am smiling too.[15]

Whatever the accent or dialect used, conversation-level human sound would not be troubling to birds; it is only movement that spooks them, and this is obscured by the hide. The etiquette of whispering in hides is for the benefit of humans—to insure that the pondlife is the dominant speaker. On this afternoon, a luminous steel-grey sky shines on a metallic pond as waves of birds arrive in jagged, dark, silhouetted clusters. Landing with splashes, they commence bobbing for food, tails upended. On the far edge of the marsh, a shadowy family of mallards glides in and out of reeds, the quietly coloured female and the iridescent male egging their floozy juveniles on to feeding acumen. We stay through sunset, a late and lurid event in these huge skies, and into the long *humeen*, the subarctic twilight. Afterwards, the pale light over the marsh will last until almost midnight.

Insects laid a spell on me
In the upstairs rooms of the Stromness Natural History Museum, there are long wood and glass cases that shelter, among other things, a nineteenth-century conception of nature: here are birds' nests arranged in sizes from tiny to huge, eggs of all colors nestled in cotton wool, and specimens of the sand-brown spiral and whorled chambered cases in which the ocean cradles its young. There are fossil fish from the Stromness Flags and the Sandwick Fish Bed, including the commonest *Glyptolepis paudicens*, crossop-

terygians, placoderms, acanthodians, and lungfish. Around the low cases are tall vertical glass houses for stuffed birds with painted beaks and painted webbed feet: there are perhaps a hundred frozen-in-flight, frozen-on-a-branch, or frozen-in-defense-of-their-young stuffed birds, among them a Snow Bunting presented by Miss Macdonald; a particoloured, Brindle-Headed Brambling with ginger and black feathers; a Kingfisher much dulled by death; a Corn Crake; a handsome Wigeon; and a Velvet Scoter, all black with a bill painted yellow and red as for a circus wagon. Along the bottom of the glass cases are fixed assemblages of voles, the tiny field creatures who star in an ongoing debate about whether one species is unique to Orkney, and if so whether it did or did not reach the island over an ancient land bridge that once connected Orkney to the Caithness peninsula. Like several other Orcadian mysteries, this one has proved satisfying enough to preoccupy a few souls for their entire lives. (How a person lets herself or himself be chosen by one of the world's questions is, to me, the greatest curiosity.) There are no snakes in the cases; the land bridge disappeared under postglacial seas too soon for reptiles or amphibians to reach the islands, and while frogs and toads are occasionally introduced into local gardens, they do not establish permanent colonies.

The museum dates from 1837, when the Orkney Natural History Society was begun "for the two-fold object of investigating the natural history and antiquities of the Country, and stimulating the inhabitants of these Island to the study of the Almighty's works." It was the time of natural theology, before the tectonic plates of science and spirit shifted and the fault opened up in modern thought. Just as the Old European culture survived longest on the peripheries of Europe, in quiet, remote Orkney it seems to have been possible for an individual to weave scientific and spiritual inquiry well into modernity. It was one Charles Clouston—minister to the parish of Sandwick and scholar of rocks, meteors, birds, plants, and most especially marine algae—who was the first president of the Orkney Natural History Society. Reverend Clouston's study of the almighty algae is commemorated by a species of kelp named *Laminaria cloustonii*. The Stromness Museum cases also hold the vast shell collection of Robert Rendall, theologian, student of the mollusca, and poet. Rendall arrived on the islands from

Glasgow as a seven-year-old, and his memoir leaves little doubt about the power of this place to nurture wholeness:

> I came to know the scalies and the curly doddies, the sea pinks, the cocks and hens, the wild white clover (sucking this for its sweetness), the seggies in the Crantit meadeows, golden dandylions run to seed, meadowsweet in the gullies of the cliffs at Scapa and Berstane, wiry 'sodgers' to slash in mimic battles. Insects, too, of all sorts laid a spell upon me: burnished beetles in the sun, cabbage butterflies in the garden, small blue ones by the roadside ditches, bumble bees in their ceremonial splendour of colour.[16]

By now the island is working its way on us, too. The openness is something like the clearing achieved in St. Magnus, a space in which awareness may rise. I wonder how much of the wholeness one detects in Rendall, Clouston, and Muir can be traced to this island geography. All islands are evocative places that owe some of their special identity to clear geographical definition; crossing to an island is often passage into another reality. In addition to the usual island gestalt, this particular place—wet, flat, wind-swept—has an exceedingly spare quality. Usually, a treeless countryside that stretches away like an uninflected life seems a prison of time, but this one is different. A place stripped of ordinary vegetation, rapturously open, strongly acted upon by the forces of nature, it engages the imagination with something at-the-bone. Like Ithaka, Orkney has been a rocky nurse, and in T. S. Eliot's assessment of Edwin Muir, one can trace the character of the island itself: "a reserved, reticent man, not fluent in conversation. Yet his personality made a deep impression upon me, and especially the impression of one very rare and precious quality . . . complete integrity."[17] Perhaps these observations will partially explain the kind of travel that happens on Orkney, where a traveler may cast a plumb line into time.

Sermons in stones

The place-names on the map of Mainland are distinguished by typographical conventions that are a subtle commentary: whereas Roman antiquities are marked by a bold, machine-made, all-caps typeface, names of Neolithic and Bronze Age antiquities are printed in the intricate, hand-drawn calligraphy of illuminated manuscripts. We are headed toward three of these elegant markings on the map. The central plain of west Mainland Island is flat pastureland with swaths of moors and bogs, surrounded by low hills. From this low inland plain the sea is hidden and there comes no sound of the *swa*, the low prolonged note of waves heard at a distance. When clouds are caught on the encircling hills, the place goes grey and moody. It was here that a prehistoric tribe chose to build three sermons in stone now named the Ring of Brodgar, the Stones of Stenness, and Maeshowe. The three works date to the late Neolithic era but they share one common bond with St. Magnus Cathedral and with the modern streets of Stromness town: for millennia, the plentiful stone in this land has invited masons to create enduring works in rock. The lands around the island's oldest ceremonial stoneworks are a patchwork of golden bere and barley fields and green-grass grazing lands, threaded lightly by a well-paved road, but these more recent human earthworks are such a modest presence on the landscape that the tall stone rings and the mound of the chambered cairn still hold sway on the plain.

The Stones of Stenness and the Ring of Brodgar stand within a mile of each other on a narrow causeway that runs between the tidal Loch of Stenness and the freshwater Loch of Harray. The stones in the two circles are enormous megaliths, hewn from somewhere, moved to the site by some ingenious means, sunk deep in the ground for stability with the precision of an engineering corps, arranged in circles with the logic of an Earth-worshipping people. Beyond the two rings of stones, there once stood other, isolated monoliths, but over many centuries they have been removed by crofters for whom the great stones were an obstacle to the plough. Approaching from the east, one comes upon the Stones of Stenness first, close by the road, on a low, flat bit of land: four tall, narrow slabs in a hundred-foot circle that once contained perhaps twenty stones. The remaining monoliths are roughly seventeen feet high, perhaps four feet wide, and about four inches thick. They are deeply and irregularly weathered, the surfaces worn into swirls like lava flows and topographical maps. Each stone glistens with silvery flecks of mica, and is veined with rust and taxi-cab-yellow strands of lichens. These growths, like the coral reefs they resemble, are sensitive to acidic precipitations; the presence of these bright veins of colour amounts to a report on the good air quality of the prevailing Atlantic winds. A pair of mute swans, white as clouds, floats on the nearby loch, and a cluster of pale yellow butterflies slowly fan their wings on the stones, lightly launching the play between brevity and the old ache for immortality. At the bases of the stones grow clumps of late summer daisies, and on two sides the menhir circle is surrounded by an oatfield, the grain shaking, rustling, shaking, rippling in the wind; the long-whiskered spears bending and waving in runnels that are, just as people have always said, like the surface of a sea. The circle is a somber, powerful place steeped in time, yet compared to what lies further up the road it is a child's wading pool.

At the Ring of Brodgar a mown path curves up around a hillside of purple heathers, and the megaliths rise against a deep blue sky. On this day, the hill is washed in the Orkney summer colours, blue and green and purple—intense, saturated shades, heartier even than the blue chicory weeds and purple loosestrifes of New England's flinty summer soils. From the distance, the megaliths rise up from the field of color as implacable, dark, spine-tingling figures: almost thirty of the original sixty stones stand in a ring cast three hundred and forty feet in diameter, fully occupying the huge hilltop over-looking the two lochs. Surrounding the megaliths in every direction are only the open space of the huge Orkney sky—the largest sky I have ever seen—and the rolling land. The individual stones stand in an arrangement fraternal but wary, like the tribal chieftains who once met on this island to plan their raiding strategies: each plinth stakes out a place with plenty of room between itself and its nearest neighbor. Around the host of stones, the hill slopes down into a moat shaped by the builders, most likely to build up the rise and surround the menhirs with water, the potent life-giving element. Signs of erosion show that the fifteen-foot megaliths were originally much taller, perhaps twenty feet tall, and perhaps they were shaped as rectangles. Whatever their original shape, the stones have weathered into asymmetrical, lean, dark, and skeletal forms that resemble the sculptures of Alberto Giacometti. These are natives whose character is the meeting of time, rock, wind, rain, and sun; the contours and surfaces and hubris wept away in undulating ripples until each stone is an unmistakable individual, dignified and acquainted with sorrow; there is a ghost, a fat one, an avuncular soul, a stooped figure bearing a baby on its back. Brodgar is the kind of place where one walks alone and silently, where there is nothing to say to another living person.

One mile east of the Stones of Stenness is the chambered tomb—or cairn, as they say here—called Maeshowe. From the slender road that connects Stromness and Kirkwall, the cairn appears as a great cone shaped mound of grass rising on the otherwise very flat plain. About twenty-four feet high and one hundred fourteen feet around, the mound is visible from everywhere on the plain, sited so as to suggest that it was the central focus of the region. On the opposite side of the road is Tormiston Mill, a handsome mill with a pair of white geese snoozing in the sun on the grassy slope of the millburn and a wooden shack where one buys tickets to the mound. The buying of tickets for places like Maeshowe and the Acropolis is at best a silly bureaucratic practice, at worst a demeaning, perhaps dangerous, insult to the powers and purposes of the places. It is of course absurd to imagine that by a cardboard ticket one gains entrance to what such places are. The walk towards the cairn is along a pasture filled with fat brown cows who push their noses through the wire fence to be stroked. When I pull my hand from a pocket to pat one warm, pungent head, the little ticket to the tomb comes out too, and spends a precarious moment fluttering on the cow's broad sculptured cheek.

It is a bright sunny day, windy, a bit chilly, in mid-August. Racing clouds are casting raggedy shadows on the pastures and on the benign, grassy mound in the distance. The entrance to the mound is guarded by an elderly gentleman with cigarette breath, who is dressed in a crisp grey uniform. We hand over the cardboard tickets and, midway in a line of some fifteen other visitors, enter a corridor that leads into the inner chamber. Immediately inside, the corridor is dark, dank, low, and cramped—an inverse of the fresh, wide outside world. We are poking, hunched over, down a narrow, mouldy passageway, thirty-six feet long and four feet six inches high. Fifteen feet down the corridor my mother makes her decision, declares the space unfit for breathing, and bucks the one-way tourist line back into the fresh air. Outside, the guard hopes to persuade my mother that once she is in the heart of the tomb she will be able to stand up straight and breathe: she smiles and will have none of it. When she has recovered, I enter the passageway again.

The corridor walls are massive flagstones: slabs about five feet wide and eighteen feet long form the roof, sides, and floor of the passageway. A pamphlet tells me to be impressed: the slabs are accurately plumbed and leveled, rabbeted to fit one another precisely and dressed by hammer stones; some joints are so fine as not to admit the blade of a knife; a slightly obtuse fracture angle has been used to make the lower courses of the oversailing smooth and not stepped. In prehistoric Britain, only Stonehenge compares to the technical achievement of Maeshowe; the cairn inspires archaeological praise for the "assured competence and mastery over building material." These feats notwithstanding, nearly blind in the dark, one feels along rough, pocked walls and over an uneven, rugged floor toward a chamber at the end. There, one enters a square, high ceilinged stone room that contains, on each of three walls, large burial cells, the surfaces covered with runic inscriptions. The guard reappears with a lamp and, standing before the middle cell, lights up a series of animals scratched in the stone. He holds the lamp under the faint drawings as a child holds a light under his face at Halloween. His voice chants rhythmically as he moves the lamp over the drawings. "The dragon"—pause, then a slow scrape of the lamp down the old stone block—"the walrus"—pause, then another slow downward scrape of the lamp—"the serpent." He lifts the lamp again to the underside of the dragon and repeats the illumination. "The dragon . . . the walrus . . . the serpent." He holds his lamp under the deeply cut runic markings on the tombs and translates them in a rough paraphrase. One inscription is a boast by a plundering Viking that his lady, Ingaborg, is the most desirable woman in all the land; another says that the inscribers have stolen a magnificent treasure from the tomb; a third message says that while an earl named Harald and some of his men were snowbound in the tomb two of the men lost their wits, which was deemed "a great hindrance to their journey." Another rune mentions "Jerusalemfarers"; that would be Crusaders leaving Orkney for the Holy Land in 1151. I'm confused about when the mound was made, by whom, and whose runes these are: Crusaders and Vikings are crashing into the prehistoric centuries, and the chamber seems to hold one time called the unknown. Maeshowe confused archaeologists, too. First, the Viking runes led them to think, for years after the excavation in 1861, that the tomb itself was Norse. In time, they came to the realization that the cairn has risen seamlessly from the plain since about 2700 B.C., that it was nearly four thousand years old when the Vikings came to steal one kind of treasure and leave another.[18]

After the guide leaves, I stand for a long while in the darkened interior, looking at the unreadable markings that wander in wavering lines like a maze of heron's footprints in mud—long pointed ends to the letters—a dense and pretty thicket of signs. It is dark and quiet, safe, earthy. Gradually one knows that this is not only a burial place, but a birth canal and womb, that the swelling on the landscape above is a green pregnancy. How artfully these people embodied in their works the intimacies and paradoxes of the wheel, planting death at the core of fertility. Summer is the wrong season to see the other sign of the idea embodied here. In late December the surrounding pastures will be covered in snow, the tomb a white lump on the landscape. The sun will be setting low and early on the horizon, and on the day of the winter solstice it will shine down the long passage, a bolt of light that creeps along the stones and turns them brilliant gold. As sunlight reaches the end of the passage, it will briefly illuminate the inner chamber. Tenderly, the Stone Age builders included their dead in the planting season, just stirring at the winter solstice when light returns to the fields that are the outer skin of the tumulus belly. Emerging is like coming out of a matinée movie: you rub your eyes in the too-bright light, and you try to adjust to a quotidian world of sidewalks and automobile horns, everything the same, but not, after the story in the dark room. In the bright light outside Maeshowe, brown cows are the only living thing in sight. The small group of visitors has dispersed, and the guard has gone, too, perhaps for lunch. As I start back to our car, from faraway a voice is calling my name; turning, I see a tall woman standing in the long grass atop the Maeshowe mound, waving at me to join her. She has the look of mountaineers atop summits and I walk up slowly, admiring her station. On top of the cairn, there is no hint of the dark interior. The wind is warm and steady, flattening the grasses, and we have to speak in voices just shy of shouts. Naturally, we can see very far.

The funerary architecture of Maeshowe is so much like the kinds built on the Iberian Peninsula and in the Mediterranean that almost everyone agrees that these are works by people who came from the south, a people intimately familiar with collective burial rites, and schooled in the techniques of tomb-building. And everyone seems to agree that although the skulls found in the tombs have a largish brain capacity of fifteen hundred cubic centimeters, they are *dolichocranial*. I am not surprised to learn that this word means long and narrow. Beyond these basics, the questions about the cairn and standing stone earthworks stretch away as far as the eye can see. What are they? Who made them? How? This is the stuff of lifelong learned debates, and because the evidence is scanty, the various proposals are portraits of epistemology, of the very idea of what knowledge is. In fitting tribute to their many-splendoured appeal to the imagination, the works are claimed by several camps. The same midwinter sun that enters the cairn bisects the circle of Brodgar, and some archaeologists propose that the standing stones are cunning computing devices to predict eclipses and perform other astronomical calculations. Others believe that they are ceremonial centers. Archaeo-mythologist Marija Gimbutas proposes that rituals of regeneration took place at Brodgar and Stenness through "energetic ring dances" of a matriarchal society. Euan MacKie thinks the rings and cairns were ceremonial complexes of a patriarchal theocracy headed by chiefs engaged in astronomical and magical work. Graham and Anna Ritchie agree that the works indicate social cohesion, mathematical skills, and a grasp of the principles of solar and lunar cycles, but wonder how a nonliterate society could make astronomical recordings. Some argue that the complexity and difficulty of the engineering indicate a stratified society; others counter that two or three farmer-hunters, in the seasons of leisure, could have easily quarried, transported, and installed the monoliths. Yet another recalls that in traditional societies neighbors come together to cooperate in large projects with ritual purposes (canoes in the Trobriands, the lodges of the Pacific Coast).[19] And, as ever, some scholars scrupulously say that we know nothing conclusive about the purpose of the stones and cairns, nothing of the nature of the late Neolithic beliefs, and probably never will.

These are delicate matters. In pondering them, how much can we credit the visceral reactions and thoughts that we have when surrounded by the stones, when we see them rise up dark and massive on the horizon, when we consider them accepting the millennia of rains, snows, and salt erosion? We do not have to decide between astronomy and ritual to know that the stones bring us intimately in touch with planet time. These beings, already old when the Neolithics plucked them from the Earth, vibrate with the slowest breath in nature. They call us to consider that time itself, born again each moment, is also tall and worn. We can know that for whatever reason the builders were a people who continually reminded themselves of time, which they figured as massive and circular. Moreover, because the stones are hewn, sited, and placed with human consciousness, they also vibrate with the newest breath in nature. The rings record an intersection of one of the most ancient and one of the most recent forms spun by the Earth. We can know by the way we feel in the presence of this intersection how fine it is when rocks and mind interact, when praise and discovery are known as a single endeavor.

I will venture, too, that we can know that the ring and the mound are variations on a theme. Both are round and made of massive stones, both are securely fixed in the Earth, and both elicit a dynamic interaction between Earth and sky. But the rings are flung-open public forms, filled with light, formed by staunchly individual, widely spaced markers. Pinioned in the Earth, these *éminences grises* emphasize verticality; they point toward the sky and might well plot its movements. Maeshowe also acknowledges the sky, indeed calculates its light and allows the sun into its chamber precisely once each year, but the cairn is otherwise dark and sealed, an interior curator of things round, horizontal, private, enfolded, and unified. Using the same materials and site, the stone-works are nearly symmetrical inverses of one another. Taken together, they form a yin/yang symbol of the bond between two realms.

In the late twentieth century we are the same species as the Neolithic builders, and we know that we are capable of Mardi

Gras, test tubes, Mount Palomar, wailing walls, and of growing reflective under the stars. (This last trait is especially reasonable: the latest tale is that exploding supernovas wash out over the galaxies, like the Nile flooding the Egyptian deltas, saturating space with the material that has become—among other things—us.) Knowing ourselves, surely we know that there were processions, dancers, rattles, newborns held up to the moon, men with antlers tied to their heads, smart women who remembered cycles and dates. We can also know that it stopped, and that for some three thousand years no tribe has come to do whatever they did in the stone circles and sheltered cairns. We can know that for all the quiet years, the intersection of rock and mind has stood as a relatively fixed point in the round of gales, stalks, and snow, yielding but slowly as seasons have cracked and splintered off small pieces for travelers to tuck in leather satchels, and have toppled megaliths into stumps on which the melancholy crofter might ponder things.

Skara Brae   A possible clue about the builders of these cunning and moving stoneworks lies midway up the western coast of Mainland on the small Bay of Skaill, a backwards C cut into the coastline. Here in 1850 a great storm blew the sand dunes away and uncovered ten skillfully constructed, interconnected huts made of thin slabs of unmortared flagstone. This settlement of chambered dwellings, so close to the sea, unsheltered from the winds and waves, turns out to be the oldest prehistoric site in Europe. It is an affecting cluster of little round homes that was the domestic place of a small kinship group for some six hundred and fifty years, from about 3100 B.C. to 2450 B.C. These dates are in the late Neolithic era, a transitional time whose artifacts always as-tonish by being at once so primitive and so familiar.

Since the big storm, a brilliant, lush green seaside grass has overgrown the tops of the excavated mounds so they now resemble cross-sectioned yurts. From the closeby sea comes the steady, howl-ing wind. A ring of visitors in bright nylon anoraks, Wellingtons, and good walking shoes huddles around the rim of one hut, looking down into the old room. In the center of the room is a stone slab that was the hearth. There are short cubicles of stone on either side which are bedchambers. Along the perimeter there are small stone recesses that served as cupboards, sideboards, and closets. On one side of the room stands a small watertight tank where, it is surmised, the tribe kept fresh shellfish, much like seafood restaurants keep tanks of live lobsters. There are small pits in the sand that are the drainage and plumbing conduits that carried wastes into the prehistoric sea.

There are no remaining roofs over the huts; because the bones of red deer, wild boar, sheep, and cattle are found in abundance in the excavation, it seems likely the tribe's roofs, like their boats, were made of skin. Whale bones are also found, presumably used for building material and kitchen utensils. By the time these pastoralists, farmers, hunters, and fishers "houked Skara Brae from the sand," the balmy Boreal climate had given way to the Atlantic Phase, a slightly more erratic but still warm, calm period. Their island yet held a hinterland of birch, hazel, rowan, and elder, red deer and wild boar. Calm fjords full of fish indented the coastline. The people already grew the primitive form of barley; they had a tiny sort of cattle, and sheep that must have been the unique seaweed-eating kind that continue to live on North Ronaldsay, the northernmost island of Orkney. In a tiny site museum is hung an artist's rendering of life inside the round huts of Skara Brae. The mural is all sepia tones; wearing skins and with long shining hair, the people are intently cooking, sleeping, scraping bones. The children are naked, warm, one believes, around the big central fire. The bedchambers are nicely fitted with corner posts and swagging curtains. "An intelligent people," concludes the National Trust guide, a burly, dapper man happy to be charmed by my mother into a private chat about the early ones. As my mother and the guide wander through the excavated rooms in deep conversation, I am once again confused about how to link peoples to works. It turns out that everyone is. Maeshowe is carbon-dated to 2700 B.C., Stenness to about 2356 B.C. The people of Skara Brae (3100 B.C. to 2450 B.C.) are contemporaries of the cairn-tomb builders, but apparently not definitively the builders themselves. Pottery shards, etc.—inconclusive.

Part of the mystery may lie in that fact that the Skara Brae people lived at a turbulent time that coincides with the very end of the Old European goddess culture, evidence of which, some scholars now propose, dates as far back as 80,000 B.C.[20] In this interpretation, prehistoric Europe had been inhabited for at least forty thousand years by peoples with an apparently peaceful way of life that predates the invasions of warlike Indo-European tribes from the southern steppes during the fourth millennium B.C. The culture originated in the Mediterranean, and its rituals centered around a female divinity who embodied the cycles of earthly realities and appeared in many forms, among them bird, boar, and deer—in the north, especially deer. The northernmost tribes were luckier than their contemporaries in other parts of Europe. They arrived on Orkney about 4000 B.C., just about the time that other parts of Europe were starting to be overrun by the Indo-Europeans with their domesticated horses, daggers, bows and arrows, their bigger, stronger bodies, and their sky god. In the face of the Indo-European invasions, the Old European culture essentially collapsed. Save for piecemeal pockets, it survived intact only on the fringes of the continent and only for a few thousand years. in Minoan Crete until about 1500 B.C., and perhaps in Orkney until the arrival of the Picts and Celts. The stoneworks may have been made by tribes with slightly more sophisticated building skills than those at Skara Brae, peoples who shared the same worldview, driven by invaders from the mainland. It is commonly said that nothing else of the culture that made these dwellings, rings, and mounds remains. This is, of course, nonsense.

My home
it is in
Suleskerry
Some days later we pay a visit to a nineteenth-century farmstead in Kirbuster in Birsay Parish. The structure is a typical longhouse of a subsistence life which, precisely like that of the Skara Brae peoples', combined farming, fishing, and hunting. A massive whale bone forms the overhead lintel of the garden gate. The longhouse is, naturally, a long and narrow series of rooms: the ben, but, byre, and stable, all filled with the sweet acrid smell and blueish smoke of burning peat. The rooms are low-ceilinged, made of stone. In the big room, the but, there is a central stone hearth and fire-back with a smoke-hole chimney located in the ceiling slightly off center from the hearth so rain will not put out the fire. There are short beds in recesses in the walls, cupboards and sideboards of stone. There is a small stone recess near the floor where geese nest,

and a place for calves to huddle just beyond the hearth. In the animals' byre there is a series of drainage holes. Hanging on a nail on the wall in the one bedroom is a pale, yellowed sampler stitched with an exacting promissory note: "He will fulfill the desires of them that fear Him." The divinity has undergone a change, but as of the nineteenth century the late-Neolithic subsistence life of Skara Brae and even the basic appointment of dwellings had endured five thousand years.

Moreover, the worldview of the Old European goddess culture has survived, if tenuously, in spite of the efforts to destroy the *pagani* that went on in Orkney, as throughout Europe, during the sixteenth and seventeenth centuries. In Sir Walter Scott's novel *The Pirate*, the sibyl Norna is based on an old pagan woman whose "principal subsistence," Scott says, "was by a trade in favorable winds, which she sold to mariners at Stromness." This woman made protective charms for whalers and was thought able to cause the sea to swallow thieves.[21] Her protective powers must have been very strong, for Orkney court records show that women who practiced the pagan religion were routinely extirpated. Although one Bessie Skebister could inform fishermen and their wives when boats were in danger, and was so reliable as to inspire an old island proverb—"Giff Bessie say it is weill it is weill"—she was strangled and burned for "riding on the back of a certain James Sandieson, and flying with him through the air to Zetland with a brindle in his mouth." For flying, for herbal healings, for the unusual behaviours of birds, cats, worms, and cows, for refusing a neighbor corn, for a cow that sickened, as punishment for men drowned at sea while an old woman was at home spinning, a typical sentence was the following, meted out to Marable Couper in 1624: "The Judge acceptis the determinatioun of the Assyse, and ordainis the pannell to be tane be the lockman, hir hands bund, and be caried to the head of the Lon, the place of exectuion, and thair to be knet to ane staik, wiried to the death, and brunt in asses."[22]

The proceedings in St. Magnus Cathedral each Sunday morning are testimony to the ongoing prevalence and virtues of the sky god culture. Still, a powerful idea is often as yielding as water, and it is hardly surprising that a worldview of one hundred thousand years' duration should continue to inform early modern and modern Western society. Most obviously, the life-giving aspect of the Old European goddess remains in Christianity as Mary, and in Scotland and Ireland as Brigit, the patron saint of childbirth, celebrated by offerings of milk and dandelions, by special cakes and holy wells, and corn-sheaf dolls that invite her to visit the hearth.[23] Beyond such official absorptions, images and rituals of the old culture occur in ordinary daily life in unassuming ways. Into the nineteenth century, the custom in Orkney was to become engaged at the rings of Stenness and Brodgar, which the peasantry commonly called the Temple of the Moon and the Temple of the Sun. Young lovers stole away from a dance at the kirk of Stenness and went first to the small ring, the Temple of the Moon, where the woman fell down on her knees and prayed to pagan divinities, asking that they help her to keep her promise. The couple then went up the hill to the Temple of the Sun, where the man prayed in like manner. Then the lovers walked to the Stone of Odin, a solitary standing stone that once stood near the Stenness circle. Standing on opposite sides of the stone, they solemnly took hold of each other's right hands through a hole worn in the stone, and swore to be faithful. The ceremony was so sacred that anyone who broke an engagement made in this way was ostracized from society.[24] When the consecrated Odin stone was destroyed in 1814 by a Ferry-Louper (a stranger from the south) who used the broken stones in building his cowhouse, the islanders attempted to burn the man's house with him in it. Supposedly the custom of trysting and becoming engaged within the stone circles has died out, but one need only glance at them to know that the rings are an ideal place to declare love and plight a troth. The ages of the Earth are your witnesses, and it is certainly worth traveling to Orkney to become engaged in the presence of these stones.

The old culture also survives in modern Orkney in households where weddings are set for days when the moon is waxing and the tides flowing. The pagan world is radiant in the farm and agricultural shows of August. Goddess emblems are found on the handsome cast-iron house signs with deer, trees, snakes, and pigs hovering over the numerals. And the pagan worldview of a holy compact between humans and the rest of nature survives in folkstories: in the stories of larger-than-life Scottish women who change themselves into deer, and deer who change into women, and in an old story particular to Orkney, the tale of the selkie-folk. Seals in this part of the world come in two categories: the common seal, which Orcadians call the tang fish, and the selkie-folk, the large seals who have the power to assume human form, among them the great, rough, Greenland, crested, and grey seals. Stories of selkie-folk survive in children's books, in sea-songs, and in the literature of modern masters; in all forms, the stories keep the idea that humans are intimately linked with animals, and they issue from the time when, as the Netsilik Eskimo poet Nalungiaq has it, "a person could become an animal, and an animal could become a person if she wanted to."[25]

This intimacy is expressed in stories as a metamorphosis that allows an erotic union between human and animal beings. Both male and female selkies can come to land as humans: the male selkies come willingly to secretly tryst with women whose husbands are straying, or disappointing, lovers; the female selkies are unwilling partners of human males. George Mackay Brown's contemporary version of the selkie-girl tale begins: "A sealskin lying on the rocks—well, he could make use of that all right. Somebody must have dropped it. . . . In the late afternoon Simon went down to the rocks for limpet bait. . . . The bucket was half full when he heard the first delicate mournful cry, a weeping from the waters. He looked across the bay. A girl was kneeling among the waves. She was naked."[26]

Those are always the basic ingredients: an unmarried farmer, a sealskin, a naked woman in the waves. In an older version of the tale,[27] an island crofter, off gathering limpets and whelks in an ebb, sees a trio of maidens sunning and singing on a skerry. Alarmed by the man, the damsels quickly scoop up three grey bundles on the rock and dive into the sea, but not before the farmer has fallen in love with one of them. For months, he pines for her at the ebb, finally despairing of her return. When he shares his woe with an old man of the village, the old man tells him a great secret. One day the following summer, the girl and her companions are back, basking on a rock at the edge of a shallow pool. Unseen, the crofter creeps up and quick as a wink steals her grey bundle. The maidens all slip back into the sea, but the crofter sees that one of them has not changed back into a seal. Grey skin under his arm, the crofter makes for his farm but is stopped by doleful weeping and lamentation. Turning, he sees the beautiful young woman following him, her hands held out in supplication as tears flow down her face. "O bonnie man! if there's onie mercy i' thee human breast, gae back me skin! I cinno', cinno', cinno' live i' the sea without it. I cinno', cinno', cinnno' bide among me ain folk without my ain seal skin. Oh, pity a peur distressed, forlorn lass, gin doo wad ever hope for mercy theesel!" The pity the crofter feels only increases the passion of love, and with much higgling he persuades the sea-lass to live with him as his wife. For good measure, he hides her sealskin.

The selkie bears five bairns, but never ceases to walk the shore looking for her skin, nor to sing along the sand calling to her ocean kin. One day when her husband and all the children but the youngest are fishing, she determines to find her long-lost skin. As she searches, her young lass asks, "Mam, what are doo leukan for?" "O bairn, deu no tell, " replies the selkie-mother, "but I'm leukan for a bonnie skin, tae mak a rivlin that wad ceur thee sare fit." The lass says, "May be I ken whar hid is. Ae day, whin ye war a' ott, an' ded tought I was sleepan i' the bed, he teuk a bonnie skin doon; he oiled it and gloured at it a peerie minute more, dan folded hid and led hid up under dae aisins abeun dae bed." Overjoyed, the mother rushes to the aisin space, calls out, "Fareweel, peerie buddo!" to her child, flings on her well-tended skin, and plunges into the sea with wild cries of joy. Rowing home, her husband passes by as the selkie's sea-lover greets her with every token of delight. The selkie looks up and cries to the crofter, "Goodman o' Orphir, farewek tae thee! I liked dee weel, doo war geud tae me; bit I lo'e better me man o' the sea!" In versions of the story written for children, the selkie returns once a year at the same time and visits her human family, but in other accounts the bonnie selkie-woman simply disappears forever, as mysteriously and silently as she came.

> I am a woman on the land
> I am a selkie in the sea,
> And when I'm far from any strand
> My home it is in Suleskerry.

Originally, the story expresses a strong, complex bond between humans and other species; reinterpreted in light of a dualistic theology, selkie-folk begin to be considered as fallen angels whose wickedness is not quite bad enough to condemn them to hell, only to animal life. The shift in the original story reflects the change from the old imaginative bond with the Earth to the belief that the natural world is "fallen," and that animals are lesser beings than humans. George Mackay Brown not only holds to the old imaginative view, he takes the usual story one step further and makes it an allegory for the artist; in his story, the child of Simon and the selkie grows up to be a musician, a shy, oddly cold man who can make the sea sound in his music.

B y rights, tea would have been the first and frequent subject of these pages, for it is the steady companion of the Scottish day, and each hotel, no matter how humble, stocks its rooms with supplies for brew-ups: electric pot for boiling water, ceramic pot for brewing, china cups and small tea-creamers, a raft of teas, honey, fresh milk, and lemons. This is a delight and an astonishment, for not only is there no such thing in American hotels, but room service even in respectable ones, when asked for tea with milk, can deliver a plastic jug of tepid water, this covered by a square of Saran Wrap, and a drinking glass of milk. To request tea in an American office is often to throw the receptionist into a swivet: he or she believes that there is tea somewhere in the corporate pantry, but where? One prefers not to ask rather than to send this person on a scavenger mission, especially because the tea, if found, is a grim bag-tea like Red Rose. Naturally, one might as well ask for a trip to Bombay as to ask for looseleaf Earl Grey, or first-flush Darjeeling, or Assam tips. Home is a fluid place: each day at four o'clock, I could easily be an expatriate. *Afternoon tea*

One afternoon we are poking up the rocky coastline from Black Craig near Stromness north past Skara Brae to Brough Head; this western end of the island is folded and fissured in a steady cascade of bays, headlands, gloups, caves, and the handsome invasions of ocean into the land that are called geos. These places are named Lyre, Nebo, Axna, Saed, Sand, and Skipi, in a succession of sounds as quirky and original as the land. We wind slowly north toward Skipi Geo just around the Brough of Birsay, stopping to walk Marwick Head. The wide plateau at the summit of the cliff tilts at a precipitous angle toward the sea, covered with great, loose, cracked plates of flagstone in thin layers: orange, grey, ochraceous rocks that will weather into fertile soil or be pried up for roofing flags if they do not first slide into the sea. The bluff is perpetually wet and glistening, and cold water pools dot the depressions and rectangular fissures in the rock. Over the exposed plateau, wind blows in steadily and coldly from the sea. This is the home of the largest and most spectacular seabird colony on Mainland; some thirty-five thousand guillemots, ten thousand kittiwakes, as well as fulmars and razorbills, who favor the eroded flagstone ledges for nesting and the abundance of shoaling fish for eating. But in this stormy weather, only a few guillemots—auks, and clumsy on land—bumble along the slabs of pitted rock cliff. For miles to the west, there is flat, grey, choppy ocean; for miles to the east, a grey, clouded sky under which low, treeless fields roll smoothly into the moors.

It is nearing four o'clock in the afternoon, and sure enough, parked just off the road, overlooking the pungent tidal flats, we come upon a small caravan camper with its aluminum door open to a late-middle-aged Scottish couple, sitting at a folding table, taking tea and biscuits. Passing by, one only has a glimpse: his thick, white socks and heavy black shoes; her plump pear form and print dress; the electric kettle on the table. The archaeologists are puzzled as to why the people of Skara Brae would locate their huts so close to the sea, and have surmised that in fact the settlement was originally located in a protected hollow, that time has eroded the shoreline inland toward the huts. That would make sense. Indeed, when presented at Skara Brae with the lure of a sparkling sea and the howling wind, we ourselves tucked into the hollow of a dune for lunch, eating cheese and apples in the sun with wind skimming our heads, blowing the sand into rippling ridges, flattening the beach grasses. Probably the archaeologists are right, but this utterly typical scene of Scottish domesticity blithely planted at the edge of harsh cliffs, afternoon tea conducted in the wind and cold, suggests another possibility.

Among the oldest artifacts of Orkney are pots that bear impressions of a primitive four-rowed form of *bere,* a variety of barley transformed as desired into meal and malt. Ever since the first Neolithic farmers sowed their treasured grain some five thousand years ago, Orkney has been farmed, and only recently have barley fields changed over to clover and grass. Now, international shipping makes it lucrative for farmers to fatten cattle for urban markets, and the new secret of Orkney agriculture is using grass exquisitely well, with the kind of efficiency directed toward water in Israel. In summer the grass is grazing food; surplus is carefully stored as silage which will be used to feed animals through the winter. Everywhere on the island, domes rise along edges of pastures; these are mounded heaps of grass, compressed under tightly drawn sheets of plastic to keep the piles inert. Smaller, more numerous, and more ephemeral than the burial cairns, these mounds are a new kind of ritual rising on the landscape. Again, rocks are the underlying story. When first formed, the landmass of Orkney was bare granite peaks, but seventy-five million years of rain, wind, cold, heat, and the steady seduction of gravity eroded the peaks in sediments washing down into plains. The sandstones not only turn into houses of worship, they crumble into a very rich, acidic soil that once supported rustling bere fields, and now, the pasturelands.

Something new from something old

Some bere is still grown and marketed. After days of strong tea, heart-stopping sweets called cluttie dumplings, and chips served indiscriminately with everything, we are eager for an herbal brew and a green salad. Many wrong turns down rabbit warrens of streets brings us to the one organic market in Kirkwall town. Here we do find ginger and orange teas, rose-scented soaps, and, if not salads, a lunch of grains. And my mother discovers a flour made from bere: "beremeal" it is called. A sack of beremeal strikes her as the perfect gift for many friends at home. As all agricultural produce must be declared at U.S. Customs, her inventory will provide drama during reentry.

By good fortune we are in Orkney during the Orkney Agricultural Society's 105th Annual Show. The smaller shows at Sanday and Shapinsay have already been held, and in the papers we read the headline news: earlier this month, the Supreme Beef-Cattle Championship changed hands at the East Mainland show, Jim Baillie's steer bowing to the animal raised by J. M. Lennie of Tankerness. One afternoon, after spending the morning at a bright blue bay watching seals swim and prepare for their pups to be born, we drive to Bignold Park outside Kirkwall, where the Mainland show is just commencing. As the poster promises, Tony the Kellogg's Tiger is there on Ronnie Marwick's model-T Ford, signing autographs and giving away badges. There is also a simulator said to capture the thrills of skiing. There is a carriage-driving competition, a musical dressage, and a turnout of vintage vehicles. There is a tug-of-war featuring four male and two female squads, and there is a 1914 gas engine. But these novelties are all fluff. Animals, plants and an incredible number of things baked and sewn by women are the raison d'être for the show. This is the world of tall gold trophies for (to name only the tiniest tip of the iceberg): Best AA Bull; Best Black Polled Cow (in milk or in calf); Best One-Year-Old Horned or Coloured Heifer, Steer Calf (calved after 31st January), and Best Yearling; Best Suffolk Ram, Gimmer, Ewe; Best Leicester Ram, Gimmer, Ewe; Best Cheviot Ram, Gimmer, and Ewe; Best Female Goat in Milk; Best Goatling (not having borne a kid); Best Light-Legged and Heavy-Legged Horses. These last are Clydesdales and Shires whose sturdy legs end in pyramidal cones of thick pristine-white fetlocks. The award for the best award must go to the Special Prize for the Best Pen of Three Fat Lambs, surely to be given out by Mother Goose herself.

Inside the fairground stalls are groaning tables of flowers, vegetables, things preserved in jars, things baked and knit. Among the things that prizes are given for are Pot Plants (this means African marigolds and busy-Lizzies, not something else) and Cut Flowers. In the latter category you will find Vase of Candytuft, which this year was won at the East Mainland show by Mrs. J. Pirie of Comely Toab, followed by Miss Mabel Eunson (who also garnered Most Points in Marigolds). There are prizewinning Beetroots, Broad Beans, Golden Garden Turnips, Six-Pod Peas, and Shallots. There is the massive Fruit category, in which Miss Mabel Eunson received Most Points, winning in Gooseberries, Black and Red Currants. As the names of entries and awards pile on they are a hymn to plenty, and the cornucopia is best simply listed, leaving it to each imagination to supply colors, clear glass jars, and plump round forms inside: Plum Jam, Rhubarb Jam, Apricot Jam, Apple Jelly, Uncooked Chutney, Lemon Curd. On the Baking Table, there are plates of Oatcakes (thick and thin), Bere Bannocks, Drop Scones, Treacle Scones, Iced Buns, Rock Cakes, Sausage Rolls, Short-bread, Egg Sponge Sandwich (no filling), Victoria Sandwich (top decorated), Currant Buns and Associated Uncooked Fancies. On other tables, awards have been given for Something New from Something Old, for Night Attire, Crochet Cushion, White Hens Eggs, Meat Rolls and Bed Socks, Jumper with a Fair Isle Yoke, Dressed Doll, and Lampshade. Tea Cosy was won by Miss Elsa Work, ditto Mittens, Lace Scarf, and Matinée Coat. Best Use of 100g of Yarn was garnered by Mrs. Alison Aitken. In a nearby wing, children have entered in these areas: Wild Flowers (pressed, named and mounted), Local Shells, Scrapbooks, and Writing (en-velope addressed to the show secretary), Nature Diary (kept for one month), Drop Scones, and Buttonhole.

For the next six weeks, on one island after another, Orcadians will be plunged into their annual round of harvest rituals: fairs and shows that praise gimmers and calves, and the skills of men and women who make things gleam in jars. After the work is done, these people can think of no finer holiday than getting together to compare and admire the fruits of their labor. It takes your breath away; it would be as though accountants held an annual festival at which they laid out their green ledger books (now spreadsheets and computers) and walked around them humming, cavorting, eating cluttie dumplings, feeling that all is momentarily right with the world.

D ays and nights are often so wet that we are driven indoors, *A chain of* physically and imaginatively, and after all this journey is *mountains* not only to islands but into the territory that mothers and daughters inhabit. One sodden afternoon my mother and I find ourselves sitting in the small hotel library in front of a peat fire. We speak of how the bright fiddle music of the islands, the songs of the "Beeswing Hornpipe," "Muddy Roads," and "Big Sandy River" remind us of Tennessee bluegrass and our mountain years; with selkies in mind, we consider the sealskin that my mother has kept in an attic trunk for forty-six years, wrapped in a protective, beautiful paper. Above all, we tell tales of Callahans, Tarwaters, Speeds, and Watkinses who make up my mother's family in Tuscaloosa, Alabama. Led by the climate, we find ourselves doing what people in Scotland have been doing for thousands of years: sitting indoors around peat fires retelling and refining family sagas. Just before our trip, a classics scholar (a good one, but not, after all, a geographer) told me that the Appalachians and the Highlands are really one mountain chain connected under the Atlantic Ocean. Considering the path of the Scots-Irish immigration, it would be remarkable if it were true, and my mother I are engaged by the thought. It can be no coincidence that we wonder about the underwater chain of mountain ranges, about whether the geography of our earlier lives together and the territory in which we are presently traveling are linked. It is well into our trip; we are traveling now between prized bonds and prized differences, feeling our way into a future where meat still loves salt.

Bog-
trotting
Years ago, I saw in the newspaper the photograph of an Iron Age man dug up from a peat bog in Denmark—flesh and hair and features perfectly intact, a little leather cap on his head perfectly preserved, even the twined rope around his neck intact. Each March, rows of bowed green heads rise up in our porch greenhouse from peat pots. Here on Mainland, I've several times seen someone pick up a small, hard, fibrous cake and toss it on a fire in the lobby of an inn or a bank. Nineteenth-century photographs on postcards in Kirkwall shops show women struggling home with great straw baskets laden with peat bricks strapped onto their backs. Everywhere, in the town streets and through the countryside, twines the sweet, distinctive smell of burning peat. Wrapped daily in its smoke and smell I realize that, as with many things one uses fairly regularly, I am not sure exactly what peat *is*.

One day we take a walk with Michael Hartley out to his peat fields in Evie, on the northwest side of Mainland Island, passing on the way a pond awash in a family of mute swans, the cygnets old enough to be white and sleek like their faery-tale parents. Michael's peat field came as part of the bargain when he and his wife Jenny bought a small farm called Inner Urrigar. Their farmhouse faces the sea and looks out toward the tiny isle of Eynhallow. It has electric baseboards, but the Hartleys' peat stove is stoked throughout the year to keep down the heating bill. The mixture of old and new fuels is a commonplace, most dramatically pictured on the island of Flotta, where peat fields are cheek-by-jowl with the terminal that handles oil from the North Sea beds. By this time in late summer, all but the very preoccupied or lazy have harvested their supply of winter peat, dried the bricks, driven them home, and stacked them up high alongside crofthouses exactly like cords of wood are piled up neatly in New England. Here the work ethic proposed to children in the tale of the Grasshopper and the Ant would find little resistance, and there are few surviving grasshopper-souls. Michael and Jenny brought their dried peats home three weeks ago.

Michael's peat field, like all the other peat fields in Orkney, looks like no other landscape on Earth: these are vast black mires, lonely uninflected swards scruffily skim-coated with tussocks of heathers, grasses, and a creeping film of liverworts, the continuous surface interrupted at intervals by long trenches from which peats have been harvested. This is blanket mire, a much drier kind of peat than the bog peat common to Ireland. Even so, the hard, crusty surface of mantle is springy and porous, and in places gives way to squelchy, saturated veins. Walking through the field, one can suddenly step in a watery puddle; here and there, little streams seep from the mire in brown-stained rivulets. Of his lifelong bog inquiry, Sir Harry Godwin, an emeritus professor of botany at Cambridge, once commented that it was "a delightful involvement with what might be called bog-trotting, although heaven knows, there can be few natural communities less adapted to sustain trotting than those of the squelchy rain-fed mires."[28] As dryly as possible, Sir Harry also recalls how as a young man just beginning his studies he was present when two great peat bog authorities, Knud Jessen and Hugo Osvald, stood in the rain while debating a bog classification point (soligenous vs. topogenous) *in situ* and slowly sank up to their knees in the soft bogland.

With a friend, Michael harvests a year's worth of peat at a time, working in early to midsummer during a run of warm and sunny days. He likes the work, cutting into the earth until it is too wet to cut, no sounds save the wind, the tools, and spare work talk. Using a tusker, the men cut off the top layer of dwarf shrubs, grasses, and lichens in long strips like sod, and set it aside. Later, when the peat has been removed, they will carefully replace this top layer of vegetation over the harvested base some ten feet below the old surface level. This practice spares the landscape from bearing such gashes as mar West Virginia and Ohio strip-mined hillsides, and as the lower level widens with the years, the strips of vegetation meld together until their borders disappear. The result is that the carpet of plants is continuous, although it undergoes startling drops in altitude here and there. Most common in the surface tapestry are dwarf shrubs of heather, then cross-leaved heath (lover of ocean air), lichens, crowberry, and tussocks of purple moor grass, adder's tongues, bell-heathers, bogbeans, cow parsleys and little sundews. Here and there on the black hill stands a bee-buzzing colony of yellow bog-asphodel, star-shaped, scented flowers with bright red stamens. In the wettest peat hummocks grow many species of sphagnum mosses, among them *magellanicum*, the source of the purple-reddish metallic luster that occasionally flashes over the dark blanket.

The plant tapestry saved, Michael and his friend slice into the peat, making a strip about twelve inches wide. They continue down the trench, essentially taking a long slice off the exposed edge, cutting down about ten to fifteen feet, and carving large brick-shaped pieces of peat off the strip. The deeper they cut, the wetter the earth becomes, and at some depth the peat becomes a slurry. Even for someone laying eyes on this operation for the first time, it is clear that digging up peatmire is elemental. As Seamus Heaney has it: "Every layer they strip / Seems camped on before. / The bogholes might be Atlantic seepage. / The wet centre is bottomless."[29] Even the topmost layer of blanket peat is somewhat wet, and all the fresh-cut bricks must be set out evenly, neatly, to dry for several weeks—first on the ground alongside the trench, then in tall beehive-shaped stacks called ruckles. As they dry, the peats harden and lighten, and in a few weeks' time they can be loaded up in a truck and driven home. Nearby are scattered remnants of some drying peats that another harvester has left by his trench. Michael snorts at the sloppiness: not only were the peats laid out to dry in random disarray rather than in a proper fashion, by now they have hardened into unusable sizes and shapes. The neighbor is not a grasshopper, but surely a marginal ant.

However alarming to live, sinking humans, the ability of peat slowly to enfold materials into itself is precisely what makes this substance occur. When conditions are right—a poorly drained soil and a wet, cold climate—vegetation becomes waterlogged and sinks to the bottom of pools or decays on the surface of rain-fed mires. With a wet climate and a mean annual temperature of about forty-five degrees, Orkney is now an ideal niche for rain-fed blanket peat. Over millennia, the decaying plants have accumulated into thick deposits, the bottom layers growing ever more greatly compressed, and finally carbonized—a process of time and pressure similar to the one that yields diamonds. Michael's peat field has been forming for three thousand five hundred years, since about 1500 B.C. That was well after the first human colonists arrived, and it was during the onset of the new colder, wetter climate. We can know these things because peat is an acidic archive. Bone is quickly dissolved, but flesh, leather, wood, and wool—all proteins—are preserved, and vegetable material can be analyzed and pollen-dated. Properly read, the peat calendar tells the story of when these islands were forested, when the glaciers melted, when the seas rose.

As we walk across the odd, ascetic moors back to Michael's Land Rover, the only sound other than our voices is a curlew down the wind. Like oil, peat requires vast tracts of formation time, but unlike oil it is at least a quasi-renewable fuel. I have heard that peat-burning pollutes the air, and ask Michael what he thinks. "People have done this for centuries," he says, "and in a way in which the countryside and its wildlife have not suffered. I would, in my opinion, be inclined to say that the burning of peat presents little threat to the environment, when compared to coal and oils. And the only threat to the peatlands is the commercial firms using machinery which claws out the heart of the hillsides leaving an ugly scar, and of course there is the question of the use of peat for horticultural purposes. This also is a threat, but ordinary cutting by hand certainly does not pose any problems."

All the while that our boots squish along the crusty surface, a wind blows steadily and a Poseidon force crashes against the sea-cliffs: two of the most stunning, reliable energies in nature are constantly hurling themselves at the island. Where are the windmills and tidal energy stations? When I ask, Michael leads me to see three huge windmills located one hundred and ninety-seven feet above sea level atop Burghar Hill. Here we are standing on one of the windiest spots in Britain. These windmills, which have the sleek, rounded look of Art Deco, are an experiment by the Wind Energy Group Consortium and the Department of Energy. Although some islanders fret about a future in which their bare landscape sprouts a forest of windmills, the experiment seems to be working: the largest of these structures, built in 1985, supplies one thousand homes, producing three megawatts of electricity. Meanwhile just north of Orkney, the sea is being drilled for oil, with fouling of these bays sure to happen. *The Orcadian* of August 9 reports that a new oil field has been found (to the west of the Scapa field which supplies Orkney's Flotta terminal) and drilled by the semi-submersible rig *Treasure Searcher*. Another newspaper article reports that Orcadians have grown uneasy about the transporting of nuclear materials through their waters, no longer believing assurances from the shipping companies. Here on a tiny North Sea island are most elements of the energy predicament of the human world at large: a plausible, but minute, energy source that was sufficient only for a smaller population with more modest energy demands; experimental works that provoke skepticism; toxic, non-renewable fuels that bring profit to a few and disaster to all; almost entirely overlooked energies of the sun and tides.

A great experiment

Like much of the world, I am thinking about energy more than usual this summer and fall because of the Persian Gulf conflict, which has continued throughout our travels in Scotland. It is a most apt time to be in the proverbial land of thrift and near the North Sea oil-drilling stations. Many nights we find a television and watch a Scottish news station, often in a hotel lounge or pub. Troop deployments are shown, pictures of British warships and American destroyers and airborne divisions setting off into the Gulf. Scottish reporters interview the young from both countries going off to war. Scottish soldiers are reflective, and not ashamed to have tears in their eyes. Their faces and voices carry an overwhelming sense of their mortality, resignation to an unpleasant duty, and a longing to return home soon. American pilots, leaning against their fighters, say, "We'll bomb the hell out of Baghdad," and (this hopefully), "The president wouldn't send us to Eye-rak and not let us pull the trigger," and, "Yeah, sure I'm excited. Nothing more exciting than the fear of combat. An exciting fear." When footage of the combat-eager American soldiers appears, or the president flickers across Scottish television on his golf cart or guzzles through Kennebunkport Bay in his cigarette boat, I want to be a citizen of, not some other country, but some other America—some other possible America whose citizens recognize that the way of life said by their president to be threatened by the invasion of Kuwait is an unctuous version of the dream.

On elemental Orkney, it is especially clear that other than devastating the planet, the only problem with the fruits of the unctuous way—jet skis, toaster ovens, *et alii*—is that none of these things comes in handy, and it is unwise to press them into service, if any of what used to be called the big questions should occur to you in the night. Great numbers of people have been misled into imagining that having things, rather than wrestling with chaos, comprises the main event of life, and by now the sheer weight of material goods suffocates the light wealths: conversation, clouds, sun on a rail, thinking on the word *scintilla*, the cool, sour smell of tomato plants. And yet. It is also fitting to be in Scotland while the latest American misadventure to maintain its profligacy unfolds, because the spare dourness of the society makes one want irrationally to cast aside restraint, to be flamboyant and careless. Being in this good, grey, courteous, workable, conserving country is at once to lament the miasmic crudity that America has become and to sympathize all the more with why America was dreamed—not the least by peoples like these northern Europeans who helped populate and fuel its radical trajectory. Between the narrow way of Scotland and the profligacy of America fluctuates not only the question about humans in nature, but about nature itself. Where else, if not from nature, do these principles, these two possibilities for habitation, arise? It seems that genuine freedom, by a law of nature, must share the world with mere license. By this pairing, you might say that nature, great experimenter, has posed—most keenly in our species—a beauty of a question.

Camera obscura

When at last we leave Orkney and head toward Edinburgh, we are keen for the pleasures of a city, and we receive an auspicious escort into the city when a young motorcycle courier, instead of merely providing directions, offers to be our guide. But something has happened to us. Within hours both of us, who live in standardly polluted American cities, have splitting headaches, burning eyes, and raspy throats. The weeks on Orkney have cleared our lungs and airways and minds: we have become used to the fresh, good air from the Atlantic and to the open stretches of land and time. Entering Edinburgh, we might as well be diving into toxic waste. Even the antics of the famous festival performers are soured by the blare of traffic and the black film that covers buildings, streets, and sills of rooms. Orkney has remained pristine through remoteness and the conserving habits of an agricultural people with lingering pagan values, the Highlands through a brutal history. But the Scots have done no better with their cities than other industrial countries. We struggle uphill, past buses spewing blue-grey exhausts, to the camera obscura lodged in the Outlook Tower.

The camera obscura is operated from within its dark room by a guide holding a long black rod. When she opens the shutter, a 360-degree picture of the outside world is cast on a big, white, concave, circular pan. We stand around the big dish alongside an extended family of elegant Italian travelers, the men and women in dark, formal clothes, their children in lacy dresses, black patent-leather shoes, and tiny tailored suits. The image projected by the camera obscura shows the city round and floating in the dark room like a planet, soundless and somewhat pale, like a dream of itself. With her long rod, the guide points out the Water of Leith river, John Knox's house, the King's Stables, and the Queen Street Gardens. And then she shows us a trick. She places a piece of plain white paper over the great image of the city: when she lifts the paper, the man walking in that part of the image lifts up out of the city block and onto her paper; he strolls above the sidewalk all by himself, high over the cars and buildings. Then she sets him down again on the sidewalk, and he glides off the paper. The children squeal at this quintessential image of lightness, a flying carpet made with mirrors. The young woman picks up a whole city bus, which streams over her paper like an airship, and then she lifts one of the grand red brick buildings of the university from its ancient foundation and lets it hang weightlessly over the Earth.

Surely it will be in the camera obscura of our imagination, the great human pans dreamed up by life itself, that we will learn, if we do, the trick of traveling lightly through the world. My mother and I go about the city for another day, sometimes with handkerchiefs over our noses against the exhausts, until we realize that we must lift ourselves out of the city and set ourselves down in the Trossachs, just north of Glasgow. In the cool foothills there we spend several days walking streams and mossy forests, and then we lift ourselves back to America. Our home country is as rude as the Edinburgh air. On the plane, a flight steward taunts a middle-aged Scotsman whose reading light is on the fritz, and barks to young girls from Glasgow whose accent he does not understand, "Speak English." Their reply—soft, astonished—that they *are* speaking English, is too quiet for his ears, and he barks again: "Speak up. I can't read lips." After landing in Logan Airport, we ask directions to the interflight transfer area: an airline staff-person snarls at us to get out of line, while outside a taxi dispatcher bellows, "Move it, move it, move it." In this brute atmosphere, I wonder how things will go at customs. Probably either prehistoric beremeal or a deep Southern accent alone would have bewildered Bostonians; the combination undoes them, and they must call for help. Soon a senior supervisor appears, and a huddled discussion commences between the uniformed men and my mother, with the soft, lumpish meal sacks being handed carefully around the group like show-and-tell items in a science class. Such diplomacies are an area in which my mother needs no help. When I join the group, she is reading aloud the recipe for bere bannocks printed on the back of the sack, and the officials are trying to decide if these will taste more like waffles or pancakes. After this experience with my mother, U.S. customs barely glances at her daughter's duffel bag—the one holding a modest sheaf of thistles, rosehips, and barley stalks.

NOTES

FIELD NOTES FROM BELIZE

The names of Caye Caulker residents, the plant biologist, and some private Belizean citizens have been changed. John Jex, Jim Baird, Dora Weyer, Winil Grant Borg, Louis, Rosita Arviga, and Don Eligio are themselves.

1. O. Nigel Bolland, *The Formation of a Colonial Society* (Baltimore: Johns Hopkins University Press, 1977), p. 197.

2. Ancient Maya civilization sustained a population of several million in what is now Guatemala, Belize, Honduras, and Mexico; the scholars' guestimate is that in Belize there were nearly one million Maya souls, five times the present population of 200,000. Modern Belize has the sparsest population in Central America, less than twenty-four inhabitants per square mile. For contrast, consider that El Salvador, only very slightly smaller than Belize, has seven million inhabitants.

3. Sydney Olivier, "British Honduras," *Encyclopaedia Britannica* (1937).

4. Fang Lizhi, "Form and Physics," *Partisan Review* 4 (1991), pp. 657–64. Translated from the Chinese by David Moser. Essay reprinted from *Wensue Pingiun* (Literary Review), May 1988.

5. The pamphlet at Altun Ha dates to the 1970s, before the recent advances in translating Maya glyphs. See Linda Schele and David Freidel, *A Forest of Kings* (New York: William Morrow, 1990).

6. Ptolemy Tompkins, *This Tree Grows out of Hell* (San Francisco: Harper San Francisco, 1990), pp. 10–11.

7. Ibid., p. 10. Tompkins suggests that the East is the fifth as well as the first direction, the place of birth and rebirth. Other sources indicate that the center is the fifth, regenerative locus.

8. Algar Robert Gregg, *British Honduras* (London: Her Majesty's Stationery Office, 1968), p. 73.

9. T. Patrick Culbert, *The Lost Civilization: The Story of the Classic Maya* (New York: Harper & Row, 1974), p. 108.

10. From a paper presented by David Stuart and Stephen Houston, 1989; quoted in David Roberts, "The Decipherment of Ancient Maya," *The Atlantic Monthly*, September 1991, pp. 87–100.

11. Quoted in David Roberts, "The Decipherment of Ancient Maya," *The Atlantic Monthly*, September 1991, p. 90.

12. J. E. S. Thompson, *The Rise and Fall of Maya Civilization*, 2d ed. (Norman: University of Oklahoma Press, 1966), pp. 4, 14.

13. Culbert, *The Lost Civilization*, p. 116. Culbert's theory is based on the results of a conference held in Santa Fe in October 1970. Eleven scholars met to "reconsider the question of the collapse." During their discussions, they moved away from the old debate about single causes and the tendency "to move from single-cause theories to theories of a domino sort, in which a starting cause [leads] to a whole series of reactions that together resulted in the collapse." What they embraced instead was a concept derived from systems theory, which suggests that "the reasons for the Maya collapse are inherent in the system and are the same reasons that for many centuries led to growth and success." All cultures, says Culbert, are complex systems. Some are stable and contain elements that counteract variations and keep values on a steady keel; some are growth systems in which changes in one part of the system amplify changes in another. At some point, a growth system (like the classic Maya culture) can stabilize and reach equilibrium, or it can go into "overshoot" mode and outstrip its resources. Culbert believes that the "Maya collapse is an exemplary case of overshoot by a culture that had expanded too rapidly and had used its resources too recklessly in an environment that demanded careful techniques of conservation." It is, he muses, an experience similar to the future foreseen by the Club of Rome in *The Limits to Growth*.

14. Tompkins, *This Tree Grows out of Hell*, pp. 25–28. Tompkin's speculative view is that as Maya civilization grew from village to metropolis, the subtle rituals of the shamans were gradually recast for the purposes of an authoritarian elite and used in crude, theatrical displays that demoralized rather than envigorated the psyche. Tompkins notes that to propose that village-scale Maya society was more benign than the later pyramid culture is not to name the villages primal paradises. Such projections, he

says, are aptly described as "modern myths, thinly disguised as nonfiction accounts" and are ironic since the myths of primal peoples commonly reveal their own vigorous search for paradise. What can be said is that ancient Amerindian spiritual experience revolved around an encounter with death and divinities that was essential to the process of becoming fully alive. By nature and training, the shaman is one who enters the disorienting world of demons and divinities, returning unscathed to publicly express the experience. By watching their shamans in trance, and by ritual dancing, fasting, and chanting, ordinary villagers might also experience the ecstatic travel that brings life-sustaining qualities into being. Having viscerally faced death, they were more alert; having greeted the Earth divinities, the creatures and lands around them were charged with meaning. They returned from their travels with the "rains and breezes of the universe rattling" through their human selves, its "moods and energies" always partly their own. If the journeys were necessarily risky, they were the coalescence of generations of experience into a process of metamorphosis: the terrors and joys of ecstatic travel could forge a soul, integrate the psyche, produce the state of being at home in the universe. It was these insights into the meaning of death and the more-than-human forces for the living that may have degenerated. If the peasants revolted, it may have been in part because the central rituals of their culture had become obstacles to life. It could be that the Maya felt they had discovered the limits of one way of life, and returned to village order, not as a retreat, but as a step forward.

15. The *Chilam Balam of Chumayel*, as quoted in Irene Nicholson, *Mexican and Central American Mythology*, rev. ed. (New York: Peter Bedrick Books, 1985), p. 19.

16. Thompson, *The Rise and Fall of Maya Civilization*, p. 13.

17. Typical are the events of 1618, when Fathers Batolome de Fuensalida and Juan de Orbita visited the village of Tipu on what is now the Belize River, a town of about five hundred Maya inhabitants who had, in the missionaries' view, undergone earlier conversion. When the fathers discovered Maya sacred emblems mingled with Christian crosses in the newly built church, they declared the local worship of *Jesu Christo* to be a sham, ordered the people flogged and their old articles of worship burned. When the missionaries left town, Tipu villagers set fire to the church, and soon afterwards another Spanish Father on his way through Tipu had the village chief and eighty others put to death in retribution. At a high cost, the Tipu villagers had made a name for themselves and were gradually left alone. Other Maya in nearby villages simply fled deeper into the forest to escape such unwelcome attentions. In Belize, the Maya never ceased

resisting European attempts to conquer them. As late as 1872, Maya villagers were engaged in armed conflict with British raiders.

18. Ralph Roys, *The Book of the Chilam Balam of Chumayel* (Norman: University of Oklahoma Press, 1933).

19. Maya have arrived in Belize from Yucatán (Yucatec Maya), from the Petén forest of Guatemala (Mopan Maya), and from the Verapez in Guatemala (Kekchi Maya). Recently, Maya refugees from the Guatemalan highlands have come into Belize to escape an oppressive political regime.

20. Elaine Elisabetsky, "Folklore, Tradition, or Know-How?" in *Cultural Survival*, Summer 1991, p. 10. Steven R. King writes, in "The Source of Our Cures" (*Cultural Survival*, Summer 1991, p. 19), that by one estimate seventy-four percent of the one hundred and twenty-one plant compounds "currently used in the global pharmacopoeia have been discovered through research based on ethnobotanical information on the use of plants by indigenous people." And yet, until very recently, such knowledge was taken from cultures without compensation, the operative theory being that it belonged to all humankind. The flaw in this view is that the medicines and commodities derived from and based on indigenous knowledge are very definitely defined as the profit-generating property of a few in the context of industrial production—an imbalance in logic compounded by the fact that science-based medicines and products are almost never available to the people from whose source knowledge they arise. It calls for a startling realignment of our thinking to realize, as Jack Kloppenburg, author of *First the Seed*, says, that "indigenous people have in effect been engaged in a massive program of foreign aid to the urban populations of the industrialized North." ("No Hunting!: Biodiversity, Indigenous Rights, and Scientific Poaching," in *Cultural Survival*, Summer 1991, pp. 14–18).

21. Gregg, *British Honduras*, p. 86. Gregg's view is that fourth- and fifth-century Maya farmers sheared away whatever the existing vegetation was in order to plant maize and a mix of trees useful to their society, among them breadnuts for food, sapodillas for fruit and gum, and cohune palms for oil and thatch material. As the ceremonial cities grew, these farmers had left off shifting-field *milpa* agriculture and invented a new, high-yield, terraced-slope and raised-field agriculture that could feed the increasing population. To reuse the same land from year to year, the farmers fertilized soils with fish bones and seaweeds; to keep tropical soils cool enough to absorb nutrients, they shaded the terrace plots, using the mahogany as the tree of choice. Then, when the cities began to be abandoned in the tenth and eleventh centuries, farmers apparently returned to *milpa* agriculture,

leaving the stands of mahogany to be gradually surrounded by other woodland vegetation.

22. Norman Ashcraft, *Colonialism and Underdevelopment: Processes of Political Economic Change in British Honduras* (New York: Teachers College Press, Columbia University, 1973), p. 33. For my understanding of the political economy of Belize, I am indebted to both Norman Ashcraft and O. Nigel Bolland.

23. Gregg, *British Honduras,* p. 17.

24. Ashcraft, *Colonialism and Underdevelopment,* p. 45.

25. And there are the cowbirds. Formerly a bird that followed the buffalo herds of the Great Plains, the cowbird reacted to the plains being opened and settled by slowly making its way east and having a population explosion. Like the cuckoo, the cowbird has the habit of laying its eggs in the nests of other, smaller birds. Among warbler and redstart eggs, cowbird eggs grow faster and hatch earlier; baby cowbirds promptly push their nestmates over the edge into oblivion.

26. Anne Sutherland, *Caye Caulker* (Boulder, Colorado: Westview Press, 1986). Anne Sutherland's anthropological study of the Caye Caulker fishing cooperative is a thorough account of the techniques of lobster fishing, the history of the cooperative, the kinship structures of the islanders, and the effects of tourism on the island. Her research confirmed and clarified many facts gleaned during my time on the island.

Of the islanders' independence, Sutherland comments that because Belize "is a political backwater, a variety of cultural groups have flourished in the absence of a strong central government. Caye Caulker, for example, has a history of ignoring power hierarchies outside its boundaries and guarding zealously its local independence. Within this context of political autonomy, Caye Caulker has also developed a society with relatively little social hierarchy. The fisherman's cooperative, with its egalitarian membership and local control of production and distribution, is a reflection of the society in which it developed" (p. 8).

In 1991, an airplane landing strip was built on Caye Caulker, despite islanders' protests and sabotage efforts during construction. This will certainly affect the pace of things.

27. Quoted ibid., p. 89.

28. "Belize Breeze" is the name for the marijuana grown in the local bush. It is an intense strain, and estimates are that Belize is the fourth largest supplier of marijuana to the United States. Belizeans resist anti-drug campaigns that do not make a distinction between marijuana, which is tolerated, and cocaine, which is known to be dangerous. The official GNP of Belize is $190 million (U.S.), and it is thought that another $85

million comes into the country through sales of Belizean grown marijuana and transshipments of cocaine through the country.

29. Eugene H. Kaplan, *Coral Reefs* (Boston: Houghton Mifflin Company, 1982), pp. 101–4.

30. Caroline Miller, "A Home for Howlers," *Sanctuary Magazine,* September 1988, p. 9. Zoologist Robert Horwich of the University of Wisconsin proposed the idea of the baboon sanctuary in 1985 to the village council of Bermudian Landing, and received help in organizing the project from botanist Jon Lyon and Ed Johnson of New Mexico. Fallet Young, a native resident of Bermudian Landing, is the full-time manager.

FOLLOWING HERMES

1. For a masterful discussion of this matter, see Neil Evernden's *The Natural Alien: Humankind and Environment* (Toronto: University of Toronto Press, 1985). As Keith Thomas writes in *Man And The Natural World: A History of the Modern Sensibility* (New York: Pantheon Books, 1983), such radical anthropocentrism dates to early modern Europe, when theologians provided for an emerging exploitative production system the moral foundations for the domination of nature by human beings. Interpretations of scripture inspired the typical belief that "all things [are created] principally for the benefit and pleasure of man." Horseflies were created to sharpen the wits of men, birds to entertain, lobsters for food and contemplation, the dog to be affectionate, the louse to inspire clean habits, weeds to provide a struggle to put fire in one's spirit. Upon learning from travelers of the respectful nature philosophies of Buddhists and Hindus, seventeenth- and eighteenth-century religious Europeans were shocked and contemptuous. Of the Eastern nature reverence, scientist Robert Boyle said it was "a discouraging impediment to the empire of man over the inferior creatures." (Still, their philosophies have not prevented Asian cultures from creating industrial pollution, deforestation, and species extinction. The world's most anthropocentric religion has contributed to present day environmental troubles, but degradation of the Earth predates and extends well beyond the borders of Christendom.)

2. Richard G. Geldard, *Ancient Greece: A Guide To the Sacred Places* (New York: Alfred A. Knopf, 1989), p. 187. For a good discussion of the Panathenaia pilgrimage, see Richard Geldard's section on the Acropolis.

3. Euripides, *Iphigenia in Tauris,* lines 476–77, trans. Witter Bynner, in *Euripides,* vol. 3 of *The Complete Greek Tragedies,* ed. David Greene and Richmond Lattimore (Chicago: University of Chicago Press, 1959), p. 391.

4. R. S. Surtees, in *Handley Cross,* 1854. All quotations from the *Oxford English Dictionary,* 1935 edition.

5. In his field guide, *Trees and Shrubs of Greece* (Athens: P. Efstathiadis & Sons, 1978), George Sfikas says that Greece has the lowest percentage of forested land in Europe; eighty-five percent is treeless scrub, fields, pasture, or barren, eroded land.

6. Carole Rubenstein, "'Like Early Mist': Five Songs of the Penan Urun," *Sarawak Museum Journal,* 1989.

7. See Lorus and Margery Milne, *The Arena of Life: Dynamics of Ecology* (Garden City, New York: Natural History Press [Doubleday], 1971).

8. Odysséas Elytes, "Selections from the *Open Book,*" translated by Theofanis G. Stavrou in consultation with the poet, in *Odysseus Elytis: Analogies of Light,* ed. Ivar Ivask (Norman: University of Oklahoma Press, 1975, 1981), pp. 27–33.

9. Odysséas Elytes, speaking on his poetry in an interview with Ivar Ivask in Athens, March 1975. In *Odysseus Elytis: Analogies of Light,* ed. Ivar Ivask, pp. 7–15.

10. Keith Thomas, *Man And The Natural World,* p. 236.

11. Odysséas Elytes, in *Odysseus Elytis: Analogies of Light,* p. 27.

12. Quotes from James Lovelock, *The Ages of Gaia: A Biography of Our Living Earth,* Commonwealth Fund Book Program, series ed. Lewis Thomas, M.D. (New York: W. W. Norton & Company, 1988), pp. 3, 19, 39, 205–8.

13. Aeschylus, *Agamemnon,* lines 1567–76. All quotations from the *Oresteia* of Aeschylus (*Agamemnon, The Libation Bearers, Eumenides*) are from the translation by Richmond Lattimore (Chicago: University of Chicago Press, 1953).

14. Henry Miller, *The Colossus of Maroussi* (New York: New Directions, 1941), quoted in Richard G. Geldard, *Ancient Greece: A Guide To The Sacred Places of Ancient Greece* (New York: Alfred A. Knopf, 1989), p. 166.

15. Henry Beston, *Herbs and The Earth: An Evocative Excursion into the Lore and Legend of Our Common Herbs* (Boston: David R. Godine, Publisher, Inc., 1990), p. 93.

16. *Eumenides,* lines 737–40, *Oresteia* of Aeschylus, trans. Richmond Lattimore.

17. Ibid., lines 841–47.

18. Christine Downing, *The Goddess: Mythological Images of the Feminine* (New York: Crossroad, 1981).

19. Donald S. Carne-Ross, to whom my own thoughts about the *Oresteia* are indebted, has persuasively argued in his beautiful essay "The

Beastly House of Atreus" (*Kenyon Review,* Spring 1981) that the two worlds may be fundamentally impossible to reconcile. A more complete discussion of the role of Artemis in the *Oresteia* can be found in an essay in my forthcoming doctoral dissertation, *Along the Border: Poetry and the Ecological Life,* Boston University, Fall 1993.

20. *Agamemnon,* line 950, *Oresteia* of Aeschylus, trans. Richard Lattimore.

21. Philo, *On the Creation,* 133, quoted in Clarence J. Glacken, *Traces on A Rhodian Shore* (Berkeley: University of California Press, 1967), p. 14.

22. Sophocles, *Antigone,* "Ode to Man" passage, lines 414–55, translation by Donald S. Carne-Ross, unpublished.

23. For a discussion of the history of early modern ecology, see the introduction in Lorus and Margery Milne, *The Arena of Life.*

24. K. S. Schrader-Frechette, *Environmental Ethics* (Pacific Grove, Calif.: Boxwood Press, 1981), p. ix.

25. The Greek word *technē* (art, skill, cunning of hand, technique, a system or method of making something) is the root of words such as *technical* and *technology.* In Aristotle, *technē* refers to anything deliberately created by humans, in contrast to things that occur in *physis,* or nature, without human influence. *Technē* is the source of paintings, music, weapons, houses, and egg-beaters, but not humans (at least not the biological component of a human being), nor stars, nor grizzly bears. *Technē* can also mean the skill to make things, and the knowledge of *how* to make (but not why). For the Greeks, fine arts, medical arts, applied sciences, and crafts were all *technē.* (Based loosely on a definition in Peter A. Angeles, *Dictionary of Philosophy* [New York: Barnes & Noble Books, a division of Harper & Row, 1981].)

26. Lovelock, *The Ages of Gaia,* p. 219.

27. "Attracting Quality Tourism," *The Athenian,* July 1989, pp. 14–15.

THE VERY RICH HOURS

1. See Jean Craighead George, *Everglades Wildguide* (Washington, D.C.: National Park Service, Division of Publications, 1988), pp. 45–46. For a full account of alligator holes, see Frank C. Craighead, *The Role of the Alligator in Shaping Plant Communities and Maintaining Wildlife in the Southern Everglades* (Maitland, Fla.: Florida Audubon Society).

2. Jean Henri Fabre, *The Life of the Spider,* trans. Alexander Teixeira de Mattos (New York: Dodd, Mead and Co., 1912).

3. Rainer F. Foelix, *Biology of Spiders* (Cambridge, Mass.: Harvard University Press, 1982), p. 138.

4. Lame Deer, Lakota shaman, quoted in "The Sacred Hoop: A Contemporary Perspective," Paula Gunn Allen, *Studies in American Indian Literature* (New York: Modern Language Association of America, 1983), p. 16.

5. Marjory Stoneman Douglas, *The Everglades: River of Grass,* rev. ed. (Sarasota, Fla.: Pineapple Press, 1988), p. 299.

6. "Three Náhuatl Poems (Aztec): translated by William Carlos Williams," in Thomas Mabry Cranfill, ed., *The Muse in Mexico* (Austin: University of Texas Press, 1959), pp. 90–91.

7. Douglas, *The Everglades,* pp. 278–79, 310–11.

8. Robert S. Chandler, quoted by Keith Schneider in "Returning Part of Everglades To Nature for $700 Million," *The New York Times,* March 11, 1991. As Peter and I glide through the swamp, Miami courtrooms are full of everglades politics: a federal lawsuit, filed in 1988 on behalf of the Everglades National Park by the U.S. Attorney in Miami, means to compel Florida to eliminate pollution in water that enters those everglades included in the National Park. Two months after our journey, in March of 1991, the long impasse in the matter has yielded a plan: to return the Kissimmee River to its original channel; to establish 25,300 acres of marshland to filter the pollution entering the glades; to breach several canals, allowing water to flow across a conservation area; to add 107,000 acres to the park; to allow water to again fill the Shark River Slough. At the same time, a one-hundred-year-old woman met with EPA head William Reilly to urge that funding for the $700 million plan be forthcoming. She wore a straw hat with a wide brim, a rope of pearls, and a look as fierce as a red-shouldered hawk: Marjory Stoneman Douglas, on the case.

9. Ernst Bloch, as quoted by Jurgen Moltmann in "The Alienation and Liberation of Nature," in *On Nature,* Boston University Studies in Philosophy and Religion, vol. 6, ed. Leroy Rouner (Notre Dame, Ind.: University of Notre Dame Press, 1984), pp. 135–36.

10. Jean Henri Fabre, *The Insect World of J. Henri Fabre,* trans. Alexander Teixeira de Mattos (1949; reprint, Boston: Beacon Press, 1991), p. 298.

11. The terms used to identify parts of the orb-weavers' webs are from Foelix, *Biology of Spiders,* and from B. J. and Elizabeth Kaston, *How to Know the Spiders* (Dubuque, Iowa: Wm. C. Brown Company, 1953).

12. Willis J. Gertsch, *American Spiders* (Toronto and New York: D. Van Nostrand Company, 1949), pp. 54–56 *passim.*

13. Charles Darwin, *The Voyage Of The Beagle,* The Natural History Library (New York: Doubleday, Anchor Books, 1962), pp. 159–60.

14. Song lyric quoted: © 1989, Peter Niels Dunn, from "United States of Genocide," *Friends and Guitars, The Spin Doctors.*

15. J. Donald Hughes, *American Indian Ecology* (El Paso: Texas Western Press, University of Texas at El Paso, 1983), pp. 3–4.

16. Marion Spjut Gilliland, *The Material Culture of Key Marco, Florida* (Gainesville: University of Florida Presses, 1975).

17. Jerald T. Milanich and Charles H. Fairbanks, *Florida Archaeology* (New York: Academic Press, Harcourt Brace Jovanovich, 1980), p. 243.

18. Douglas, *The Everglades,* p. 91.

19. Father Juan Rogel, Jesuit priest among the Calusa, quoted in Jerald T. Milanich and Charles H. Fairbanks, *Florida Archaeology* (New York: Academic Press, Harcourt Brace Jovanovich, 1980), p. 249.

20. "Three Náhuatl Poems (Aztec): Workings by William Carlos Williams," *The Muse in Mexico,* pp. 90–91.

21. Mark Twain, *Life on the Mississippi* (New York: Heritage Press, 1944).

22. Virgil, *Eclogues,* lines 79–83, after a translation by Paul Alpers, *The Singer of the Eclogues: A Study of Vigilian Pastoral* (Berkeley: University of California Press, 1979), p. 15.

SOUTH OF THE ULTIMA THULE

1. It is less likely that the Tennessee storytellers were recounting Shakespeare's *King Lear* than "The True Chronicles of King Lier," the comforting Christian folktale upon which the Bard based his existential version.

2. James Lovelock, *The Ages of Gaia* (New York: W. W. Norton & Co., 1988), p. 10.

3. John Prebble, *The Highland Clearances* (London: Secker & Warburg, 1963). The historical information in this section is drawn from general reading, but especially from John Prebble's thorough account.

4. Ibid., pp. 31–32.

5. Samuel Johnson, from the combined edition of Johnson's *Journal to the Western Isles of Scotland* and Boswell's *Journal of a Tour to the Hebrides,* ed. Peter Levi (London and New York: 1984), as quoted in *The Story of English,* Robert McCrum, William Cran, and Robert MacNeil (New York: Penguin Books, 1987), p. 137. My knowledge of Scots imports into English comes from *The Story of English,* which includes a fine account of the relationship of Scots and English.

6. See Carolyn Merchant, *The Death of Nature: Women, Ecology and the Scientific Revolution* (San Francisco: Harper & Row, 1980). Not only population increase, but inhumane practices preceding the outbreak of the bubonic plague were the root cause of the poor condition of the European

soils. Heavy taxation had unravelled the medieval economy and eco-system: because peasants were unable to reinvest in their land or to plow and properly manure, the soils became exhausted. Marginal soils were cultivated; crop yields and nutritional values decreased, and there was not enough land in production to ward off famine in bad years. Between 1300 and 1350, the bubonic plague hit the already malnourished populations very hard. 1450 saw the low point of the population. By 1550, the lands, forests, and soils were recovered.

7. That I even think to muse whether a near-genocide benefitted the land suggests how values will be challenged as we seek a new balance with a changed Earth. If our species enjoyed an effortless equilibrium (with itself and with its surround), both pristine landscapes and decent societies would be common enough, and if sound habitation were less elusive, we would not be tempted to try to wrest it at any cost. Sadly, the clearances cannot be dismissed as a bit of historical barbary. It has recently been proposed that a small, wealthy human population—achieved by draconian means—could be a solution to human overpopulation and stressing of the Earth. Garrett Hardin's "lifeboat ethics" is a triage approach to over-population that calls for rich countries to disallow immigration, to eschew medical, food, and economic aid to poor countries—to become isolated, relatively comfortable lifeboats, leaving the rest of the world to drown. Like the clearances episode, lifeboat ethics reminds us that in times of extremis, many moral compasses will spin. Even so, one can hope that Hardin's harsh proposal may serve as a stimulus toward decency. Curi-ously, conventional humanists often peg biocentric views—"Earth First" literature and "deep ecology" philosophy, for instance—as misanthropic. Yet, paradoxically, a shift from anthropocentrist to biocentrist values—putting the Earth first, identifying with the deeper Self of the living planet—will likely sustain the envelope of human life.

See Garrett Hardin, *Exploring New Ethics for Survival* (New York: Viking, 1972), and Hardin, "Living on a Lifeboat," *BioScience* 24 (October 1974): 561–68. See also Paul R. Ehrlich, *The Population Bomb* (New York: Ballantine, 1968), and D. Meadows et al., *The Limits to Growth* (New York: New American Library, 1974).

8. This map feature must date from at least 330 B.C., when a Greek explorer, Pytheas of Marseilles, circumnavigated Orkney and said that he had seen the edge of the world. See R. J. Berry, *The Natural History of Orkney* (London: Collins, 1985), p. 18.

9. Edwin Muir, *An Autobiography* (New York: William Sloane Asso-ciates, Inc., 1954), p. 62. The poet Edwin Muir grew up on a Wyre Island farm. His *Autobiography* is not enough known, yet there can be no better

account of a place than Muir's memoir of rural late nineteenth–century Orkney.

10. V. Gordon Childe, *The Prehistory of Scotland* (Hertford, England: Paul, Trench, Trubrer & Co., 1935), p. 59.

11. Patrick Bailey, *Orkney* (London and North Pomfret, Vt.: David & Charles, 1985), p. 16.

12. Marija Gimbutas, *The Language of the Goddess* (San Francisco: Harper & Row, 1989), pp. 196–97.

13. Berry, *The Natural History of Orkney*, p. 36. See also Jacquetta Hawkes, *A Land* (Boston: Beacon Press, 1991); her geological history of Great Britain is essential reading.

14. McCrum, Cran, MacNeil, *The Story of English*, p. 145. See also W. L. Lorimer, trans., *New Testament in Scots* (Southside, 1983). Also W. W. Smith's *New Testament* (1901).

15. Just for fun, here is a passage of Gaelic and the English translation, from a story called "The Fairy Queen in the Form of a Frog." The complete story appears in *Folk Tales and Fairy Lore, in Gaelic and English, Collected from Oral Tradition*, by Rev. James Macdougall ("Sometime Minister of Duror"), ed. Rev. George Calder, B.D. (Edinburgh: John Grant, 1920), p. 270.

Bha uair eigin a' fuireachd, aig ceann Loch Raonasa an Arainn, bean tuathanaich a bhitheadh a' deanamh aite mna-gluin d'a banchoimhearsmaich. Air latha boidheach fogharaidh thuit dhi fein agus do mhnaoi eile a bhi mach air an achadh ag gearradh coirce. Romh fheasgar leum muile-mhag mhor, bhuidhe gu h-eigineach a rathad a corrain; agus, an uair a chunnaic i an creutair truagh 'ga slaodadh fein a cunnairt, thubhairt i: "Tha thusa an sin, a luideag bhochd; b'fheairrde thu mise mu d' thimchioll an uine ghorid," "O! am beathach mosach, ma thig i an rathad agamsa, cuiridh mi barr mo chorrain troimpe." "Cha chuir, cha chuir," arsa bean an tuathaniach; "cha'n 'eil an creutair bochd ach a' magaran mu 'n cuairt a' trusadh a cuid mar tha sinn fein." Agus leigeadh air falbh a' mhuile-mhag le a beatha.

At the head of Loch Ransa, in Arran, there once lived a farmer's wife who used to act as midwife to her neighbours. On a fine day in harvest she and another woman happened to be out in the field cutting oats. Before evening a large yellow frog leaped with difficulty out of the way of her sickle, and when she saw the poor creature dragging itself out of danger she said: "There you are, poor clumsy thing; you would be the better of my help soon." "O! the nasty beast," said the other woman, "if she comes my way, I'll put the point of my sickle through her." "No!

No!" said the farmer's wife, "the poor creature is only crawling about gathering her portion like ourselves." And the frog was let away with her life.

16. Robert Rendall, *Orkney Shore* (Kirkwall: Kirkwall Press, 1960), quoted in Berry, *The Natural History of Orkney*, pp. 204–5.

17. T. S. Eliot, in the introduction to Edwin Muir's *Collected Poems* (New York: Oxford University Press, 1965).

18. Archaeological dates and information about Maeshowe are from our visit to the site itself, supplemented by data from Bailey, *Orkney*, pp. 208–10; and Berry, *The Natural History of Orkney*, pp. 166–67.

19. Childe, *The Prehistory of Scotland*, p. 55.

20. See Gimbutas, *The Language of the Goddess*. Introducing *The Language of the Goddess*, Joseph Campbell comments that "the first recognition of such a matristic order of thought and life antecedent to and underlying the historical forms of both Europe and the Near East appeared in 1861 in Johann Jakob Bachofen's *Das Mutterrecht*, where it was shown that in the codes of Roman Law vestigial features can be recognized of a matrilineal order of inheritance." In addition to *Das Mutterrecht*, a few other sources are: J. J. Bachofen, *Myth, Religion and Mother Right: Selected Writings*; T. Jacobsen, *The Treasures of Darkness: A History of Mesopotamian Religions*; R. G. Wasson, C. Ruck, and A. Hoffman, *The Road to Eleusis: Unveiling the Secret of the Mysteries*; Carolyn Merchant, *The Death of Nature*; M. Stone, *When God was a Woman*; Vincent Scully, *The Earth, The Temple and the Gods: Greek Sacred Architecture*; M. Robbins, "The Assimilation of Pre Indo-European Goddesses into Indo-European Society," *Journal of Indo-European Studies* 8; Eric Neumann, *The Great Mother: An Analysis of the Archetype*, Bollingen Series 47; R. G. Levy, *Religious Conceptions of the Stone Age and Their Influence upon European Thought*.

21. Lord Teignmouth, *Sketches of the Coasts and Islands of Scotland* (London: 1836), vol. 1, pp. 286, 287; reprinted in G. F. Black, *Examples of Printed Folk-Lore Concerning the Orkney and Shetland Islands*, vol. 3 of *Country Folklore* (London: David Nutt, 1903).

22. "Trials for Witchcraft, Sorcery, and Superstition in Orkney," printed in *Miscellany of the Abbotsford Club*, vol. 1, pp. 135–42; reprinted in Black, *Examples of Printed Folk-Lore*.

23. Marija Gimbutas, *The Language of the Goddess*, p. 110.

24. George Low, *A Tour through the Islands of Orkney and Shetland, Containing Hints Relative to Their Ancient, Modern and Natural History*, collected in 1774 (Kirkwall: 1879), reprinted in Black, *Examples of Printed Folk-Lore*.

25. The Netsilik Eskimo, who call themselves "people of the seal" would well understand the selkie stories of another northern culture. Nalungiaq is a Netsilik woman whose poetry was collected by Knud Rasmussen. Here is the complete text of her poem "Magic Words":

> In the very earliest time,
> when both people and animals lived on earth,
> a person could become an animal if he wanted to
> and an animal could become a human being.
> Sometimes they were people
> and sometimes animals
> and there was no difference.
> All spoke the same language.
> That was the time when words were like magic.
> The human mind had mysterious powers.
> A word spoken by chance
> might have strange consequences.
> It would suddenly come alive
> and what people wanted to happen could happen.
> All you had to do was say it.
> Nobody could explain this.
> That's the way it was.

From Edward Field, *Eskimo Songs and Stories*, collected by Knud Rasmussen on the Fifth Thule Expedition, selected and translated by Edward Field (New York: Delacorte Press/S. Lawrence, 1973).

26. George Mackay Brown, "Sealskin," *A Time To Keep and Other Stories* (New York: Vanguard Press, 1983), pp. 172–73.

27. This account of the selkie story is based on several versions, including one given in W. Traill Dennison, "Orkney Folklore: Sea Myths," from papers published in the *Scottish Antiquary*, vol. 5, pp. 171–77, and reprinted in Black, *Examples of Printed Folk-Lore*.

28. Sir Harry Godwin, *The Archives of the Peat Bogs* (Cambridge: Cambridge University Press, 1981), p. 1.

29. Seamus Heaney, "Bogland," in *Door Into the Dark* (London: Faber & Faber Ltd., 1969).

SOURCES AND
SUGGESTIONS FOR
FURTHER READING

FIELD NOTES FROM BELIZE

Ashcraft, Norman. *Colonialism and Underdevelopment: Processes of Political Economic Change in British Honduras.* New York: Teachers College Press, 1973.

Bollard, O. Nigel. *The Formation of a Colonial Society.* Baltimore: Johns Hopkins University Press, 1977.

Clancy, Flora S., and Peter D. Harrison, eds. *Vision and Revision in Maya Studies.* Albuquerque: University of New Mexico Press, 1990.

Coe, Michael D. *The Maya.* Rev. ed. London: Thames and Hudson Ltd., 1966 and 1980.

Culbert, T. Patrick. *The Lost Civilization: The Story of the Classic Maya.* New York: Harper and Row, 1974.

Cultural Survival Quarterly, Summer 1991. 53A Church Street, Cambridge, MA 02138.

Evernden, Neil. *The Natural Alien: Humankind and Environment.* Toronto: University of Toronto Press, 1985.

Goetz, Delia, and Sylvanus G. Morley, from the translation of Adrián Recinos. *Popol Vuh: The Sacred Book of the Ancient Quiche Maya.* Norman: University of Oklahoma Press, 1950.

Gregg, A. R., *British Honduras.* London: Her Majesty's Stationery Office, 1968.

Kaplan, Eugene H. *A Field Guide to Coral Reefs.* Peterson Field Guides. Boston: Houghton Mifflin, 1982.

Kohák, Erazim. *The Embers and the Stars: A Philosophical Inquiry into the Moral Sense of Nature.* Chicago: University of Chicago Press, 1984.

Lewis, Norman. "A Letter from Belize." In *A View Of The World: Selected Journalism*. London: Eland, 1986.

Lizhi, Fang. "Form and Physics." *Partisan Review* 58, no. 4 (1991).

Mahler, Richard, and Steele Wotkyns. *Belize: A Natural Destination*. Santa Fe, N. Mex.: John Muir Publications, 1991.

Merleau-Ponty, Maurice. *Phenomenology of Perception*. London: Routledge & Kegan Paul, 1962.

Nicholson, Irene. *Mexican and Central American Mythology*. New York: Peter Bedrick Books, 1985.

Pendergast, D. M. *Excavations at Altun Ha, Belize, 1964–1970*, vol. 1, Toronto: Royal Ontario Museum, 1979.

Roys, Ralph C. *The Book of the Chilam Balam of Chumayel*. Norman: University of Oklahoma Press, 1967.

Sanctuary: The Journal of the Massachusetts Audubon Society, vol. 27, no. 9 (September 1988).

Sutherland, Anne. *Caye Caulker: Economic Success in a Belizean Fishing Village*. Boulder, Colo.: Westview Press, 1986.

Thompson, John Eric Sidney. *The Rise and Fall of Maya Civilization*. Norman: University of Oklahoma Press, 1966.

Von Hagen, Victor W. *World of the Maya*. New York: New American Library, 1960.

Walcott, Derek. *The Star-Apple Kingdom*. New York: Farrar, Straus and Giroux, 1979.

FOLLOWING HERMES

Aeschylus. *Oresteia*. Translated by Richmond Lattimore. Chicago: University of Chicago Press, 1953.

Carne-Ross, Donald S. "The Beastly House of Atreus." *Kenyon Review*, new series vol. 3, no. 2 (Spring 1981).

Elytes, Odysséas. *Anihitá Hártia (Open Book)*. Athens: Asterias, 1974. Selections translated by Theofanis G. Stavrou appear in *Odysseus Elytes: Analogies of Light*. Edited by Ivar Ivask. Norman: University of Oklahoma Press, 1975, 1981.

Evernden, Neil. *The Natural Alien: Humankind and Environment*. Toronto: University of Toronto Press, 1985.

Geldard, Richard G. *Ancient Greece: A Guide To the Sacred Places*. New York: Alfred A. Knopf, 1989.

Glacken, Clarence J. *Traces on A Rhodian Shore*. Berkeley: University of California Press, 1967, 1973.

Lovelock, James. *The Ages of Gaia: A Biography of Our Living Earth.* Commonwealth Fund Book Program, edited by Lewis Thomas, M.D. New York: W. W. Norton & Company, 1988.

Milne, Lorus and Margery. *The Arena of Life: Dynamics of Ecology.* Garden City, N.Y.: Doubleday, Natural History Press, 1971.

Schrader-Frechette, K. S. *Environmental Ethics* 9. Pacific Grove, Calif.: Boxwood Press, 1981.

Thomas, Keith. *Man And The Natural World: A History of the Modern Sensibility.* New York: Pantheon Books, 1983.

THE VERY RICH HOURS

Connell, Evan S. *A Long Desire.* San Francisco: North Point Press, 1988.

Darwin, Charles. *The Voyage Of The Beagle.* New York: Doubleday, Natural History Library, 1962.

Douglas, Marjory Stoneman. *The Everglades: River of Grass.* Rev. ed. Sarasota, Fla.: Pineapple Press, 1988.

Fabre, J. Henri. *The Life of the Spider.* Translated by Alexander Teixeira de Mattos. New York: Dodd, Mead and Company, 1912.

Foelix, Rainer F. *Biology of Spiders.* Cambridge, Mass.: Harvard University Press, 1982.

George, Jean Craighead. *Everglades Wildguide.* Washington, D.C.: National Park Service, 1988.

Gertsch, Willis J. *American Spiders.* Toronto and New York: D. Van Nostrand Company, 1949.

Gilliland, Marion Spjut. *The Material Culture of Key Marco, Florida.* Gainesville: University of Florida Presses, 1975.

Kaston, B. J. and Elizabeth. *How To Know The Spiders.* Dubuque, Iowa: Wm. C. Brown Company, 1953.

Milanich, Jerald T. and Fairbanks, Charles H. *Florida Archaeology.* New York: Academic Press, Harcourt, Brace, Jovanovich, 1980.

Virgil, *The Eclogues.* Translated by Paul J. Alpers in Alpers, *The Singer of the Eclogues: A Study of Virgilian Pastoral.* Berkeley: University of California Press, 1979.

Twain, Mark [Samuel Clemens]. *Life on the Mississippi.* New York: Heritage Press, 1944.

SOUTH OF THE ULTIMA THULE

Bailey, Patrick. *Orkney.* London and North Pomfret, Vt.: David & Charles, 1985.

Berry, R. J. *The Natural History of Orkney*. London: William Collins Sons & Co., 1985.

Black, G. F. *Examples of Printed Folk-Lore Concerning the Orkney and Shetland Islands*. Vol. 3 of *Country Folklore*. London: David Nutt, 1903.

Brown, George Mackay. *A Time To Keep and Other Stories*. New York: Vanguard Press, 1983.

Childe, V. Gordon. *The Prehistory of Scotland*. Hertford, England: Paul, Trench, Trubrer & Co., 1935.

Gimbutas, Marija. *The Language of the Goddess*. San Francisco: Harper & Row, 1989.

Godwin, Sir Harry. *The Archives of the Peat Bogs*. Cambridge: Cambridge University Press, 1981.

Hawkes, Jacquetta. *A Land*. Boston: Beacon Press, 1991.

Heaney, Seamus. *Door Into the Dark*. London: Faber & Faber Ltd., 1969.

Levi, Peter, ed. *Johnson's "Journal to the Western Isles of Scotland" and Boswell's "Journal of a Tour to the Hebrides."* Combined edition. (London and New York: 1984).

Lorimer, W. L., trans. *New Testament in Scots*. Southside: 1983.

Lovelock, James. *The Ages of Gaia: A Biography of Our Living Earth*. Commonwealth Fund Book Program, edited by Lewis Thomas, M.D. New York: W. W. Norton & Company, 1988.

McCrum, Robert, William Cran, and Robert MacNeil. *The Story of English*. New York: Penguin Books, 1987.

Merchant, Carolyn. *The Death of Nature: Women, Ecology and the Scientific Revolution*. San Francisco: Harper & Row, 1980.

Muir, Edwin. *An Autobiography*. New York: William Sloane Associates, Inc., 1954.

Muir, Edwin. *Collected Poems*. New York: Oxford University Press, 1965.

Prebble, John. *The Highland Clearances*. London: Secker & Warburg, 1963.

Rendall, Robert. *Orkney Shore*. Kirkwall: Kirkwall Press, 1960.

Scott, Sir Walter. *The Pirate*. Ivanhoe ed. New York: Waverly Book Co., 1898.

Earlier versions of these essays appeared in the following publications: "The Very Rich Hours" in *The Southwest Review,* "South of the Ultima Thule" in *The Georgia Review,* and "Field Notes from Belize" in *The Boston Globe Magazine* and in *Orion* magazine.

"What is an Orcadian" from *An Orkney Tapestry* reprinted by permission of John Murray Ltd.

"Magic Words" from *Songs and Stories of the Netsilik Eskimo* translated by Edward Fields from text collected by Knud Rasmussen, courtesy Education Development Center, Inc., Newton.

Excerpt from "Questions of Travel" from *The Complete Poems, 1927–1979* by Elizabeth Bishop. Copyright © 1979, 1983 by Alice Helen Methfessel. Reprinted by permission of Farrar, Straus & Giroux, Inc.

Excerpt from "The Schooner Flight" from *The Star Apple Kingdom* by Derek Walcott. Copyright © 1977, 1978, 1979 by Derek Walcott. Reprinted by permission of Farrar, Straus & Giroux, Inc.

Excerpt from *The Book of Chilam Balam of Chumayel* by Ralph L. Roys. New edition copyright © 1967 by the University of Oklahoma Press.